UFO ABDUCTION

FROM

UNDERSEA

By

Virgilio Sanchez-Ocejo

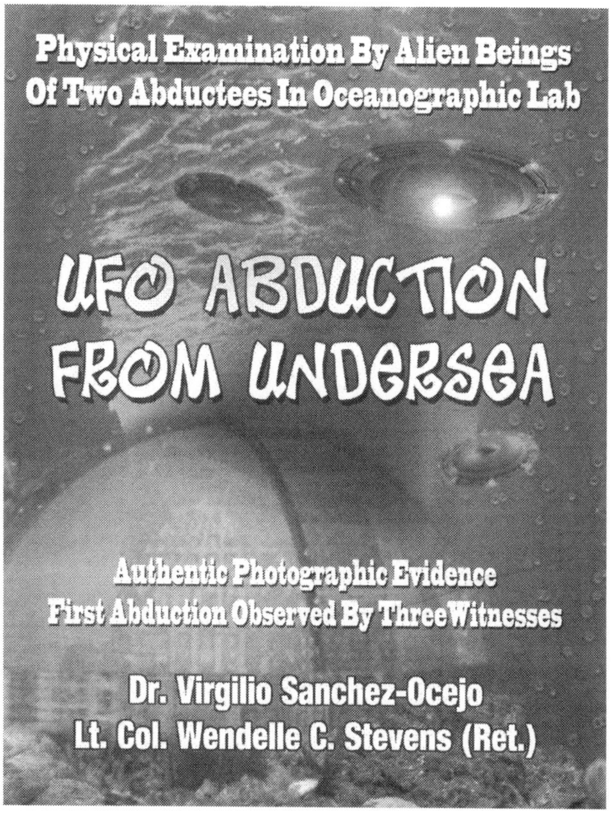
Physical Examination By Alien Beings
Of Two Abductees In Oceanographic Lab
UFO ABDUCTION
FROM UNDERSEA
Authentic Photographic Evidence
First Abduction Observed By Three Witnesses
Dr. Virgilio Sanchez-Ocejo
Lt. Col. Wendelle C. Stevens (Ret.)

GLOBAL COMMUNICATIONS

GLOBAL COMMUNICATIONS
EX LIBRIS
POST OFFICE BOX 753
NEW BRUNSWICK, NJ 08903

UFO Abduction From Undersea

By Virgilio Sanchez-Ocejo

Special Updates
by
Sean Casteel & Lt. Col. Wendell C. Stevens (Ret)

Nonfiction

Timothy Green Beckley: Editorial Director
Carol Rodriguez: Publishers Assistant
Sean Casteel: Associate Editor
Tim Swartz: Editorial Assistant
Cover Art: Tim Swartz

Printed in the United States of America

For free catalog write:
Global Communications
P.O. Box 753
New Brunswick, NJ 08903

Free Subscription to Conspiracy Journal E-Mail Newsletter
www.ConspiracyJournal.com

CONTENTS

Part One

Part Two

UFO Contact From Undersea by Virgilio Sanchez-Ocejo

By The Sea. . .By The Sea. . .
By The Beautiful Sea

By Timothy Green Beckley – "MR UFO"

They come by land, sea and air.

They come in all shapes and sizes.

UFOs have been appearing in the heavens since the beginning of recorded history. Thousands of sightings have been made. Hundreds of credible witnesses have experienced close encounters of the first, second and third kind. Yet, forgotten amongst the many dozens of always fascinating accounts are the sightings made at sea.

USOs have following our ocean faring vessels, and have been known to light up the sea at night as they head for their "home away from home."

This book by Wendelle Stevens and Dr Virgillio Sanchez-Ocejo proves that under water UFOs have taken abductees to hidden, oceanic bases for examination and reprogramming. They have shown them other-worldly scenes and events that are set to transpire. The occupants of these USOs seemingly feel safer as they navigate the depths of the oceans out of the way of our military and spying media eyes. Come along on this exciting voyage.

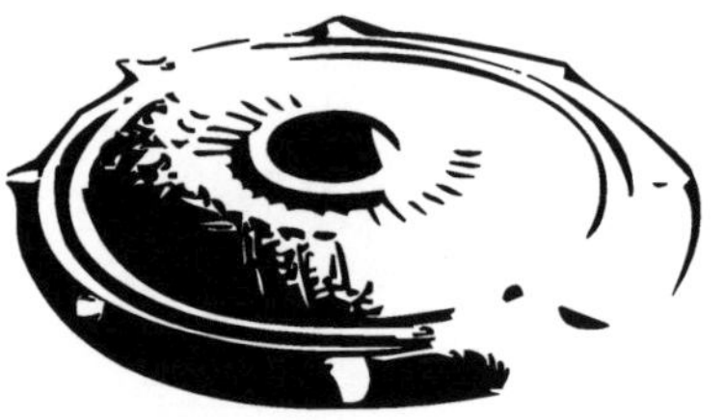

So What Is A USO?

By Sean Casteel

- Read interviews with researchers and authors Stanton Friedman, Don Ledger and Chris Styles as they recount the many mysteries of USOs and case reports of impossible underwater maneuvers.
- What happened at the Canadian port of Shag Harbor in 1967? Why is it one of the best-documented cases in the history of USOs?
- What motivates the USO occupants to make their presence felt in and around the oceans and lakes of Planet Earth? Do they maintain undersea bases there, or are they simply hiding from the prying eyes aboveground?

What exactly is a USO? The acronym stands for Unidentified Submerged Object, or alternately, Unidentified Submarine Object. USOs have been reported throughout history, dating as far back as the journey across the Atlantic of Christopher Columbus. While they are seen much less frequently than the aboveground Unidentified Flying Objects, they are nevertheless observed often enough to warrant extensive study as a related phenomenon.

According to the online encyclopedia Wikipedia, "A USO is defined as any object or optical or mechanical detection phenomenon of unknown origin observed underwater that remains unidentified even after thorough investigation. Many sightings of USOs constituting 'typical' UFOs emerging from the water are seen as a subset of the latter rather than the former. Although identifying unidentified flying objects and dispelling mistaken ideas about them have typically been important to the military as a national security issue, the comparatively rare USO sightings have not been reported as national security threats or caused the form of sensation that typical UFO sightings often have."

In other words, USOs are not viewed by the government with the same uneasiness that their flying counterparts are. Why that is so is one of those mysteries of the classified world that remains unknown at this point, though the USO phenomenon itself clearly springs from the same source as UFOs. (Conversely, it can be argued that there are several USO cases in the files of the now defunct Project Blue Book that do indicate an awareness and interest on the part of the government.)

In an interview conducted by this writer, nuclear physicist and world-renowned UFO researcher Stanton Friedman put the USO phenomenon in a nutshell this way:

"There have been a number of reports over the years of objects that do several things," Friedman said. "Navy submarines have apparently seen things moving along much faster than they can underwater, without coming in or going out. Others have seen UFOs come down in the water and move around and then take off from the water. And there have been reports of things that just come bursting forth out of the water."

Researcher and author Don Ledger, best known for his book on the Shag Harbor incident, called "Dark Object: The World's Only Government-Documented UFO Crash" (2001) and coauthored with Chris Styles, also spoke openly. Ledger talked about his early days, some thirty years ago, when he was taking courses in marine navigational aids and radar.

UFO Abduction From Undersea

In the course of his training, Ledger spoke to a man at a sonar shop in Shearwater, at a naval base in Halifax, Canada.

"He was working as a repairman for the navy on sonar," Ledger recalled. "I asked him, 'Did you ever see anything unusual down there, like whales or something besides submarines?' And he said, 'Oh, yeah, every once in a while we'll run across something that seems to be moving way too fast for a submarine.' I said, 'What do you mean by fast?' and he said, 'Well, one time we recorded one going about 150 miles an hour underwater. That's impossible.' So I said was there something wrong with the equipment? He said, no, the equipment all checked out.

"But he says, 'That's not the first time, and it won't be the last time that's happened. I said, 'What do you make of it?' And he said, 'I don't know what to make of it.'"

The sonar repairman also commented on the great depths the USO had reached.

"This thing seemed to be down a couple of miles," Ledger said, "and the guy said that there's nothing we have that can get even close to getting down there that far let alone travel at 150 miles an hour. So they're more than hydrodynamic. They're also able to maintain that pressure without killing their occupants."

Ledger offered the opinion that the objects are likely surrounded by an energy field that operates equally well both in the air and underwater.

"They're probably in an envelope all their own," he said. "It doesn't really matter how deep these things go. It probably doesn't affect them whatsoever."

According to Wikipedia, USOs are also known to have flown into and out of bodies of water that are choked with heavy ice coverings as if the ice itself presents no barrier at all. Large holes have been observed that do not appear marked by catastrophic impact, and it has been theorized that the USOs are able to melt ice at the speed of transit.

Examples of this have occurred in frigid Norway, Sweden and Russia, where these objects have been reported flying into and out of the water in the area.

THE SHAG HARBOR INCIDENT

We also spoke to Chris Styles, Don Ledger's research partner and coauthor, who provided a brief description of the Shag Harbor incident, probably the most famous water-related UFO case ever reported. Shag Harbor is located on the southern coast of Nova Scotia in Canada.

"On October 4, 1967," Styles began, "around 11:20 pm, several people called the nearby RCMP detachment and reported seeing simply lights. Some reported an aircraft had crashed into the Sound, as they called it, Shag Harbor. Three RCMP officers arrived on the scene. When they got there, they found a pale yellow light floating on the water. After several minutes, it was observed moving under its own power and leaving a heavy, dense trail of yellow foam on the water. It sank, at which time they commandeered a local boat and went out to look but could find no physical evidence.

"The search resumed at first light," Styles continued, "and eventually involved ships from the Canadian navy and seven divers. After five days, the search was canceled by Maritime Command in Halifax, reporting nil results to the search effort. No aircraft were ever reported missing, and the belief was that this was in fact the crash of an unidentified flying object."

Styles said that the significance of the Shag Harbor case lies in the fact that it is the only UFO crash scenario in the world that's supported—*in that interpretation*—by government documents that are freely available in Canada.

"And there's no controversy," Styles said, "unlike with the MJ-12 documents, as to their origin or authenticity. It's quite clear that when they interviewed the witnesses and the military personnel, the three officers, some of whom saw it in the air as well as on the water, and the fact that after an extensive naval search there was no trace, no aircraft reported missing, no missing space junk, that the conclusion was that although they didn't find it, they believe that it was a crash of a UFO."

Before it disappeared into the harbor, the object was reported by several witnesses to be at least 60 feet across.

"Most people reported seeing four flashing lights," Styles said, "that went in sequence, like one, two, three, four, and then they would all flash together once. This pattern would repeat, which is not a typical pattern seen on commercial air traffic. What's interesting is that no one reported a UFO. All simply said, 'Look, you better get down here by the shore. We think that an aircraft has crashed,' or they simply said they saw lights going into the water. It was the authorities the next morning that started referring to it as a UFO search, which is quite different from what one expects."

OVERTAKEN BY THE UNKNOWN

In the course of his many years of researching USOs, Styles ran across a very interesting case in which an Englishman named John Fairfax encountered moving "stars" as he rowed solo over the Atlantic Ocean in 1969.

"At first, he's just watching what he thinks are the stars," Styles recounted. "Of course, he's been using them for navigation, and from rowing day after day, he's extremely familiar with the sky. He's made a point to really familiarize himself in case he ended up navigating solely by dead reckoning. He had a very good boat that he had custom built. He was a little odd in that he'd come across the Atlantic the other way, against the wind and tide, so he had a troublesome journey.

"But at midpoint," Styles went one, "he thought one night that he'd seen lights that looked like stars but were much larger and brighter that just started moving in the sky. Then these things seemed to come at him, then they would back off or go down in water and come back out. He's all alone. You can't call them in or report or expect any assistance. Then he just starts to stare at them, and he feels as if he's in a trance or been taken over by this presence."

Fairfax snapped out of the trance when the cigarette he'd been holding in his hand burned down to the point that it hurt his fingers.

"This sort of broke the concentration," Styles said, "and he just went back to rowing and realized he'd been almost overtaken by whatever these lights were that continued to dog him and hound him for a while."

Fairfax recorded the incident in his logbook and later included it in his book on the journey, called "Britannia, Rowing Across the Atlantic."

"It's interesting," Styles said, "because it really documents well an aspect of this thing, how it was almost like a seduction process operating, taking over his consciousness. I've heard of these cases at sea before."

WHAT USOs LOOK LIKE

Styles said he generally runs across USO reports when he is investigating other cases. He will be interviewing a witness about a more standard UFO case when the person will volunteer a USO story without prompting by Styles.

"Most of the cases that come to my attention," he said, "have simply been lights emerging from the water. They could be sizable, but they're often not. They're often small. They could be spherical, often orange orbs or spheres. I've certainly seen cases where there have been cylinders, and there have been traditional discs. But the most common thing I hear reported would be orange spheres, very strongly orange or a deep red—what some Europeans call 'amber ramblers' emerging from the water. They're fairly well represented in the police reports on file."

Styles particularly likes to find cases in police reports that didn't get media attention.

"Where somebody has a position in the water," he said, "and they report a sighting. Then you go and check and perhaps find a record of it in the ships' logs from other vessels or something. So you'll get some good corroboration. And that happens. But again, usually I find illuminated objects or spheres or simply lights in the sky. Sometimes I've had reports of these things coming to the surface and the word I often hear is 'sizzling' on the water, as if it's a hot object. That's another one that's fairly commonly reported."

WHY GO UNDERWATER?

All three interviewees were asked their opinion as to why the USO/UFO occupants seem to feel the need to operate underwater.

"I think water provides a perfect medium for hiding," Chris Styles replied. "It's great for stealth. You're out of sight and out of mind. I mean, off the coast of Nova Scotia, so many feet down, there's not a whole lot of traffic there, right? I think there's that. There's been a lot of speculation. I know some people have wondered, is there a base there? Is there this, is there that? These things are always fun to speculate about, but I'm more into getting the data. We'll find something, and then we'll worry about the interpretation.

"It's fun to theorize about point of origin," he continued, "and ask what are they doing here? What could it mean? I think if you're going to do that, you have to open your mind to all the possibilities. That's why I like to look beyond the North American interpretation of these things, where we solely look at it in terms of the extraterrestrial hypothesis. There are other possibilities."

Styles made reference to the work by researcher Ivan Sanderson and others who have said, yes, the USOs are down there, but they're from here.

"The truth is," Styles said, "we don't know the answers, and like Dr. J. Allen Hynek said, that there are no experts on these things and that until we dredge up the hard data or the wreckage or get the door off the damn thing, we are just simply groping in the dark."

Styles' partner and coauthor Don Ledger was equally hesitant to draw conclusions.

"I don't know if there are underwater bases or any such thing," Ledger said. "We hear about these things. To me, if they're intelligently controlled by something extraterrestrial, a life form, then I think they're so far ahead of us that I don't think they think in such terms as having bases and so on. If they're in the water, they're in there for a reason. I think there's a purpose to everything they do, whether it's in the air or it's underwater. They have a reason, but God knows what that is. Anybody's guess is as good as another's, I suppose. Their purposes are entirely unknown to us and we wouldn't understand it even if they tried to explain it to us."

For Stanton Friedman, it's a matter of exploiting what's down there of value.

"Besides just hiding from the guys above, there are a lot of resources at the bottom of the ocean," Friedman said. "There are nodules of all kinds of metals, almost pure metals. There are loads of diamonds, for instance, off the coast of Africa that are underwater. There are nodules of manganese and cobalt and other things at the bottom of the ocean, besides all kinds of strange sea creatures from which they may extract some very interesting biological or chemical things.

"It's a great place to have lunch," Friedman joked. "We'll have grilled eel!"

UFO Abduction From Undersea

USOs--Silly And Serious

By Sean Casteel

§ Are the USO occupants a playful, mischievous lot? Read how they toyed with a Mississippi fisherman and quickly drew the attention of official Navy investigators, who declared the case unsolved!

§ Betty Andreasson Luca is a famous UFO experiencer who believes the abducting grays are angelic creatures. Did those same angelic grays take her on a surprise trip below the ocean with a heavenly purpose in mind?

§ What is the true nature of the relationship between the USO occupants and humankind? Are they an aspect of our kindly creators? Or do they merely catalog us as an inferior species? Luca's underwater abduction offers some meaningful clues!

While USOs are reported much less frequently than their aboveground counterparts, there still remains a core of very interesting cases, including abduction by UFOs that enter the water and take the abductee to a whole other world inside the ocean. What follows is a pair of reports on human interaction with water related unidentified objects.

UFO Abduction From Undersea

MISS THE MISSISSIPPI AND YOU

An Internet posting called "Submerged Object, The Pascagoula USO of 1973" tells the story of a pair of Mississippi families who encountered a USO while fishing together on the night of November 6, 1973.

The families' experience occurred soon after the much better known alien abduction of Calvin Parker and Charles Hickson, who claimed to have been taken while they also were fishing near Pascagoula.

No author is credited with the online account, but the story begins, "Just off the coast to the southwest of Pascagoula, between the ship channel and Round Island, are some old oyster beds where fishermen go in the evening and fish for mullet with nets from small boats, usually catching about a ton of fish per boat."

The two families, the Ryans and the Rices, were at the beds fishing.

"It was a clear night," the article continues, "with not much moonlight. At about 8 pm, Rayme Ryan spotted an object under the water near his anchored boat in about five feet of water. The object, whatever it was, was about five feet in diameter and had an amber light that seemed to come from a light source that was about three inches in diameter.

"Rayme tried to poke the object with an oar several times," the posting goes on. "When he did, the light would dim, the object would move away a few feet and stop, and then the light would brighten again."

Rayme Ryan alerted the others, and the activity continued for about 30 minutes. In his frustration at apparently being toyed with by the object, Rayme struck violently at the light, which then disappeared completely. Meanwhile, all the fishing nets came up empty.

"Rayme moved off about a half mile from the spot for thirty minutes and caught the only fish that anyone caught that night," the posting said, "about 400 pounds. When he returned to the buoy that he used to mark his 'spot,' however, he found that the object had returned and was sitting beneath the surface."

THE FISHERMEN GO TO THE COAST GUARD

Rayme again called the others over and showed them. It was at this point that two of the fishing party went to the nearby Coast Guard station, arriving at around 9:30 pm.

"It was noted in the Coast Guard report that the two fishermen 'appeared sober and extremely concerned about the object.' Guardsmen Lawrence Nations and Charles Crews were dispatched to investigate, arriving at the scene at approximately 9:40."

The Coast Guard later sent a teletype that stated, "Station personnel did in fact locate object, which had an amber beam approximately four to six feet in diameter and attached to some bright metal object moving at four to six knots. Object did in fact cease illuminating, changed to a different course, and re-illuminated itself. Subject object traveled several courses while illuminated. Station personnel could not identify object and have never seen anything like it."

The object then vanished. A daylight search of the area the next day yielded no results.

"An indication of how seriously the incident was taken by the Coast Guard," the article said, "is the fact that they sent E.A. Wilbanks and Lt. Commander C.E. Dorman from the Naval Ship Research and Development Laboratory in Panama City, Florida, to investigate."

The two Navy officials interviewed the witnesses on November 9 and concluded:

1. At least nine persons witnessed an undetermined light source between the hours of 1930 and 2200 on the night of 6 November, 1973, at two locations separated by approximately one half mile.
2. The characteristics and actions of the light source are not consistent with those of known marine organisms or with an uncontrollable manmade object. The object cannot be identified at this time.
3. The presence of the light was associated with a significant variation in the fish catch in the area.

This case has many of the classic elements of a typical USO sighting, including the maddeningly playful way it toyed with the bemused fishermen. The fact that the object remained unidentified after a thorough naval investigation is further testimony to the authentic nature of the incident. As with the Shag Harbor case in the preceding chapter, there is more than the usual paper trail, with the Coast Guard freely admitting to being just as much in the dark as everyone else while making no obvious attempt to keep any relevant facts secret. Although we may never know everything about what the high level Navy officials were able to discover in their investigation, this USO incident seems to have mystified everyone who had a part in it.

TAKEN BELOW BY A USO

Betty Andreasson Luca is a housewife, mother and grandmother and also one of the most important alien abduction abductees ever to be investigated and documented. Researcher and author Raymond Fowler has written a series of books about Betty, which tell the continuing story of Betty's mind-bending encounters with diminutive gray aliens she believes to be angelic servants of Jesus Christ.

In April 1980, Betty volunteered to undergo the process of regressive hypnosis in an attempt to retrieve the buried memories of some of what happened to her at the hands of the aliens. As recounted in "The Andreasson Affair Phase Two," Betty was abducted into an alien spacecraft, which may seem fairly routine at this point.

But this time something different happened.

"Betty seemed to describe a glass dome above her," Fowler writes. "She appeared to be in a flying object that was hurtling toward a body of water."

The transcript of the hypnosis session picks up here.

Betty: Oh, and there's some water. We're going to crash into some water. Ohhh!

(Betty cringes in terror, bracing herself for an impact. At that point, the hypnotist interrupted the session and worked to calm Betty down. A few days later, the hypnotist returned Betty to that same moment.)

Betty: It's going so fast, oh! It feels like I'm staying still. I'm tilted a little. Oh, there's water coming up! Oooh! Oooh! It's like water is rolling around and around, and it's all white up there. Round and round, and it's stopping now and it's just water. But now I'm going the opposite way. Oooh!

(At this point in the transcript, Raymond Fowler makes the statement, "If Betty's hypnotically relived experience had any basis in physical reality, where had she been taken and why? The only known planet in our solar system with large bodies of liquid water is our own Planet Earth. Because of the apparently short time that elapsed between Betty's kidnapping and the alien craft entering the water, it's hard to conceive how it could have traveled anywhere except to one of our own oceans."

Betty resumes, saying, "That whole window is water, like in water. I don't know how to explain it. It looks like we're coming above some water. We are out of that water and we're into some place that looks like ice all around. It's just a big, big—looks like a big cave or tunnel of ice with icicles all over, but there's light around it."

Betty continues.

"And it's going through this icy place and getting into a bigger place where it's lit up. But the light doesn't seem to help light the room. I see like big, big icicles. Big ones all over the place. It's like I'm riding in a car and looking out the window. I'm just moving along besides these odd—I don't know what you would call them—icicles, square icicles or glass things. And there is light there. We keep on going and there's another room of them coming up.

"Oh, wait a minute. There are people there, there's some people in there. There are some people inside those things."

Her hypnotist asks, "You mean people-people?"

"Yeah, people like me," Betty replies. "Inside those glass things. But they're not moving."

BETTY SEES THE MUSEUM OF TIME

What Betty next reports is astounding in the extreme. She is seeing what Fowler called "The Museum of Time," living people encased in the ice in what we call "tableaux" in earthly terms. Each museum person on display has his or her own scenery appropriate to their time, wearing the correct clothes, etc. The figures look neither dead nor stuffed, and include babies and children as well as many different races. Betty repeatedly calls the clothing worn by the figures "funny and old-fashioned." There are too many of the cubicles for Betty to count.

"The thing [craft] is just slowly moving," Betty said, "through the tunnel of ice, and there are all these different frozen, or something or other, people there. There's even a dog and a cat and some animals too. There's a whole bunch of stuff there, but I can't see it all."

Fowler adds this further comment: "Several days later, when I received a cassette tape of this session, I found my mind rebelling. How could such things be true? And yet, how could Betty spontaneously and emotionally relive such detailed and intricate experiences unless they were true? A cold chill coursed through my body when Betty was describing people and animals enclosed in glassy cubicles in an icy cavern. Perhaps Betty was privy to the aliens' Museum of Time!"

One would like to conclude that Betty's experience offers a clue as to what the USO occupants are really up to down there. In any case, they seem to be the same entities as the airborne UFOs, with the same proclivity for abducting their Chosen Ones and subjecting them to frightening confrontations with as yet unknown and perhaps ultimately incomprehensible alien truths. Do the aliens maintain a kind of museum of human history? Are they proudly and lovingly displaying specimens of their creation, humankind? Or is there a darker mockery at work here, a kind of contemptuous collecting of samples of a shamefully lower form of life?

Betty tends to feel her encounter experiences have been with loving, God-believing creatures, and we can only hope that she is indeed on the side of the angels, even as they take her deep into our oceans to get a glimpse of eternity.

UFO Abduction From Undersea

Strange USO Encounters In Norway And Russia

By Sean Casteel

§ The Royal Norwegian Navy has long kept classified records of USOs, which they categorize as instances where something unequivocally "not a U-boat" has been sighted. Read about some of their most fascinating cases!

§ Do USOs have the ability to withstand missiles and grenades unscathed? Are our earthly weapons of destruction mere toys to them?

§ What strange form of life did Soviet frogmen encounter during what had been a routine training exercise? Who were the nearly ten-feet-tall swimmers they saw, strange divers who were impervious to cold and extremely dangerous depths?

Norway has a long history of USO sightings, with records dating back to before World War II. According to a website called ***UFO Evidence,*** the Royal Norwegian Navy takes the reports very seriously and classifies them in four categories:

1. "Certain U-boat," when it is clearly observed visually by competent personnel, unequivocally registered on electronic localizing equipment, or photographed.

2. "Probable U-boat," when there is no reason to doubt it is a U-boat, but the requirements for a certain U-boat have not been met. Twelve such reports are known from 1975 to 1989.
3. "Possible U-boat," 120 reports from 1975 to 1989.
4. "Not U-boat."

From 1969 to May 1983, the presence of unknown U-boats in Norwegian territorial waters was reported on some 200 occasions. By correlating the reports, it is possible to reduce the actual number of objects to 175, of which the Navy classified 75, or 42 percent, of the cases as "not U-boats." These are the sightings of greatest interest to Ufologists.

A GHOST ROCKET SPLASHES DOWN

Some of the earlier reports include a case involving a "ghost rocket" that crashed into Lake Mjosa, in southeastern Norway, on July 18, 1946.

"Between 12 and 12:30 pm," the website says, "several witnesses observed a V1-like object coming in low from the west, at about 50 meters height. The witnesses first heard a strong whistling sound, not exactly like that associated with aircraft. The object flew so low as to cause the trees to sway. It impacted in Lake Mjosa, about two kilometers from the western shore. It was cigar-shaped, about 2.5 meters long, with about one-meter-long wings placed one meter behind the nose. The front and back parts were shining like metal, but the middle section, including the wings, was dark. The wings seemed to flap a little, as if made of fabric. No fire, exhaust or light was seen.

"When it hit the lake," the report continues, "the water splashed several meters into the air. There was no explosion. The sky was clear and the water quickly calmed. Some witnesses thought they saw two objects, one in front of the other."

The Norwegian Defense High Command conducted an investigation, according to press reports of the period, but the documents have never been recovered. While the object witnessed could indeed have been extraterrestrial, when one observes the timing and location of the event, one must ask if perhaps we are dealing with a manmade object, perhaps even a postwar demonstration of secret Nazi technology first intended to defeat the Allies. The fact that Project Paperclip, in which many Nazi scientists were secretly brought into the U.S. to make use of their classified military technology, occurred around the same time as the Norwegian sighting adds a little fuel to that particular fire.

Another case, more readily identifiable as a USO, happened shortly before 7 am one Thursday in October 1952. Johannes Nordlien was waiting for coworkers when he suddenly heard a howling, jet-like sound. A moment later a saucer-shaped object, four meters in diameter, came at high speed from the west and passed by him 100 meters away. It impacted with a violent splash in the river Lagen. The object was white as snow, the online report says, and Nordlien clearly observed its flat and round shape as it hit the water. When his fellow workers showed up, the water was still boiling. The loud howling sound ceased as soon as he saw the object.

In this instance, we see the more familiar disc-shape and the frequently reported boiling water, similar to the sizzling sound that Chris Styles talks about in chapter one. What kind of propulsive power causes such an extreme change in the temperature of the water, even the icily cold waters of Canada and Norway? One of the many questions about USOs to which there are still no easy answers.

CLOCKED AT AN IMPOSSIBLE SPEED

UFO Abduction From Undersea

"Between November 12 and 22, 1972, an extensive search was conducted in the 1300-meter-deep Sogne fjord. Thirty naval vessels, plus NATO forces, participated. The excitement began when the military received a report of a U-boat. The next day, the 13th, two witnesses watched an 'aircraft-like object' maneuver along the fjord. The same night, four other witnesses observed a 'bright object' on the water. On November 20, at 1 pm, a U-boat was seen near Kyrkjebo, just as it headed away from Marenlandet toward the fjord's southern end. Fifteen minutes later it was seen by five police officers at Kvamsoy, a small island about 50 kilometers north of Kyrkjebo. Here frigates dropped mines on the object. If these were two observations of the same object, we have a speed of 200 kilometers per hour, a speed of which no known submarine is capable."

No wonder the Norwegian military and even NATO forces took such an interest. Like the sonar target reported on by Don Ledger in the first chapter, the speeds at which the USO were clocked cannot be duplicated by anything manmade at this point, and we are forced to look to something extraterrestrial or at least otherworldly as the object's source.

On the night of November 22, the report continues, four witnesses sighted four "rockets" shooting up from the water at Hermansverk. The rockets were silent and resembled small red balls of light. On the afternoon of the next day, an antisubmarine missile was fired at the intruders. The water's depth at the site was only 25 meters, and the shock waves of the explosion were so powerful as to throw small boats onto land ten kilometers away. Any conventional submarine would have been severely damaged and forced to surface; yet this vessel escaped apparently unscathed.

So along with incredible speed, the objects seem impervious to our attempts to attack them with weapons like missiles, which may seem like mere toys to an advanced alien race. But there is even more to the story.

At the same time, says the ***UFO Evidence*** website, other odd events were occurring. Aircraft experienced unexplained electronic problems. Yellow and green objects were seen flying along a mountainside. Navy vessels registered sonar contact with something in deep water. Surveillance craft encountered unidentified "helicopters" which executed breakneck maneuvers in fierce storms.

It seems the mysterious powers-that-be were laying siege to the area, creating several high strange events all at once, events that the Norwegian Navy was diligently investigating at the time in an earnest effort to find out what was going on.

Another example of a USO speeding through the Norwegian water at an impossible speed happened on July 4, 1973. Erling Bakke and his wife sighted a peculiar vessel on the water. It was 25 feet long and six feet high and had a protrusion on top.

"When we first spotted the strange object," Bakke reported, "which had a speed of at least 100 kilometers per hour along the water, we at first thought it had to be some sort of speedboat. And we were amazed at people going that fast. But suddenly the object rose up at a 45-degree angle and a moment later it was gone. Then my wife and I became aware of having witnessed a UFO up close. And it was a wonderful experience."

The object was black and thus clearly visible, the ***UFO Evidence*** website says.

On September 19, 1990, a Norwegian ship had a sonar contact with an "unknown U-boat" in the waters off Ona lighthouse, about 30 kilometers outside of Molde. The Norwegian ship sent international warning signals but got no response. In an effort to get the U-boat to surface, hand grenades were dropped in the water. When that failed, the ship shot off three Terne rockets. The sonar contact ended at that point, and the next day the search was called off. The Norwegian ship did manage to make a recording of its sonar contact with the unknown object.

The website posting concludes by saying that the Norwegian Defense Forces have never managed to force even a single submarine to the surface. The strange incursions are most likely tolerated for diplomatic reasons, given that Norway is situated in a sensitive area both geopolitically and militarily. The Norwegian defense authority regards a U-boat search as successful whenever the U-boat leaves the area, or at least that is what is said for public consumption.

Which again echoes what's been said earlier—out of sight, out of mind. Perhaps the Norwegians are simply grateful to be left alone by whoever pilots the "unknown U-boats."

USOs AMONG THE RUSSIANS

A fascinating story of USOs and their alien occupants comes from a website called ***UFOinfo.com.*** There is an article posted there called "Russian Underwater Encounters: What Lurks Beneath The Surface" by Paul Stonehill in which the following account appears:

"In the summer of 1982," Stonehill begins, "Mark Shteynberg, along with Lt. Colonel Gennady Zverev, were conducting periodic training of the reconnaissance divers, or frogmen, of the Turkestan and Central Asian military regions."

The two officers received a surprise visit from a very important official, a Major General named V. Demyanko, the commander of the military diver service of the Engineer Forces of the U.S.S.R. defense department. Demyanko informed the two junior officers that previously, during similar military training dives, "the frogmen had encountered mysterious underwater swimmers, very humanlike, but huge in size, almost three meters in height. The swimmers were clad in tight-fitting silvery suits, despite icy-cold water temperatures. At the depth of 50 meters, these 'swimmers' had neither scuba diving equipment—'aqualungs'—nor any other equipment, only sphere-like helmets concealing their heads."

The commanding officer, quiet understandably disturbed, sought to capture one of the creatures. He dispatched a special group of seven divers.

"As the frogmen tried to cover the creature with a net," Stonehill writes, "the entire group was thrown out of the deep waters to the surface by some powerful force."

The frogmen were ill-equipped to surface from such depths without decompression, and were thus rendered sick by the sudden resurfacing. The only way to treat the condition, called an "aeroembolism," was to put the ill-fated frogmen into a decompression chamber. There was only one such device in the region and it could contain no more than two persons. When the commander forced four frogmen into the chamber, three of them died. The remaining frogmen were made invalids, all of which Stonehill blames on "the usual Soviet military bungling."

"The files of the Russian Ufology Research Center contain much more information," Stonehill says, "about Russian underwater sightings, including statements of naval officers and intelligence operatives. It is safe to conclude that the Soviets before and the Russians now are preoccupied with the strange and sinister creatures lurking in their waters."

EYEWITNESS REPORTS

While Stonehill admits that most of these USO events are still classified by the Russian government, even after the fall of the USSR, he has managed to collect quite a few good cases.

For instance, in August of 1965, a crew of the steamship RADUGA, while navigating in the Red Sea, observed an unusual phenomenon. At about two miles away, a fiery sphere dashed out from under the water and hovered over the surface of the sea, illuminating it. The sphere was 60 meters in diameter, and it hovered over the sea at an altitude of 150 meters. A gigantic pillar of water ascended upwards as the sphere emerged from the sea and collapsed some moments later.

Another example took place in December 1977, not far from the Novy Georgy Island. The crew of the fishing trawler VASILY KISELEV also observed something quite extraordinary. Rising vertically from under the water was a doughnut-shaped object. Its diameter was between 300 and 500 meters. It hovered at an altitude of four to five kilometers. The trawler's radar station was immediately rendered inoperative. The object hovered over the area for three hours and then disappeared instantly.

Still another incident took place in June of 1984. A ship called the GORI was in the Mediterranean, twenty nautical miles from the Straight of Gibraltar. Two sailors were on the left bridge extension wing when both men observed a strange multi-colored object. The object stopped suddenly. One of the men grabbed his binoculars and said, "It's a flying saucer, a real saucer, my God, hurry, look!" The other sailor looked through his own binoculars and saw, at a distance, over the stern, a flattened out looking object that reminded him of an upside-down frying pan. The UFO was gleaming with a grayish metallic shine. The lower portion of the craft had a precise round shape, its diameter no more than twenty meters.

Around the lower portion of the object, one seaman saw "waves" of protuberances on the outside plating. The base of the object's body consisted of two semi-discs, the smaller being on top; they slowly revolved in opposite directions. At the circumference of the lower disc were numerous shining, bright, bead-like lights. At the edge of the UFO's bottom, which was easily visible, was something that looked like a pipe. It glowed with an unnaturally bright rosy color, like a neon lamp.

Suddenly the UFO jumped up several times, as if moved by an invisible wave. Many lights illuminated its bottom portion. The crew tried to attract the object's attention using a signal projector. By that time, the commanding officer was on the deck, watching with his men. The UFO seemed to be distracted by another ship, which turned out to be an Arab cargo ship on its way to Greece. The Arabs confirmed that the UFO hovered over their ship as well.

A minute and a half later, the object changed its flight trajectory, moved to the right, gained speed and ascended rapidly. The Soviet seamen observed that when it rose through the clouds, appearing and disappearing again, it would at moments shine in the sun's rays. The craft then flared up, like a spark, and was gone instantly.

The USO phenomenon is an international one, spanning the globe with its bizarre comings and goings and always two steps ahead of anyone who tries to bring it close enough to actually understand its ways and purposes. From speeding undersea objects detected by sonar to underwater alien swimmers ten-feet-tall, the mysteries continue to pile up on themselves, eluding, at least for now, our complete understanding.

UFO Abduction From Undersea

A Remarkable Deep Sea Adventure

By Sean Casteel

- § A sighting of a USO was reported more than 500 years ago by Christopher Columbus. Did the mysterious disc-shaped object have a message for the intrepid explorer?
- § Filiberto Cardenas' USO abduction took place before startled witnesses who saw him lifted into the air and taken to a waiting ship. Read the synopsis of what happened next!
- § What does the Cardenas case have in common with the celebrated abductions of Betty Andreasson Luca and Travis Walton? Exactly where do the USO occupants take their captives?

There are numerous cases from right here in America that deserve serious attention. For instance, as mentioned earlier, Christopher Columbus himself spotted an object on October 11, 1492, on the Santa Maria. As he passed over one of the deepest parts of the Atlantic Ocean, in an area that is now notoriously called the Bermuda Triangle, strange lights were seen flashing deep under the water. Then a large, disc-shaped object rose out of the water and sped off into the night sky. A few hours later, Columbus would discover the New World. Perhaps the USO in that case was a welcoming party and an acknowledgement that a new phase of human history was beginning.

According to researcher Carl Feindt, Columbus's log described the object as being like "the flickering of a wax candle," rising and falling. Campfires on the shore could not be used as an explanation as land was far beyond the horizon.

"Indeed," says the website ***UFO Experiences***, "Columbus' logbooks describe many bizarre occurrences witnessed during their long voyage to new lands. These included seeing birds that should not have been so far from land, yet they were far out to sea."

The logbooks also recorded seeing a ship's mast weighing 120 tons floating in the ocean, though Columbus' were thought to be the first European ships in the area. There is also mention of stars that "danced in the sky."

On the other side of the American continent is the Santa Catalina Channel, which separates mainland California from the Island of Catalina.

"This stretch of water is as deep as Mount Everest is high," the same source continues, "and objects have been seen both entering the water and emerging."

Preston Dennett, a California UFO investigator with impressive credentials, reports that in 1992, hundreds of unexplained objects were sighted near the Santa Monica Mountains.

"Many of these objects were seen, not descending from the sky, but rising up, as though emerging from the water nearby. Over 200 craft were seen emerging silently from the ocean on June 14, 1992. They hovered for several seconds before shooting off into the sky. Witnesses filed reports with police as far away as Malibu. A wealth of reports filtered up to the Coast Guard, but they refused a request to search the area of the sightings."

UFO Abduction From Undersea

One cannot help but observe that the two sightings, Columbus' "wax candle" and the Santa Monica Mountains armada, took place almost exactly 500 years apart. The timing is at least interesting though difficult to interpret.

In 1989, a large object was seen by multiple witnesses and picked up on sonar, resting on the surface of the water in the Pacific Ocean. It released several smaller objects before submerging. It was tracked on sonar heading towards the Santa Catalina Channel prior to disappearing.

Several researchers, such as the well-known Bill Birnes and Stanton Friedman, continue to investigate reports of USOs, assessing their intentions or threat level. It seems that one thing USOs do more frequently than UFOs is to "split apart" or release large numbers of smaller craft. UFOs have been known to do this also, but with the underwater variety it appears to be more common.

THE STRANGE CASE OF FILIBERTO CARDENAS

Having given an overview of many of the most reputable and some slightly less well known USO cases, we now come to the abduction of Filiberto Cardenas, the primary subject of this work. As we will discover, not only was Filiberto abducted by a USO, he was also given many strange prophecies by his captors, which came electrifyingly true shortly thereafter. There are many similarities, as we can clearly determine, to other abductions, and in many respects we could call this the Hispanic version of Travis Walton's abduction from the rural town of Snow Flake, Arizona.

It all began on the evening of January 3, 1979, when Cardenas was in his gift shop in Hialeah, Florida, and received a phone call from his friend, Fernando Marti. Marti asked Cardenas to accompany him to buy a pig from the local merchants to roast the next Sunday. Marti and his wife and daughter arrived at Cardenas' place of business. They then set out on their errand. After stopping at two different farms, they were still unable to find an acceptable *puerco* for their feast. As they went along looking for another possible source, they turned off on to a rural road that was in poor condition. At that point, the car began to lose power.

After checking the engine, the two men could not figure out what the problem was. The engine next began to reflect red and violet lights in sequence. At the same moment they heard a strange noise, like a "swarm of bees," according to Marti. Both the sound and the lights illuminating the engine increased and the whole car began to shake. Marti's wife began to scream in panic, believing it was an earthquake. Filiberto, who was in the process of examining the engine, intended to go over to the open car window to comfort her, but became paralyzed instead—frozen under the hood of the car. Then the same force that paralyzed him began to lift him and suspend him in the air. Marti was able to observe the moment, hearing Cardenas shout, "Don't take me! Don't take me!" The noise and the light ceased and everything seemed to return to normal. Marti next looked up and saw a UFO ascending into the sky. Fearing for his wife and child, he shouted "They have taken Filiberto!" He tried to start the car, which took several attempts before the engine turned over.

Marti felt compelled to tell the police, but feared he would not be believed or worse that he would be accused of having done something to Cardenas. He decided to inform the police anyway, and also called Cardenas' wife, saying "A light took Filiberto away."

Meanwhile, Cardenas awoke onboard the UFO, in a seat that seemed to hold him in place by some kind of suction and restrained all his movements. He saw three strange figures, one of whom placed a strange helmet on his head and spoke to him in a language he thought sounded like German. He was shown projected images, as on a television, of scenes from the past, present and future of mankind. He was then taken to a smaller ship that discharged from the mother-ship. He saw a beach approaching, and then the UFO plunged into the sea. All was obscured by the incredible velocity at which the ship moved.

A DROP IN THE OCEAN

The ship veered to the right and began to lose speed. In front of them, Cardenas could now see a tunnel with walls that seemed illuminated as if they were phosphorescent. The ship entered the tunnel and then emerged in a place that was completely dry. It looked like a large cavern, but he noticed there were no stalactites or stalagmites. The area was huge. He noticed two symbols, one of them being a serpent, as large as "an electric light pole," Cardenas later said. The other image was similar but smaller. His captors took him from the ship and told him to sit down on a large rock.

The comparison here to the Betty Andreasson Luca case revealed earlier should be considered. Like Luca, the UFO that transported Cardenas quickly plunged into the sea and emerged in a dry alien environment. While in Luca's case the surroundings were icy, it is still remarkably similar to the large cave to which Cardenas was taken.

In the cavern area, Cardenas was welcomed by a human-looking figure who said he was from earth and had long worked with the UFO entities. He seemed to be saying that Cardenas was most fortunate to be receiving instructions from "beings like us." After some further conversation, and a quick trip to what commonly is accepted as being an undersea alien city, Cardenas was returned to a pasture near where he had been originally abducted.

UFO Abduction From Undersea

THE FUTURE FORETOLD

Along with the trip beneath the sea, Cardenas received several predictions from the aliens in 1979 that have come unerringly true in the years that followed.

Those predictions included everything from the succession of the popes to the 1985 earthquake in Mexico City, the election of President Ronald Reagan, and the demonstration by Chinese students in Tiananmen Square in 1989. Cardenas also prophesied the assassination in 1981 of Anwar Sadat and the Gulf War against Saddam Hussein in 1990.

All of these prophecies are included in this expanded edition of "UFO Abduction From Undersea" by Sanchez-Stevens. Unlike many abductees who become fearful of their own shadow after their initial confrontation with other-worldly forces, Cardenas has encountered everything that is good about the abduction phenomenon—benevolent, welcoming aliens, "television" images that imply a deep and abiding interest in the future of mankind, as well as displays of human courage that serve to thrill and inspire us fellow earthlings. With all of this in mind, now is the moment to take a breather and then proceed to read on!

UFO Contact From Undersea
by
Virgilio Sanchez-Ocejo

GLOBAL COMMUNICATIONS
EX LIBRIS
POST OFFICE BOX 753
NEW BRUNSWICK, NJ 08903

UFO Abduction From Undersea

UFO Abduction From Undersea

DEDICATION

I dedicate this work to my beloved wife, Maria Elena for her courage and valor during the difficult times of this investigation. Her faith in our sincerity of purpose never failed.

ACKNOWLEDGEMENTS

My appreciation and thanks to Sr. Mario Rodriguez who favored me with his gracious support. Also to all the professionals and friends who intercommunicated and assisted directly or indirectly in this investigation. Also to Don Pedro Perriz, Sr. Fabio Zerpa, Dr. J. Allen Hynek and Mr. Allen Hendry, and for the cooperation and interest of the innumerable others who contributed in so many necessary ways which made this effort a success.

Virgilio Sanchez-Ocejo

UFO Abduction From Undersea

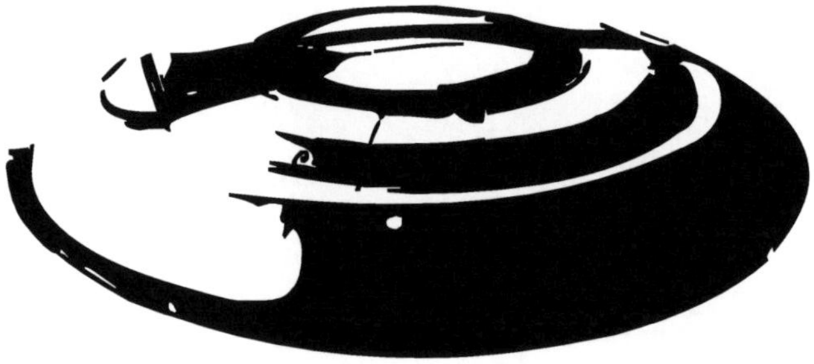

UFO Abduction From Undersea

PUBLISHERS PREFACE

The UFO abduction of Filiberto Cardenas of 60 East 38th Street, Hialeah, Florida, is an important contribution to the body of UFO literature because this may be the first case on record where the original abductee was able to successfully introduce another person into the contact events and to actually take them aboard an alien spacecraft with him.

An important aspect of this case is Cardenas' willingness—after six weeks of recovery from the first shocking experience—to come out in public and tell the details in his own name and identity. The reason for this position is his absolute conviction, after an unbelievable amount of proof of the reality of the physical experience in full waking reality, that it is essential that the public be made aware of what is really going on and how much we are all affected by it. He has a message to tell and is impelled to disseminate it as widely as possible for him to do.

He has been advised, and shown, that he is not the only human being to be contacted by these particular space entities. He was told that he would recognize the others as he came in contact with them. There is some indication that one of these others has already been turned up in Brazil.

Another feature of this case that is becoming more evident in substantial contact cases, is considerable indication that he was identified a long time ago, earlier in his life, and that his life experiences may have been guided to some degree up to this point.

He has been a very honest, hard-working man and a determined husband and father. He was not particularly interested in the UFO phenomenon until this chain of events came about. But his fortune took a turn for the better after the contacts began and he is now rearranging his life to give himself more time to devote to the study of what is happening to him, and to others, and to tell the sleeping world what is really happening.

When the contacts began he owned a small gift shop called

Zarabanda, at 4150 East 4th Avenue, Hialeah. He sold that and bought out a small filling station and automobile service shop called Barbara Service Center, Inc., at 4105 East 4th Avenue, which was then no big money maker. He developed the service station business into a highly successful operation, but it took all of his time, and most of his wife's, all days of the week and Saturdays and Sundays. He needed more time to conduct his own investigation into what was happening to him and to tell others who would listen to what was going on. He sold the business on his birthday, the 31st of October, and began to make plans to visit UFO conferences and investigators around the country to see how much was happening to others. That is the day I met him for the first time.

Filiberto's experiences actually began on 3 January 1979, and investigation of the case was most ably undertaken by Dr. Virgilio Sanchez-Ocejo, Jr., an Attorney and local UFO investigator and researcher who was working diligently on a number of substantial UFO cases already. Sanchez entered the case on 4 January, the day after the first abduction, while Cardenas was still in the clinic, and began the long and highly detailed debriefing. He developed details and tested the data. He arranged for medical and psychological, and even neurological examinations of the witness and provided a hypnotherapist and expert on the subject to conduct regressions of the witness back to the actual contacts to develop details. The witness was found to be perfectly normal in every respect, except for the body marks, skin abrasions, and systemic disfunctions resulting directly from the UFO contact. Sanchez was assisted by Mr. D'Agustino, an electronic Engineer, for many years a UFO investigator and MUFON representative in his country Uruguay, South America. Mr. D'Agustino is now living in Miami.

On the 3rd of January, at about six PM, a Thursday evening, Filiberto Cardenas, then 46 years old, was snatched by a buzzing object that emitted a beam of violet-bluish-white light which caused him to float up the beam and out of sight of his three friends with him. He seemed to go into a darkish bag-shaped (later described as roughly football-shaped) object which then flew away to the west with Cardenas aboard.

Filiberto and three members of the Marti family, Fernando 46, his wife Elizabeth 36, and daughter Mirta 13, of 8632 NW 35th Court, were returning from an unsuccessful effort to buy a suckling pig for a Sunday-night supper. The farmer they had gone to see had no more pigs for sale and they were returning to U.S. Highway Route 27, also known as Okeechobee Road, to go back home. Cardenas' 1970 Chevrolet Station Wagon developed electrical problems. The headlights and all other lights went out and the engine stalled, and the car came to a stop near Florida's Turnpike Extension. When Fernando tried the starter there was no electrical current al all. Fernando, who was driving at the time, and Filiberto got out and opened the engine hood and looked in at the engine to see what was wrong, Cardenas said.

"At that moment the engine began to reflect different colors, red, violet, blue, orange and then a bluish white." They heard an intense buzzing noise, "like many thousands of bees," Cardenas said. "I tried to move but I was paralized in position, unable to do anything—even unable to move my arms. I could hear the screams of the women in the car. I looked down and saw that I was suspended in the air and rising. When I was 8 to 10 feet above the car everything went dark, and I don't remember what happened.

"The next thing I remember is waking up to consciousness on my hands and knees, and two bright lights rushing at me. I heard brakes screeching and tires skid, and the lights swerved and came to a stop. I was helped from the road by a man taking my collar and leading me off the road. I learned later that this was near 137th Avenue on the Tamiami Trail, some 16 miles from where my car stalled."

A motorist called Police and Patrolman William Christian of the Fifth Precinct Station came and picked Cardenas up. This was about 8:15 PM, two hours after he had been elevated up the beam of light before the eyes of his friends. The police officer later said that Cardenas told him he had no idea what had happened. When I interviewed Cardenas he told me that he did not dare tell the policeman what he knew for fear of being considered crazy.

Meanwhile, Fernando Marti, who was also looking under the hood with Cardenas, saw the engine reflecting the various light colors and then saw Cardenas' feet ascending above the hood, to his left. He also felt weightless and jumped further into the engine area, on top of the hot engine, and grabbed hold—which probably saved him from Cardenas' fate. When the light dimmed and he felt weight again he looked out and saw Cardenas rising and shouting, "Let me go, let me go!" He watched Cardenas float up the beam of light until he entered the dark bag-shaped form that then flew west.

Fernando ran around the car to comfort the screaming, trembling women and told them, "They took Filiberto—they took Filiberto!" Fernando's wife Elizabeth had been in an earthquake in California, and fearing the same thing when the car started shaking had grabbed Mirta and pulled her across her lap, putting her arms around her for protection.

Fernando jumped into the car and tried the ignition again and this time there was spark and the engine truned over and started but ran very roughly—like it was not getting enough gas or something. The car chugged forward slowly and then began to improve a little, finally running all right again. Fernando stopped at the nearest facility and called the police to report the problem, but they told him to go to a pay phone and call back. He got back into the car, which started OK this time, and they drove to Hialeah to a pay phone. He called the police again and reported what had happened and Cardenas' disappearance. Then he called Cardenas' wife, Iris, and told her that an object with a large light had taken Filiberto. She wanted more details and he tried unsuccessfully to explain something he himself didn't understand. Mrs. Cardenas began to cry.

When Fernando hung up the phone, Iris got a nephew to drive her to where Filiberto had disappeared, and after checking with the police and finding that they knew nothing more than Marti's call, she and the nephew set out to see what they could find out. They didn't find anything at the scene.

When Cardenas was found about 8 PM, the police notified Mrs. Cardenas and she rushed to the station and took him to a local clinic for treatment.

"I would find it hard to believe if I read about it in a newspaper," admitted Marti, "but I was there with my wife and daughter. We were all terrified by the light and the noise," he said. "When it ended Filiberto had vanished."

"Before this happened," Cardenas said, "I scoffed at UFOs. Now I know differently."

Someone said that a checkup should be made for radiation if this was in fact UFO related. The local clinic was unable to treat or examine for such effects and Cardenas was taken to Miami's Jackson Memorial Hospital about 01:30 in the morning of the 4th to see what they could do. His medical records show that he complained of pains in both knees and out-of-focus vision in the last hour. Following X-rays and a general examination, the hospital noted, "Stable vital signs," a 0.2x0.2 centimeter abrasion on his forehead and a 2x2 centimeter yellow lesion on his right shoulder. He was also checked for radioactive contamination at the hospital by an Air Force team sent up from Homestead Air Force Base, south of Miami. The tests were negative and he was released and sent home.

UFO Abduction From Undersea

Cardenas developed various odd symptoms, i.e. excessive thirst, profuse sweating, sulphurous body odor, short memory, hot and cold flashes, and sexual disfunction. His urine was a very dark yellow-brown and had a bad odor.

Homestead reported no unusual air activity observed by RADAR during the time of this abduction.

Dr. Jose Yedra, a local hypnotherapist who had no personal position on UFOs, pro or con, regressed Filiberto into the experience 4 times to develop details and help restore the lost memory. This had to be done in Spanish as Cardenas is not fluent in the English language. Cardenas spoke of being taken by 3 human-like alien entities dressed in tightly fitted bluish-white one-piece suits. He was taken to a beach someplace totally unfamiliar to him where he saw deep blue water, a narrow sand beach and reddish-brown to reddish-purple rocks rising steeply away from the beach sand. While the spacecraft hovered at ground level the aliens worked some kind of a lock on a rock. One of the aliens got out of the small craft they were in and pointed a "flashlight" kind of instrument at a large rock abutement. The rock parted and revealed a tunnel or a large cavern. More of the same or similar craft came out and they all took off and flew out over the ocean waves. Suddenly they all tilted down and descended into the water and went underneath the surface. He remembered being seated near the "glass" of the windshield, or port and seeing the sea water rush by at great velocity but it didn't seem to be touching the "glass".

One of the entities, Kiostros, spoke to Cardenas in good Spanish with a kind of Portugese or Italian accent, which the Cuban did not understand easily. Kiostros talked about the higher energy of the sexual organs, the need for a different religion, the sinking of California into the Pacific, the future disability of an actress who will become the First Lady of the White House, and the disastrous end of President Sadat's rule in Egypt before the end of 1981! More predictions included the death of another very famous actress, a cure for cancer, the Peoples Republic of China fighting Russia for control of Asia, an Arabic war in the middle east, eventually involving Saudi Arabia and Israel as well. But most important of all was that 6 people from Earth were coming back in a UFO craft in public to deliver a message. (This was supposed to occur after 3 months, April 3rd, and so far as is known it may have happened.)

(NOTE: we have a case in Brazil that happened exactly three months after Mr. Cardenas adbuction. Also when Cardenas said in his hypnotic regression, "after 3 months", we came up with

April 3 date.)

Cardenas returned to the abduction site several times, and each time he arrived there his expensive gold electronic watch would run very rapidly and gain time. He could audibly hear it whirr inside. For some time after returning, each time he touched it with his right index finger it would speed up and whirr again, and he demonstrated this for his wife, Dr. Sanchez and other friends. He took it to be repaired.

At the abduction site he would hear "their" voices in his head and he would be given information. Later he could do this without going to the site.

On 21 February 1979, about a month and a half after the first abduction he was directed to the same site again. By now he was asking if his wife, Iris, could accompany him, and this time he took her along. At around 03:00 a top-shaped UFO arrived and he and his wife were BOTH taken aboard the ship and did not return until nearly 06:00 AM the following morning! This time they were both aboard in full waking consciousness and remained fully aware and alert the whole time. They could both remember the whole experience without hypnotic regression.

These UFOnauts were described something like the beings encountered by Herbert Schirmer in Nebraska in 1967. The aliens wore tight-fitted blue-white one-piece suits covering everything except the face. The Cardenases observed a serpent-like emblem on the right breast of the garment and a button-like earphone over the right ear with a small antenna sticking out the top. The main physical difference was the smaller 4-foot size of the beings. They spoke telepathically to the Cardenases, and conversed among themselves in a language that sounded like Arabic.

The two male and one female crew members seemed fascinated by Iris Cardenas' painted fingernails and toenails. The aliens suffered from sneezing throughout the experience, and explained that there was something that emanated from human bodies that caused this in close proximity.

The control room in the spacecraft was surrounded by one wall of small 3-dimensional TV-like screens showing a great many things. Another wall was covered with illuminated colored buttons of many shades.

Mrs. Cardenas said that she pinched herself to be sure she was not dreaming. She also asked one of the aliens if she could touch him and he agreed. The material of his suit felt slick in one direction and rough in another, like tiny fish scales. His body was firm under the material of the suit.

UFO Abduction From Undersea

"They spoke to me of universal LOVE," Cardenas said, "And I have learned from them that this is what I must do—LOVE and help my fellow man." Cardenas experienced a period of time after the first abduction where he was telepathically influenced to say meaningless words and numbers for 5 minutes each night. He now reports heightened telepathic sensitivity toward others. He once sensed that his father-in-law need aid, and drove automatically to the spot where the man's car had broken down.

Although no spacecraft was actually seen on the first abduction, one was clearly observed by Filiberto and Iris the second time as it approached and hovered near their parked car in almost the same place as the first when Filiberto was snatched. The ship did not actually touch down, but hovered a few feet above the ground. It was as large as a refrigerated railroad car, roughly mushroom-shaped, and had a smaller gondola on the bottom. It was a dull silver-gray in color in the air until it "landed", and then a row of colored lights of blue, violet, silver and white came "on" and blinked all around the side of the mushroom-shaped larger upper part. More lights of the same colors blinked around the bottom of the gondola.

The Cardenas couple walked up to what looked like a plate-glass window, and then suddenly they were through the "glass" and inside the ship. They saw several narrow one-legged chairs with tall backs. The chairs could turn around. Then they saw the very human looking occupants of the ship. They were from 3½ to 4 feet tall (smaller than Filiberto) and were dressed in the tight-fitted silvery bluish-white one-piece suits previously described by Filiberto. The emblem worn on the right side of the chest looked like an "X" lying down with a raised serpent in the center. The aliens have big eyes that are oblique, like orientals, but they were longer and came farther around to the side of the face. They had a normal straight nose and a small mouth that never moved.

Iris lighted a cigarette inside the craft and Mr. Cardenas told her not to smoke "so that she would not contaminate the atmosphere inside the ship".

When Cardenas, telepathically advised of this second meeting, asked if he could bring his wife to the contact, he was told that "they" considered Iris and him a unity or that she was one with him and therefore could accompany him. Iris asked the aliens if they were the ones who had abducted two little girls from Puerto Rico (she had heard the story from a nurse when she was in the clinic with Filiberto), and they answered that they do not abduct little girls..., which relieved Iris of the fears for her 3-year-old daughter, Barbarita.

UFO Abduction From Undersea

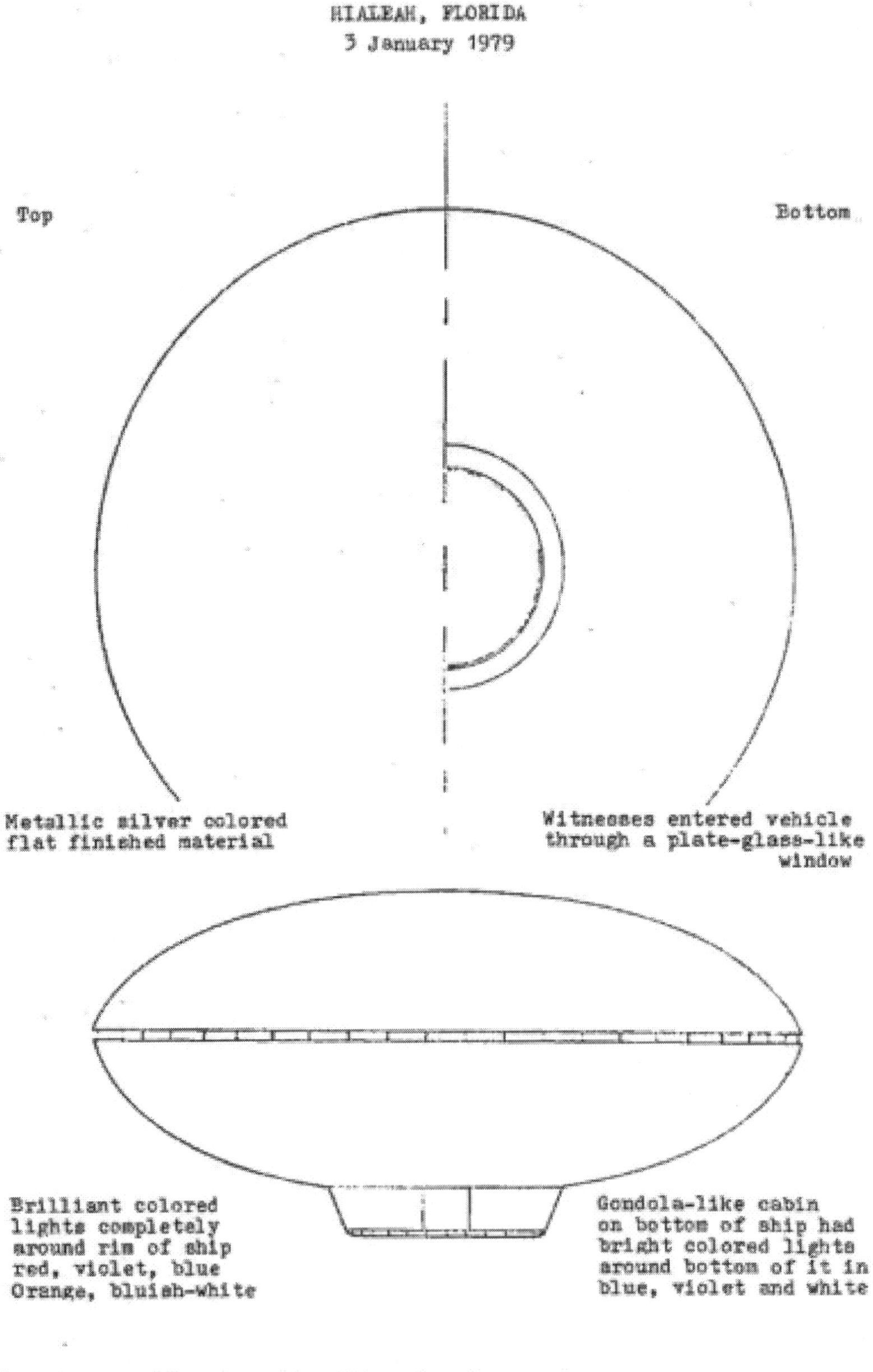

An erected drawing of the ship used on the second abduction, and believed to have been used on the first one also. From an original sketch by Iris Cardenas.

UFO Abduction From Undersea

The alien beings all had an identical arrangement of 5 thin cables that came from the lower waistline up to the neck of the suit and went inside. These cables did not hamper the movement of the beings in any way.

Filiberto says the aliens spoke of many things, but he does not want to elaborate on them at this time. Some things are best left to the future, that there is a time for everything. He and his wife were in the ship from about 04:00 to 05:15 AM. When they returned home—about 05:30—Filiberto immediately called Dr. Sanchez-Ocejo and told him of the second contact but that he couldn't say anything until after 10:00 AM. He would call Sanchez back later.

At exactly 10:00 AM a large mother-ship with 2 smaller disc-shaped objects flying around it was seen by hundreds of witnesses at Miami International Airport (10 miles from this most recent encounter). Mrs. Julia Gonzales and Mr. Ricardo Sanchez, airport employees working in the center of the airport runway area, stated that they observed all 3 objects clearly for several minutes. They also saw passengers who were boarding a flight for departure stop and stare at the unusual spectacle, and saw other airport employees watching the ships in the sky overhead. Gonzales called a local radio station to report the strange phenomenon and was referred to Dr. Sanchez-Ocejo, the same one who investigated the Cardenas case, whom they then called and reported the sighting, almost while it was still going on.

When Sanchez hung up the phone from that call, the second call from Filiberto, who was also trying to call him (on his instructions from the aliens to wait until after 10:00— to report the details of the second abduction aboard the spacecraft. Filiberto knew nothing of the airport sighting until Sanchez told him at that time, and then he began to wonder about the strange instructions to wait until after the specific time.

When Sanchez interviewed the airport workers from their particular sighting point and ascertained the exact position of the spacecraft, said to be about 11:00 o'clock from magnetic north and high in that direction, he could easily see that that position is DIRECTLY over the place where the Cardenas couple was taken aboard 5 hours earlier!

During the 4 hypnotic regressions on the first abduction, it was discovered that the alien beings first told Cardenas what they were going to do, and then they installed two very small (electronic) devices in his head—one behing each ear. After that they could transmit the same 3-D physical projections of scenes suspended in the air in front of him that they showed him in the

"TV panels" in the control room aboard the spacecraft. He received full sight and sound, as well as other sensory sensations such as heat and cold and smells. The scenes are just as real to him as waking reality experience except that they take place completely withing the "frame" of the scene, like a very sophisticated picture frame suspended freely in the air. His scenes of future events are shown to him in this way.

He was told that the only reason he is being shown future events is to demonstrate, in time, the reality of his contacts, so that people will believe him and will accept the "message" on universal LOVE which he has been given.

The aliens have their place and we have ours, except that WE have forgotten the real law of Universal Love—REAL LOVE FOR ONE ANOTHER, that is the key to solving all of our own self-generated problems of existance...

The contacts continue and Filiberto is being prepared for a larger mission. He wonders if the world is ready for, or wants help...

When I joined Dr. Sanchez-Ocejo in his investigation of this case, I was particularly interested in four special aspects of this phenomenon which I had found prominent in another very secret investigation I had been carrying on in that part of the world for some years. The secrecy was necessitated by the position of the contactee in his society and the harm that could come to him if it got out. Nothing was ever released on this case and no part of it was ever transmitted by mail. There was little likelyhood that the contactee in Hialeah could have known anything about the contactee in Puerto Rico, and I knew that the man in Puerto Rico had never heard of Filiberto Cardenas.

The four points in common were:

1. Material devices implanted in the bodies of the contactees by the extraterrestrial beings.
2. The contactees were taken to deep underwater bases by the extraterrestrial beings in both cases.
3. In both cases the witness was shown a sequence of dire events in store for Earth in our near future, and this was done with picture panoramas projected in the air by some mechanical means.
4. Both contacts have been going on for a long time and are still going on!

In both cases the time for release of this information to the world is NOW. I have inserted the summary report of the Puerto Rican case in the back of this book as an appendix. There are still other similar cases that mutually support these two cases also.

They will be detailed in future releases.

Here then are the complete details of the sensational UFO abduction of Filiberto Cardenas as revealed by the very able investigation of Dr. Sanchez-Ocejo and his special investigation team. It is a pity that more such investigations are not undertaken and published for those who seek to know.

A very pertinent point of interest; when I called the local newspapers about this case when I first found out about it, some three to four weeks after the first abduction, I was told that they considered the case suspect and not worth wasting any time on. Another paper said that it was very suspicious and they had ceased following it. A third said some nutty organization had gotten hold of the witness and was trying to exploit it. This piqued my personal interest because this was almost exactly what happened in the Bill Herrmann abduction case in Charleston, South Carolina, which ultimately turned out to have a vast amount of supporting evidence in it that was completely overlooked in the cursory interviews conducted by the media there.

We will have more of these and we encourage those new witnesses to come forward with their information as soon as possible.

Wendelle C. Stevens

UFO Abduction From Undersea

PROLOGUE BY THE AUTHOR

From the time I began studying UFOs in 1956, I always wished that some day I would come to discover everything about the phenomenon. I never could imagine how complex and complicated this might be. Though sometimes we felt discouraged, always something would come up to renew our interest, a note in the newspaper, someone would call to tell us of their experience or they were witnesses to another sighting, or something else. These things fired anew in us sparks of returning interest. The disbelief in the unknown, the fruitless search for some real evidence, a screw, a bolt of the strange apparatus so generalized, that which we call Unidentified Flying Object.

There are many and very good arguments that makes us think that we may be being visited by intelligently controlled vehicles, piloted or not, that do not belong to this terrestrial plane, our three-dimensional world. We call them extraterrestrials because they do not belong to our contemporary world. Their origin offers various possibilities: They could come from space. They could be travellers in time, or travellers from a parallel world. Our personal hypothesis is that the phenomena treats of perhaps a synthesis of all these possibilities, and perhaps even more.

Of the whole UFO phenomenon, what is most intriguing, astonishing and disconcerting are the cases of direct contact. Most of these occur unexpectedly and without notice. Also is the apparent lack of announcement by the contacted a disconcerting problem.

Here in Miami, on the 3rd of Juanuary 1979, there occurred one of the kidnappings, an abduction of a human being by a UFO. One difference in this one from many others is that it presented a wealth of information. There were tests and predictions given by the contactors. Up to now, all those who have participated in this investigation have been astonished. Finally they accepted it as it is.

For those who investigate the phenomenon, like myself, Dr. J. Allen Hynek, scientist and astronomer, and president of the Center For UFO Studies (CUFOS), has given us a form of classification for the distinct kinds of sightings. He has also provided some terms that have come into common usage.

NL - Nocturnal Lights. Unexplained lights seen in the night sky.

DD - Daylight Discs. Disc-shaped objects seen in daylight.

RV - Radar/Visual. UFOs seen by witnesses and also painted by RADAR at the same time

CE-I - Close Encounter Type I. UFOs seen at more than 500 feet distance.

CE-II - Close Encounter Type II. Physical evidence encountered at the place of the UFO contact. Marks on the ground. Broken branches, etc.

CE-III - Close Encounter Type III. Contact of some kind with the occupants of the UFO. This is the most extraordinary of the Close Encounters. The actual sighting and contact with the beings from the UFOs.

The UFO phenomenon decidedly contains physical aspects. It can be painted (registered) on RADAR, they emit light and sound, make marks on the ground, break branches from trees, stop automobiles, and cause psychological traumas in animals as well as in human beings.

But when a UFO case treats of a contact it becomes isolated in a short time. One reason is the fear that the witnesses feel of being ridiculed, fear of being ridiculed in front of their friends and family. This fear is paramount if the degree of strangeness is high. For this reason the witnesses to such a case isolate themselves. They feel confused in their experience and withdraw for fear of ridicule. This tendency to isolation is also abetted by the strangeness of the event.

It is relatively easy to inform oneself about the sightings of nocturnal lights and daylight discs. These do not expose the witness to critical judgement of his mental condition. To see a strange light in the night or a ship, aparently metallic, flying in the heights of the sky, generally does not expose the witness to ridicule. But, on the contrary, if he has seen a disc-shaped ship land with flashing lights near the patio of his house at 02:00 in the morning, and he sees small beings similar to humans, it is another thing entirely. This opens the invitation to ridicule it.

At first, some people frankly related their experiences, not only to their friends, but also to authorities. They encountered blank faces and even laughter and some of them were even persecuted as if they were possessed of the devil. Others confided in their spouses and in some intimate friends. In this case their experiences ultimately came to light after a time producing a delay in informing those interested. A sophisticated person, conscious of the reaction and the inclination to ridicule, will tell of a nocturnal light or a disc, but never an encounter of the third kind. Scientists and professionals have related their encounters with lights and discs, but they haven't reported a single case of humanoids or abduction. The curtain of ridicule effectively remains.

Today one must be endowed with valor, integrity and a high sense of responsibility to report experiencing an encounter of the third kind. He must be prepared to defend the truth of his experience, not only against ridicule, but also against skeptics and some religions. He also exposes his family to a type of attack that requires great personal honesty to endure, not only for himself but for his family as well. These conditions were faced and the responsibility was assumed by Filiberto Cardenas and his family. Thanks to them we are able to offer you this report of his experiences.

The experience of this man has been investigated by a special team of professionals including engineers, doctors, psychologists, neurologists, attorneys and a professional hypnotist. Also it received the special attention of Dr. J. Allen Hynek who maintained contact, and advised in difficult moments when we needed his cooperation. We are actually in communication with the Center For UFO Studies through his associate Mr. Allen Hendry. Likewise we have maintained contact in this process with Licenciado Don Pedro Ferriz of Mexico, with Sr. Fabio Zerpa, President of ONIFE of Argentina, and with Sr. Carlos Paz Garcia, President of IPRI of Lima, Peru.

The major part of this book, concerning the whole story of the experience, has been taken directly from the four hypnotic regressions performed on Sr. Cardenas. From an editorial point of view we have arranged them to offer a chronological sequence of the experience.

Almost all of the UFO abductions have a minimum common denominator. Usually the witness only remembers having seen a UFO, and very slowly, little by little, he begins to remember having been in the presence of "creatures" who are very different. The experience is normally blotted from the memory of the witness for a time. Later, by means of a dream or by vague recollections he begins to re-illuminate some details that the witness has suspected are involved in the unusual occurrence. The details of his experience almost always are found accumulated in the most profound depths of his consciousness.

UFO Abduction From Undersea

In the Cardenas case there were witnesses at the moment of abduction in the form of the Marti family. When they reported his disappearance to authorities a state of alert was imposed and a search for the missing man was begun. When he was returned two hours later he was discovered an impossible distance across the Everglades from his abduction point, in a confused and traumatic condition and was picked up by police authorities at the return site. The conditions evident produced a state of general anxiety to know what did occur. The police dedicated much time and attention interrogating everybody involved trying to verify the realities of these circumstances. Exhausted, the police investigator came to the conclusion that this must indeed have been a close encounter of the third kind, and to our astonishment he made this entry on the official police report under Type of Offense.

Other data that tended to corroborate what had happened was the physical marks left on the body of Mr. Cardenas. These have been described in the medical report of Jackson Memorial Hospital which we have a copy of, but which for ethical and professional reasons we will not reproduce here. Also we have been asked not to publish the names of some of the professionals who gave time and energy to this project. My gratitude to all of those whose only interest has been the scientific investigation of a phenomenon that concerns us all equally.

For those who believe in the existence of UFOs (more than 57% of the North American population, according to a recent Gallup Poll made in 1978) it will be easier to accept the story of what happened to Mr. Cardenas. For the minority, the skeptics, who refuse to accept the conclusions derived from our investigation, I am sure they will encounter substantial information they will find difficult to refute.

Is this experience of Mr. Cardenas real? For the moment each must draw his own conclusions. But there is no doubt that a time will come when we will know more about these CE-III cases. For now, it all seems incredible and even in part incomprehensible, but of one thing there is no doubt; the witness believes in what occurred, and I consequently do also.

Virgilio Sanchez-Ocejo
Miami, Florida

UFO Abduction From Undersea

BIOGRAPHY OF THE WITNESS

Filiberto Cardenas was born in the city of Santi Espiritu in the province of Las Villas, Cuba on 31 October 1933, to a family of scarce resources. He began his schooling in the Colegio "El Maja." Later he passed to el Colegio Clara Luz Farina, where he studied to the fourth grade. Later at Colegio La Salle he graduated from primary school. Moving with his family to Havana, Filiberto continued his education at the Instituto de Mariano to his third baccalaureate year. He studied physical culture and physical therapy and became an electrocardiac technician.

He enlisted in the Cuban Army in 1951. He survived the Communist revolution of Fidel Castro in 1959 in the grade of sergeant and shooting instructor. Persecuted by the new government, he was obliged to seek refuge in the mountains and from there fought until made prisoner in 1961. He carries nine bullet wounds in his body. He was imprisoned from 1961 to 1970, a time full of incidents such as head of a hunger strike for 21 days to obtain improvements in the prison.

Freed from prison, he arranged his departure from there to the United States, where he arrived on 6 February 1973. At the beginning of his exile he dedicated two years to the exercise of his profession in massage and physical therapy at a private clinic operated by some doctors. From 1975 until the beginning of 1976, profiting by the boom in construction he worked at a number of different tasks and jobs trying to get ahead. Saving his money, he bought near the end of 1976 a gift shop and botica business that he operated under the name of Zarabanda Gift Shop. In September of 1979 he sold this business and bought a gasoline station in the city of Hialeah which he owned and operated during the initial investigation in this case.

UFO Abduction From Undersea

CHAPTER 1

The Experience Begins

The first time we made contact with Filiberto Cardenas was on Friday the 5th of January, in the evening. When we arrived at the Cardenas house we were received by Sr. Fernando Marti, a friend of Cardenas. He took us to the living room of the home where we were surprised to see at least 30 other people. In a short time someone came and indicated that we could pass on back to another room where we could find Filiberto. There, in his bed, we found him surrounded by members of the press. We took a seat in the corner of the room and for several minutes dedicated ourselves to observation of what was going on in that house. A state of indescribable excitation, not only of Filiberto but also of the reporters, reined. The reporters were constantly bombarding the witness with questions, from all parts of the small bedroom. Filiberto tried to answer honestly to some, though to the majority he responded, "I do not know what happened to me".

We knew some of his story from the press and though it seemed at first a little fantastic we decided to proceed with necessary caution as he related bit by bit, in that room full of people, trying to be responsive to all, a story when he really had no idea of what all had occurred. We were absorbed in what was happening when suddenly Filiberto turned toward us and asked in a routine manner, "What paper are you form?". "We are not newsmen," I answered, "We are here because what has happened to you has already happened to other people." He did not let me continue. Filiberto raised up in his bed and looking straight into my eyes he said to his wife Iris, who was sitting in another corner of the room, "Mami, don't let them go. Don't let these people go."

He said nothing else and we remained there observing the developments in the interviews. When the last of the newsmen had gone and we were alone I began to explain who we were and what we investigated. Filiberto interrupted me with the same question, "But, this has happened to other people? I thought that mine was a unique phenomenon." We talked until after 01:00 in the morning and we decided to investigate this case to try to understand what had occurred. At this time we did not go into great detail because we did not want to influence in any way the truth that we were beginning to suspect, that we had before us a real case of extraterrestrial abduction.

We had to prepare our equipment for investigation and begin as soon as possible. It was clear that for this kind of case there were no rules or procedures to follow. We had to make up a team of investigators with professional references established who would work voluntarily. This took me several days.

Meanwhile we had asked Filiberto to discontinue his contact with the newsmen as soon as possible because we couldn't work with interruptions nor pressures from outside. Filiberto did as requested. He cancelled his interviews and only finished those already promised. This gave me time to form a team. Filiberto demonstrated a tremendous interest in finding out what had in fact happened. However, the first thing he wanted to do was go through with a planned reunion with friends and acquaintances the following Sunday to raise his spirit. They had planned a small get together with music, songs and some food which we also attended Sunday the 14th. In the evening we got together with Filiberto, Mario and I in his house, and we asked him to relate quietly and in great detail all he could remember of his experience.

In the evening of 3 January 1979, Filiberto was in his shop when he received a call from his friend Fernando Marti. Fernando asked to be accompanied to the outskirts of the city to buy a pig that he wanted to roast the following Sunday. Fernando had not been able to buy one from the local merchants because the fiestas of Christmas and the New Year had taken them all. Also because Filiberto owned a station wagon that he thought to use so as not to get his own autmobile dirty. In a short time he appeared at the business of Filiberto with his wife Mirta and their daughter Isabel, 13 years old.

Fernando agreed to drive the station wagon after Filiberto said he was tired. With Fernando at the wheel, Filiberto on the passenger's seat in front and Mirta and Isabel seated in the back, they drove out of the city by Highway 27, also known as Okechobee Road. Along the road they went to two farms where they failed to find any pig for sale. Still further on, and losing

UFO Abduction From Undersea

Above—The Cardenas Service Station in Hialeah, Florida.
Below—The Cardenas home in Hialeah with the station wagon from which Filiberto was abducted parked in front of the gate. Reporters had taken over this place by the time Filiberto got back from the Police Station and Hospital after his abduction.

patience, they saw another sign indicating a farm with pigs for sale. It was already about 6:00 in the evening. They turned off on a lateral road, following an arrow that marked the desired direction, and from there another rural road, in bad condition, until they arrived at the farm. The farm was operated by Sr. Jose Hernandez, then in charge of the property, who informed them that he did not have a single pig left for sale.

Confronted with another failure, they decided to terminate the search and return to the city. As they came off the bad road onto the lateral road, the automobile began to lose force and the engine quit. They coasted around the turn and came to a stop on the right side of the road. Mrs. Marti said while they were checking she would get out and cut some branches with flowers that grew alongside that road, which she proceeded to do. After collecting various branches and putting them in the trunk, she and Isabel got back into the automobile. Fernando, at the wheel, tried to start the engine but there was no response at all. From the time she got out to cut the flowers, Mrs. Marti heard a sound in the air, but nobody paid any importance to it because small aircraft were common in that area. It was later in the investigation that the witnesses remembered that the sound had been heard before the abduction also.

Fernando exclaimed, "What is the matter with the car?". The men looked at each other and they got out of the car again. Fernando opened the hood over the engine and they both looked in trying to see what could be wrong, to localize the failure. Fernando insisted, "I can see nothing that is abnormal for which the car has no electricity." He returned to the seat and tried to crank the engine again. Nothing, not even the lights would function. "Anything happen?", he exclaimed. Filiberto was in front of the car looking under the hood near the battery. He didn't know much about mechanics and tried to see if the cables were loose or grounding, but they seemed to be firmly connected to the battery. Fernando got out of the car again and looked down past the hood near the windshield thinking that the problem could be in the general electrical connection situated near the steering column.

They were like this, Filiberto under the hood in front and Fernando under the hood on the right hand side, laying over the top of the engine so as to see behind the engine, when suddenly both of them came to realize that the engine was reflecting red and violet in sequence. At the same time they commenced to hear a strange sound. Fernando later described it as "Like many bees". The sound as well as the light that illuminated the engine

UFO Abduction From Undersea

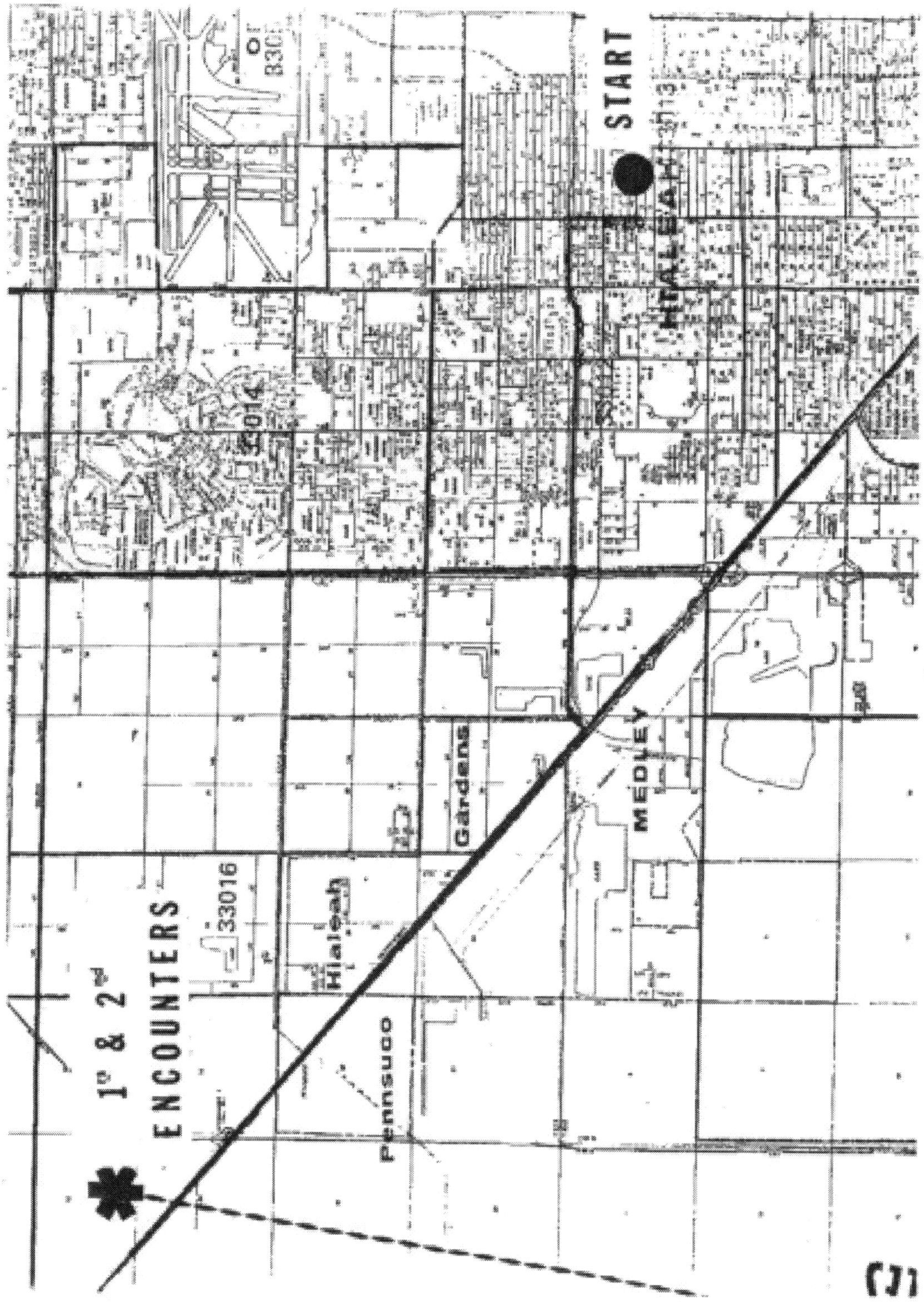

increased and the whole car began to shake. At this time Mrs. Marti was sitting in the posterior seat with her daughter Isabel at her side who began to shout in panic. The Marti family came to live in Florida from California because of a bad earthquake. This had left in Mrs. Marti a profound impression, and her first thought, upon hearing the sound and seeing the light, was that they were facing a similar phenomenon. She pulled Isabel down across the seat of the car and covered her with her body as she screamed in panic.

Upon hearing the shouts in the middle of the sound and the lights, Filiberto, who could see no cause of the problem with the motor, tried to run to the women's aid but he felt paralized and could not move. He could not move from his position nor could he change it. He felt as though something restrained and impeded his movement. Fernando, in fear, tried to crawl further into the engine compartment, seeking protection under the hood of the engine, until he also found himself immobile with his feet sticking out from under the hood in the air. He could not move.

Filiberto felt as though the force that paralized him began to lift him and suspended him in the air. Fernando, inside the motor compartment, could see Filiberto as he began to rise. At the same time he could hear Filiberto shout, "Don't take me... Don't take me". Filiberto could see the car going down as he ascended. "I was about 3 feet above the ground when I felt like everything was becoming dark and I lost track of what was happening."

The noise and the light, which had become an intense white, ceased and everything seemed to return to normal. According to the witnesses, everything related so far occurred in fractions of seconds. Fernando came out from under the hood of the car and looking toward the sky saw "Like a bulky object that ascended and then moved away." Full of fear, and after remembering that his wife and daughter were still in the back seat of the car, he shouted, "They have taken Filiberto... Mama, they have taken Filiberto." He went into the car and looked under the seat for something to defend himself with, but couldn't find anything. Then he got in the driver's seat and tried to crank the engine again. After several attempts the engine began to start but it ran very poorly, "Such as when it is out of gasoline." He also saw smoke coming from the engine area. When he got the car to move he returned toward the highway. The auto little by little began to function more normally. Along the way he thought he should advise the police, but he was afraid they would not believe him and would think he had done something to Filiberto. Then he

UFO Abduction From Undersea

Above—The station wagon stopped in the exact place where it had stalled when Filiberto was abducted. The men were inspecting the engine.
Below—Filiberto started out from under the hood of the car to see why the women were screaming inside.

UFO Abduction From Undersea

Filiberto had taken one step when the beam of light was turned on him and he became completely paralyzed. He ascended up the beam of light in this position yelling for help.

decided he had to run the risk, and near the edge of town he stopped at a service station on upper 29th Street. From there he called the police, but they told him that he would have to call them back from a private number so that they could verify the call.

He then called Mrs. Cardenas and said that, "A light took Filiberto away." Mrs. Cardenas thought that he was trying to tell her that they had run a red light and had an accident and that Filiberto was injured. Fernando got back into the car and he, Mirta and Isabel continued along the road and as they came into the town of Hialeah they saw a police car stopped in a commercial zone. He stopped and explained to the Sergeant in the patrol car what had just happened.

Meanwhile, Mrs. Cardenas got into another car and headed for the service station from which Fernando had called, trying to find at every corner the supposed accident with her husband injured. She spotted the station wagon stopped in the commercial zone, together with a number of police cars that had been summoned to that place.

There she found out what had really happened. At first, the police presumed that Filiberto would be found lost or unconscious in the outskirts. Fernando, in his confusion, thought that he might be mistaken about what he had seen, and decided to go back and look. Since it was already night and dark, the police tried to make contact with the Air Base at Homestead, to send an airplane or a helicopter with lights to the place.

While all this was taking place, Filiberto first became aware of a sound of tires running on pavement. That was his first reaction. Then he observed some very bright white lights near him, moving. These came from a car that had almost run over him. He was in the middle of a different highway, the Tamiami Trail, later found to be some 16 kilometers south of the place where he disappeared, and two hours later. He was half-unconsious, exhausted, and sweating profusely. The driver of the car got out and spoke to him in English, which he did not understnd. Filiberto was crawling on hands and knees and the driver tried to stop him. The stranger grabbed him by the jacket and almost dragged him toward the shoulder of the road. There he left Filiberto and later made it to a telephone and called the police. He reported that he had encountered a man crawling along the median between the two lanes of highway, and the danger he ran of being hit by some unsuspecting driver. The first officer to arrive on the scene was Partolman William Christian, who at first thought that he had a drunk or someone who had

UFO Abduction From Undersea

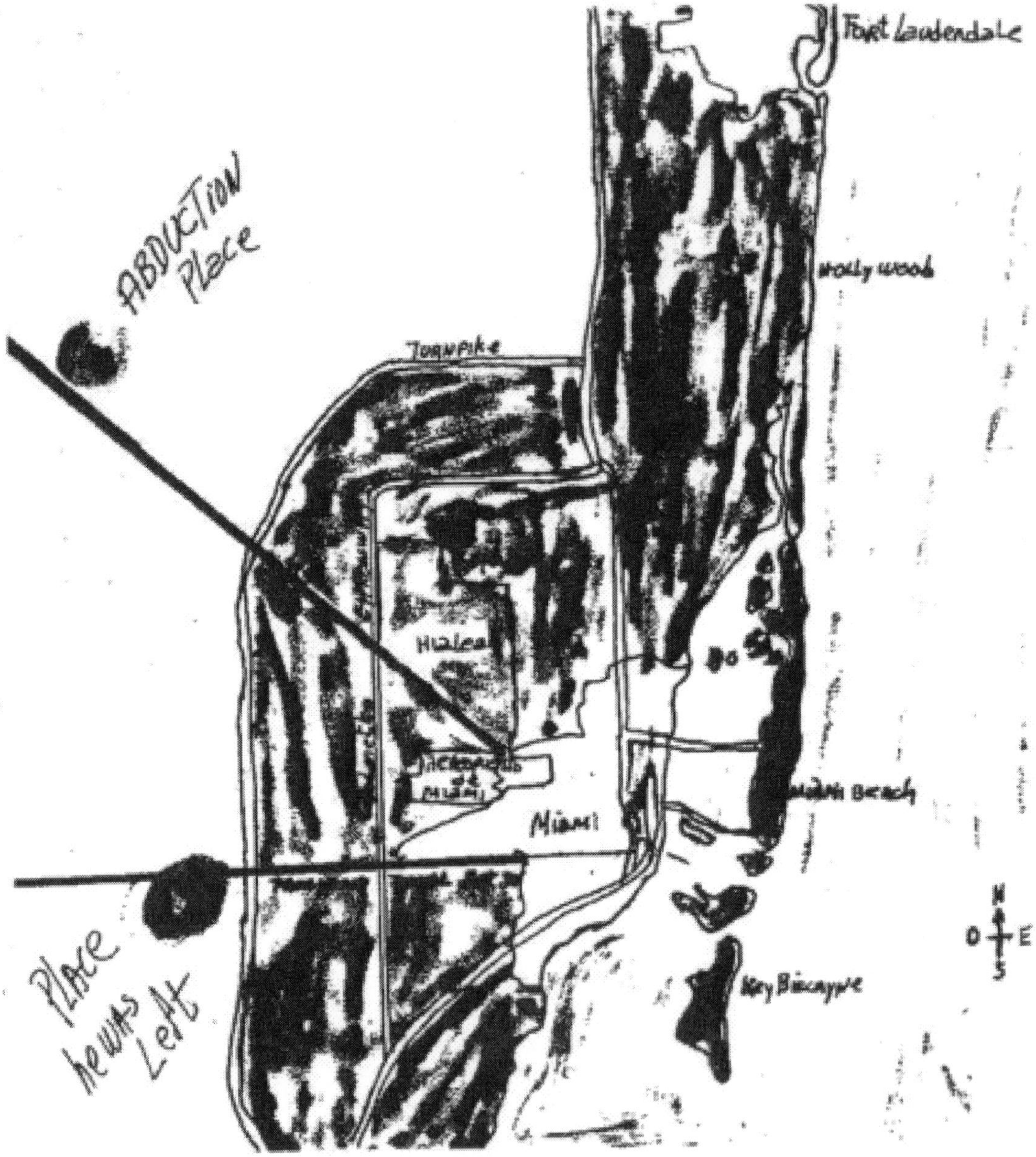

This hand drawn sketch of the event sites was made by Sanchez-Ocejo during the initial investigation.

UFO Abduction From Undersea

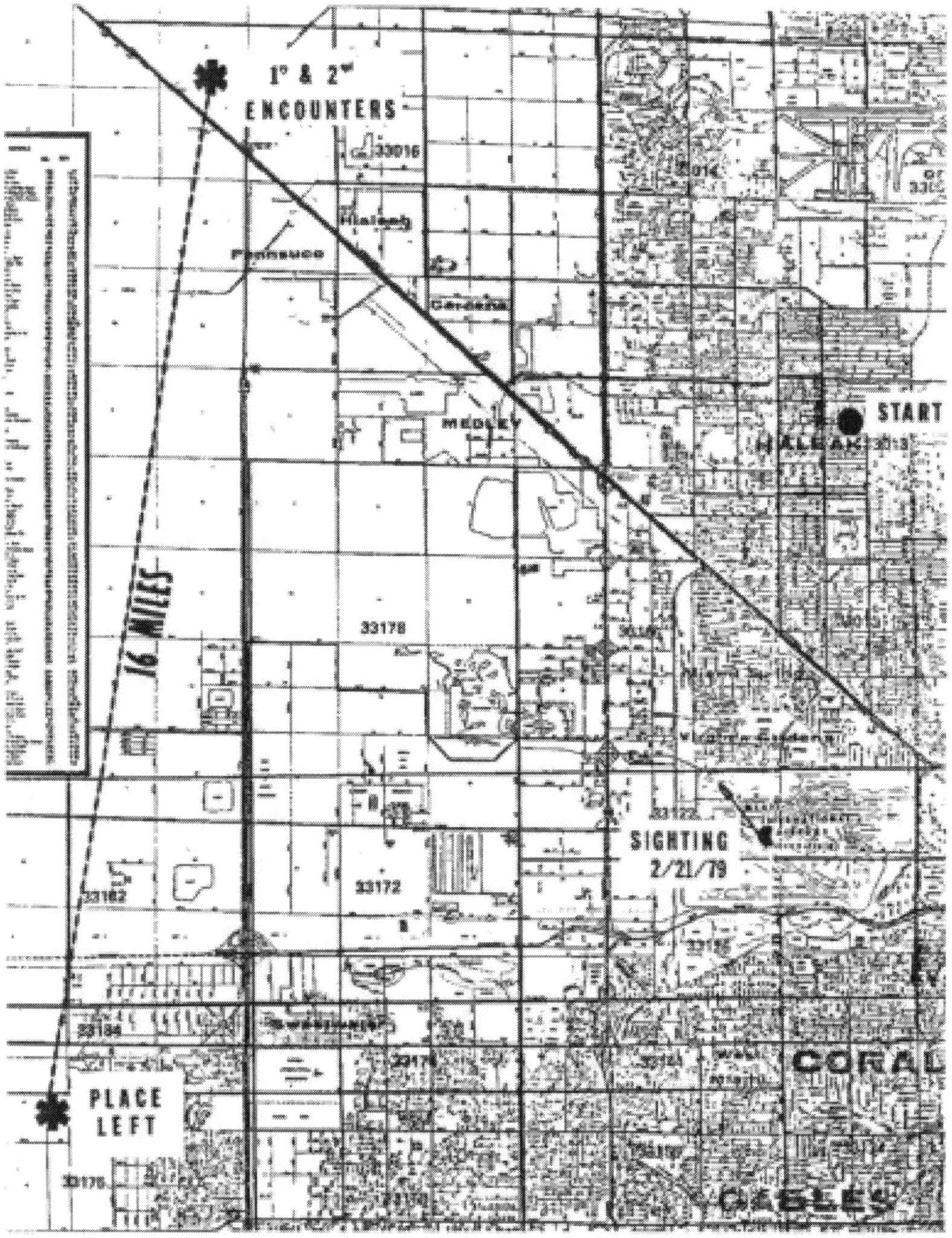

UFO Abduction From Undersea

Above—Filiberto and Iris Cardenas standing in front of the landing site where Filiberto was let out of the ship after his abduction. He was let out at the tree-line beyond the swampy meadow.
Below—The NTV Television crew examines the site.

been assaulted and left on the highway. Other patrol officers arrived, but they couldn't communicate with Filiberto because of a language problem and also the condition in which they found him. Filiberto does not speak English, but is fluent in Spanish, having been raised in Cuba. They searched his pockets and found his identification papers. They decided to take him to the police station. On the way Filiberto began to recuperate. From the identification papers found on him the police radioed a general description of what was happening ahead to the police dispatcher.

Meanwhile, in Hialeah, the police were getting ready to go out and search for the missing man when they received his description over the radio. They suspended their search plans and took Mrs. Cardenas and Fernando and family to the police station. When they arrived, the station police had Filiberto in a room where they were interrogating him. These are separate and distinct police sections and so the newcomers also interrogated Filiberto. It took almost an hour for the various police to complete their separate interrogations. A Sergeant Sanchez came to Filiberto and gave him a card which would authorize him to get an analysis for radio-activity. According to one official, something very strange and very uncommon happened to Filiberto. On the official report, under Type of Offense, he wrote: CLOSE ENCOUNTER OF THE THIRD KIND. This may be the first time a police agency admits an abduction by a UFO on an official report here in these United States.

They all left the police station, and without exchanging words, headed for the Clinica Pasteur in Hialeah, of which Filiberto is an associate member. There, in the emergency room, they were received by one of the nurses who, after hearing what had happened and seeing the note from the police, called the medical officer of the day, Dr. Fernando Grosso. When we interviewed the nurse, who prefers to remain anonymous, about her personal feelings, knowing the protagonists in this case, she said: "At first, I dint't believe it, but later after carefully observing the patient, and hearing the events that transpired, I am changing my opinion and believe that they are telling the truth. They had some experience. What impressed me most was the daughter. Though she didn't say anything her face reflected much fear."

Dr. Fernando Grosso told us that at first he thought that this was some drunk or perhaps a drug addict. When he came into the emergency room and saw the protagonists and the daughter, he began to find out what had occurred. They related the events and details described here. Dr. Grosso told us that his interest was

UFO Abduction From Undersea

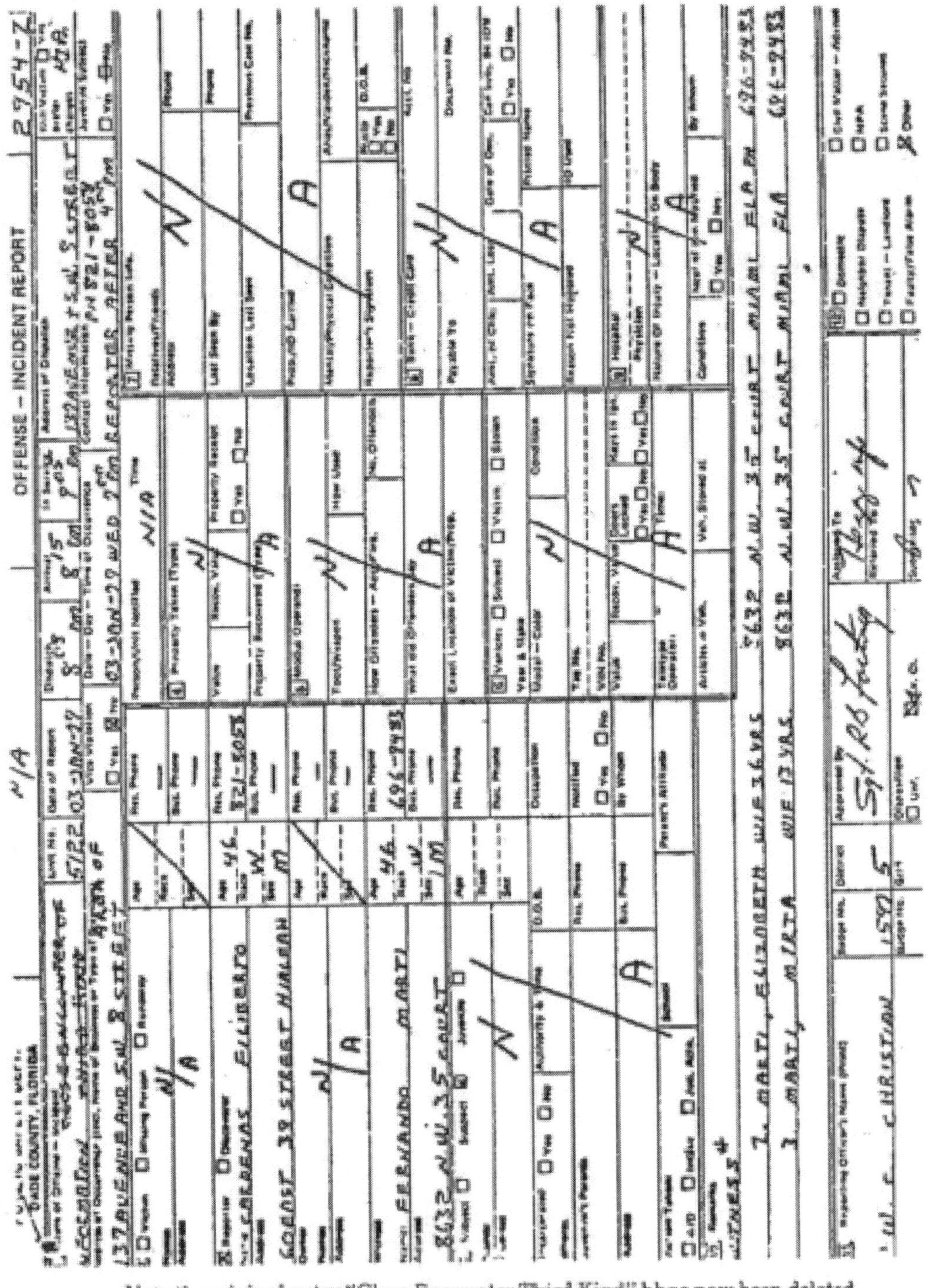

OFFENSE – INCIDENT REPORT

2954-Z

DADE COUNTY, FLORIDA

CARDENAS FILIBERTO

FERNANDO MARTI

8632 N.W. 35 COURT

1. MARTI, ELIZABETH W/F 36 YRS 8632 N.W. 35 COURT MIAMI FLA PH 696-9483

2. MARTI, MIRTA W/F 13 YRS 8632 N.W. 35 COURT MIAMI FLA 696-9483

Note the original entry "Close Encounter Third Kind" hhas now been deleted by lining through it in ink.

UFO Abduction From Undersea

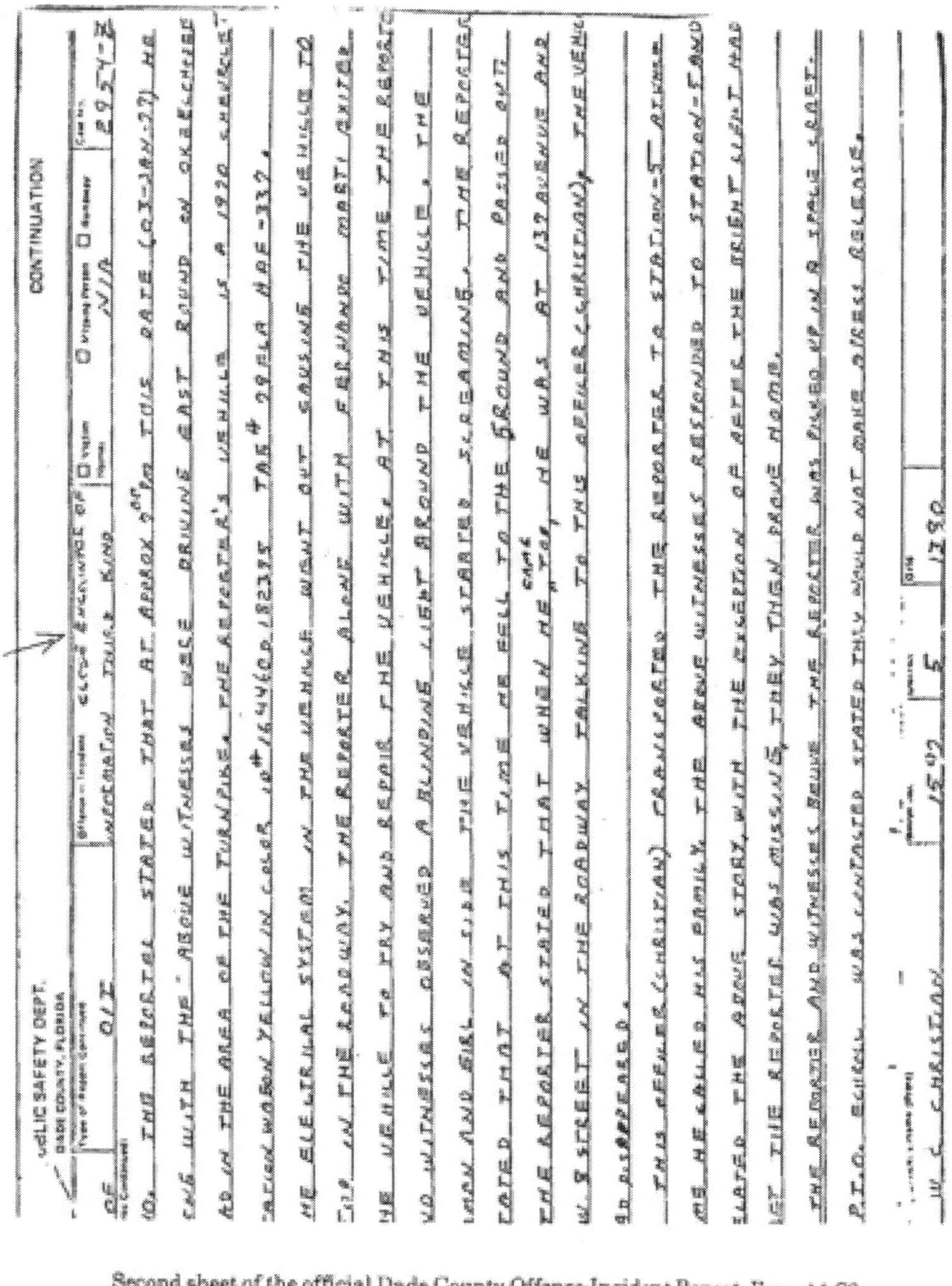

UBLIC SAFETY DEPT.
DADE COUNTY, FLORIDA

CONTINUATION

Type of Report Continued	Offense or Incident	Victim Name	Case No.
OII	CLOSE ENCOUNTER OF INFORMATION THIRD KIND	N/A	2954-Z

10. THE REPORTER STATED THAT AT APPROX 9PM THIS DATE (03-JAN-79) HE
ING WITH THE ABOVE WITNESSES WERE DRIVING EAST BOUND ON OKEECHOBEE
AD IN THE AREA OF THE TURNPIKE. THE REPORTER'S VEHICLE IS A 1970 CHEVROLET
ATION WAGON YELLOW IN COLOR ID# 1644 CD 182395 TAG# 79 FLA HOE-337.
HE ELECTRICAL SYSTEM IN THE VEHICLE WENT OUT CAUSING THE VEHICLE TO
TOP IN THE ROADWAY. THE REPORTER ALONG WITH FERNANDO MARTI EXITED
HE VEHICLE TO TRY AND REPAIR THE VEHICLE. AT THIS TIME THE REPORTE
WO WITNESSES OBSERVED A BLINDING LIGHT AROUND THE VEHICLE. THE
MAN AND GIRL IN SIDE THE VEHICLE STARTED SCREAMING. THE REPORTER
TATED THAT AT THIS TIME HE FELL TO THE GROUND AND PASSED OUT.
THE REPORTER STATED THAT WHEN HE CAME TOO, HE WAS AT 137 AVENUE AND
W 8 STREET IN THE ROADWAY TALKING TO THIS OFFICER (CHRISTIAN). THE VEHIC
AD DISAPPEARED.
THIS OFFICER (CHRISTIAN) TRANSPORTED THE REPORTER TO STATION-5 AT WHIC
ME HE CALLED HIS FAMILY. THE ABOVE WITNESSES RESPONDED TO STATION-5 AND
ELATED THE ABOVE STORY, WITH THE EXCEPTION OF AFTER THE BRIGHT LIGHT HAD
EFT THE REPORTER WAS MISSING. THEY THEN DROVE HOME.
THE REPORTER AND WITNESSES BELIEVE THE REPORTER WAS PICKED UP IN A SPACE CRAFT.
P.I.O. ECHOLL WAS CONTACTED STATED THEY WOULD NOT MAKE PRESS RELEASE.

W. C. CHRISTIAN | 1592 | 5 | 1390

Second sheet of the official Dade County Offense-Incident Report, Form 14 C2 95, Number 2954-7, dated 3 January 1979.

aroused by an expression of Fernando Marti when he said, "They did not take me because I pushed myself into the engine."

Meanwhile, Mrs. Iris Cardenas said, "You understand how this is doctor, that someone calls and says that a light has carried my husband away. I thought "una grua" (a crane) had carried him away. (Here in the United States, when there is an automobile accident, one of the first to arrive on the scene is a wrecker truck to retire the damaged vehicles. From this the expression "una grua".)

Dr. Grosso told us, "I looked at them and asked, 'Are you telling me the truth or is this all a big lie?', but it was the word of one endorsing another that made me think the four were not in collusion to perpetrate a fraud. From the beginning Filiberto had been telling me that he felt bad. Then I took his blood pressure and it was normal. I noticed some superficial abrasions and burns, three, one in the middle of his forehead and the others on the sides. He had some debility in his knees, and he told me he felt very weak. I noted that he was a little nervous and excited. The Marti family seemed more tranquil now. Mirta Marti told me about something like a light, very bright, that enveloped them as she screamed to Fernando and Filiberto: "Careful... Careful...". Suddenly remembering something else, Dr. Grosso told us, "They came here with a card from the police indicating that they suggested only a test for radioactivity. However, since I couldn't make it, I sent them on to Jackson Memorial Hospital." "Did you form any conclusions, doctor," I asked him, and he replied, "I do not think it is a fraud."

The witnesses left the Clinica Pasteur and drove to Jackson Hospital. It was now 11:30 at night and they arrived there about midnight. There they were met by the medical officer of the day who informed them that they likewise had no aparatus to test Filiberto for radiation exposure, however they would get in touch with Homestead Air Force Base to see if they had such equipment. A little later they were informed that an expert from the Air Base was on his way to the hospital to conduct the necessary tests. Meanwhile, they gave Filiberto a general examination. Filiberto felt very thirsty, and he felt like his body was projected in front of him. They were seated in a reception room when the chief of the floor advised them that the hospital was receiving telephone calls from radio stations interested in them. Filiberto said that he didn't want to reveal anything and he didn't want to see anybody. They were then conducted to a room where they were assured that they would have privacy and they could wait there for the technician from the Air Base. They waited there until nearly 04:30 AM when a man dressed in civilian clothes arrived with a large case.

He said he was the technician from the Air Base as he extracted an instrument from the case and commenced to pass it over Filiberto's body. In a little while he advised them that he could not find any type of radio activity on Filiberto but that this does not necessarily mean that Filiberto was not exposed to some kind of radiation, "Many times the reactions appear in a few days," he said. The hospital recommended that Filiberto stay several days for observation but he refused to consider it. He preferred to rest in his house. So it was "thumbs up" on condition that if he felt anything abnormal, or if he felt bad, he would inform them immediately. They all left the hospital at 05:00 AM Thursday the 4th of January and returned once again to Hialeah, to Filiberto's home.

But instead of peace and tranquility, there was waiting an army of reporters from newspapers, radio and television. The news had traveled like dust. Some had even forced doors to enter the house. "The surprise I received upon arriving at my home was greater than the surprise at what had happened to me," Filiberto later commented to me. "The lights of the television crews hurt my eyes." Filiberto was many days overcoming the pain in his eyes and for a time could only go out in the night. "I was trapped in my house like a fly," he said, referring to the reporters.

Filiberto began to experience erotic pressures and entertained sensual thoughts. He wanted to make love to his wife, and when he commenced to do so he experienced a large and prolonged orgasm. His erection was so hard that it hurt him while at the same time there seemed to be no end to his sexual appetite. Another thing that most attracted attention was the amount of water that he injested. While he was in Jackson Hospital, he confessed, he had drunk more than 25 normal glasses of water, and in the following first days he drank water constantly, though later the anxieties of thirst began to disappear. Also in those first days, when he would lie down upon his bed, he could see through the wall, something like a figure that carried something in his hands. This manifestation lasted only seconds and he could not define what it was. Later we supposed that this was his first impression when an extraterrestrial came near and put on a headcover that he carried in his hands.

In this conversation that we carried on with Filiberto, he seemed more relaxed and deliberate. When we first met him, he could not maintain conversation with the newsmen. They continually changed the subject, and sometimes talked at length without stopping, or he changed the question in the middle and asked for another. He was suffering from the irritation in his eyes and it bothered his vision. Bright lights, like automobile headlights, caused him considerable discomfort. By now a week had passed with him remaining in seclusion and he still could not see clearly. The clinic found his pulse and blood pressure normal as well as his reflexes.

The marks on his body that were discovered and described by the doctor at the hospital, as well as by our own doctor, looked like floor burns or abrasions though they did not form scabs. The smaller ones on his hands and feet disappeared in a few days. I photographed those on his hands when I visited him on the 14th. They looked superficial, like bug bites. He had a large one on his forehead, two at the hairline on the sides of his forehead, one on each foot, two on his shoulders near his chest and others. He had two large ones on the muscles of his legs near his genital area. There were small marks all over his hands and feet as well as his legs, like bug bites. He also had them on the backs of his fingers.

Earlier, on Friday the 12th of January, we returned in the evening to visit Filiberto and to introduce him to the doctor who was a part of our investigation team. The doctor performed a preliminary examination and made these notes:

In the days immediately following the abduction Filiberto slept very little. Only a few hours was sufficient and he did not feel tired. Also during this time he felt very active and was surprised that he did not tire.

In the first days, he informed us, his urine had a very strong penetrating odor and was of a dark color.

He could pass almost all day without taking food or drink and still did not feel tired or debilitated. He defacated normally.

He confessed that he sweated heavily and that his sweat also had a bod odor as well as his whole body. He could not overcome this odor with any deodorant he tried. He tried using different kinds of soap with no more success, and he could not get rid of the smell. He said the odor smelled sulfureous.

He passed the first days resting on his bed because he felt his knees weak and he was afraid he might fall. He said he felt like his lower leg, from knee to foot was separated from the rest of his body. He said this sensation began when he was in Jackson Memorial Hospital that first night. At one point, while they were waiting for the arrival of the radiation technician, he wanted to go to the bathroom, and he felt like his body was projected ahead of him and he could feel nothing from his knees to his feet. This sensation made him afraid and he continued to stay in bed most of that time.

He felt changes in body temperature. At times he felt hot in his chest and cold in his feet at the same time. This sensation would not last and the temperature would change; cold on his chest and heat on his feet. At other times he felt very hot all over and would sweat with the sulfureous odor though the temperature in the house, through the central air conditioning system, remained the same.

With respect to the strange sex drives, he told us that in the first days he did not seem to have any interest. His head hurt like he had hundreds of needle points pricking him, evidently produced by the helmet that the alien extraterrestrials placed on him when he was aboard the ship. The size of the marks on his body ranged from 2 centimeters down to almost invisible.

Before terminating this preliminary examination, it was suggested that a neurological examination should be performed before we initiated any hypnotic sessions. We should be sure of his physical and mental condition and know that there are no deficienceis before we begin. A neurological examination was scheduled for Monday the 15th.

After an intense neurological examination lasting three hours the neurologist pronounced the patient normal, with no deficiency, in normal mental condition, and of average intelligence. He had no detectable nervous afflictions.

We had to be sure that Filiberto was in good health and normal in every way before we could proceed We knew that any one with any defect, psychological or mental, with epilepsy for example, could imagine such an abduction. In such a case a hypnotic regression might reveal a product of his epileptic condition and not a real experience. We had to be as certain as possible. We finished the physical examinations and decided to commence the hypnotic sessions on Saturday the 27th.

As he began to recover from the trauma of the initial experience, Filiberto was overcome by curiosity and felt impelled to return to the abduction site again and again. He went back there several times. He noticed that every time he went back there his watch gained a lot of time. Then on site at the abduction location he noticed that his watch was running very fast and was making a whirring noise, which stopped as soon as he left. He went to Dr. Sanchez-Ocejo and told him of this strange development and pointed at the expensive gold-cased quartz chronograph on his wrist in gesture, and as he did so, it again began to whir and run

UFO Abduction From Undersea

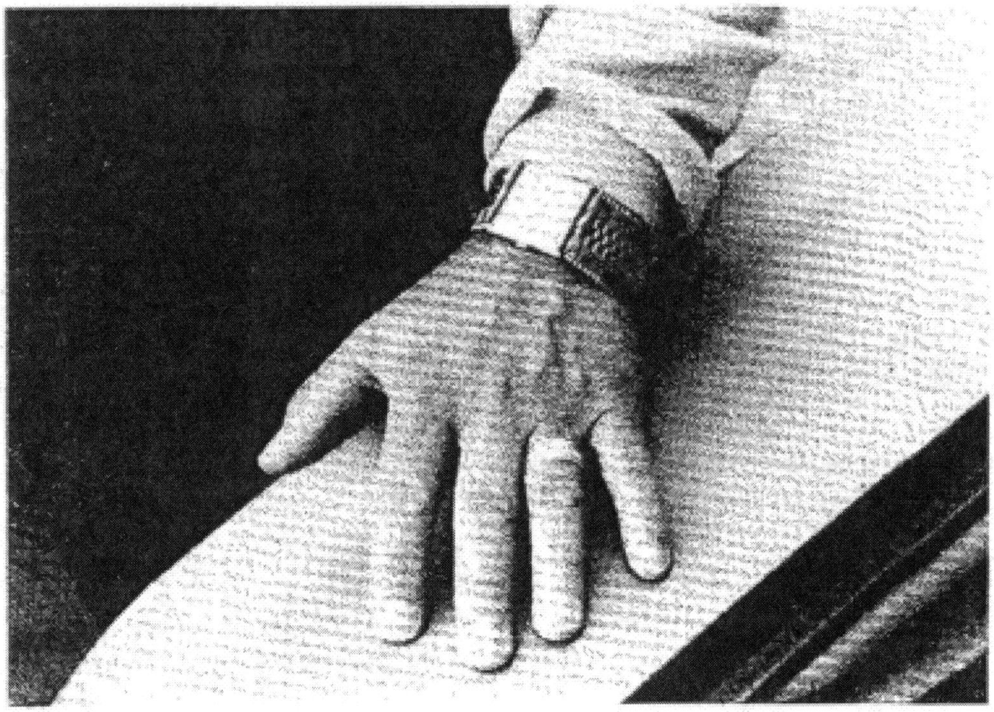

This is the gold-cased quartz chronograph worn by Cardenas during the abductions. This watch would speed up time and make a fast whirring noise the first few times Cardenas returned to the initial abduction site.

fast before their very eyes. For some time every time he pointed his right index finger at the watch it would speed up and make the whirring noise. This phenomena finally diminished and went away. Several other witnesses observed this phenomena.

14C 94U3

RECEIVED

FEB 1 1979

MEDICAL RECORDS
CORRESPONDENCE

REQUEST FOR RELEASE
OF
MEDICAL RECORDS

TO: Jackson Memorial Hospital
(PHYSICIAN'S NAME)

ADDRESS

Miami Fla
CITY STATE ZIP

I hereby request that my medical records be released to:

(PHYSICIAN'S NAME)

ADDRESS

Miami Fla 33142
CITY STATE ZIP

SEEN IN E.R. 1-3-79
DATE

Filiberto Cardenas
PATIENT'S SIGNATURE
FILIBERTO CARDENAS

These are Filiberto Cardenas' patient treatment records from Jackson Memorial Hospital.

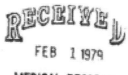

JACKSON MEMORIAL HOSPITAL

EMERGENCY ROOM GENERAL CONSENT FOR TREATMENT

Believing that I have a condition requiring hospital care, I do hereby voluntarily consent to all tests and procedures in the course of the study, diagnosis, and treatment of my illness by the medical staff, medical students, and other agents and/or employees of the Public Health Trust and the University of Miami School of Medicine. I am aware the practice of medicine and surgery is not an exact science, and I acknowledge that no guarantees have been made to me as to the results of treatments or examination in the hospital.

I specifically consent to the administration of whole human blood, human blood derivatives, or fractions thereof as deemed advisable by my physician, or his designee.

I hereby authorize Hospital and/or University representatives to take such still photographs, motion pictures, television transmission, and/or videotaped recording as they may wish.

I authorize use and disposal of any specimens or tissues taken from my body during my hospitalization for scientific, research, therapeutic, or teaching purposes.

Exceptions to above are: ______

Witness ______ SIGNATURE OF PATIENT

Witness ______ DATE: ______ TIME: ______ AM PM

If patient is unable to consent or is a minor, complete the following:
Patient (is a minor ______ years of age) is unable to consent because: ______

DATE ______ CLOSEST RELATIVE OR LEGAL GUARDIAN

JACKSON MEMORIAL HOSPITAL

HOJA DE CONSENTIMIENTO GENERAL PARA TRATAMIENTO EN LA SALA DE EMERGENCIAS

En la creencia de que estoy en un estado que requiere atención en un hospital, por este medio consiento voluntariamente a que se me hagan todas las pruebas y procedimientos para el estudio, diagnosis y tratamiento de mi enfermedad, por el cuerpo médico, estudiantes de medicina y otros agentes y/o empleados del Fideicomiso de Salud Pública y la Escuela de Medicina de la Universidad de Miami. Estoy conciente de que la práctica de la medicina y cirugía no es una ciencia exacta y reconozco que no se me han dado garantías en cuanto a los resultados de los tratamientos o exámenes en el hospital.

Yo, específicamente consiento a que se me administre sangre humana o sus derivados así como fracciones de la misma, según lo estime conveniente mi médico o el que él designe.

Por este medio autorizo al hospital y/o a los representantes de la Universidad a tomar fotografías, películas, transmisiones para televisión y/o porciones pregrabadas para televisión, si así lo desean.

Autorizo el uso y disposición de cualquier muestra o tejido tomado de mi cuerpo durante mi hospitalización, con propósitos científicos, de investigación, terapéuticos o de enseñanza.

Las excepciones a lo anterior son: ______

Testigo ______ FIRMA DEL PACIENTE

Testigo ______ FECHA: ______ HORA: ______ A.M. P.M.

Si el paciente está imposibilitado de dar su autorización o es menor de edad, favor de llenar lo siguiente:
El paciente (es un menor, de ______ años de edad) está imposibilitado de dar su autorización porque ______

FECHA ______ PARIENTE MAS CERCANO O TUTOR LEGAL

UFO Abduction From Undersea

JACKSON MEMORIAL HOSPITAL
UNIVERSITY OF MIAMI SCHOOL OF MEDICINE
MIAMI, FLORIDA

1409403

CARDENAS FILIBERTO

60 E. 38 St HIALEAH

821803

IRIS CARDENAS

'79 JAN -4 AM 1 31

DIAGNOSIS

PATIENT INSTRUCTIONS

MEDICATION – MEDICINA

ACTIVITY – ACTIVIDAD

DISPOSITION – ORDEN AL PACIENTE

CARDENAS, FILIBERTO

9004024-7

1409403

I certify that the above care was needed and that the above patient instructions are correct.

EMERGENCY DEPARTMENT MEDICAL RECORD

G-1210

UFO Abduction From Undersea

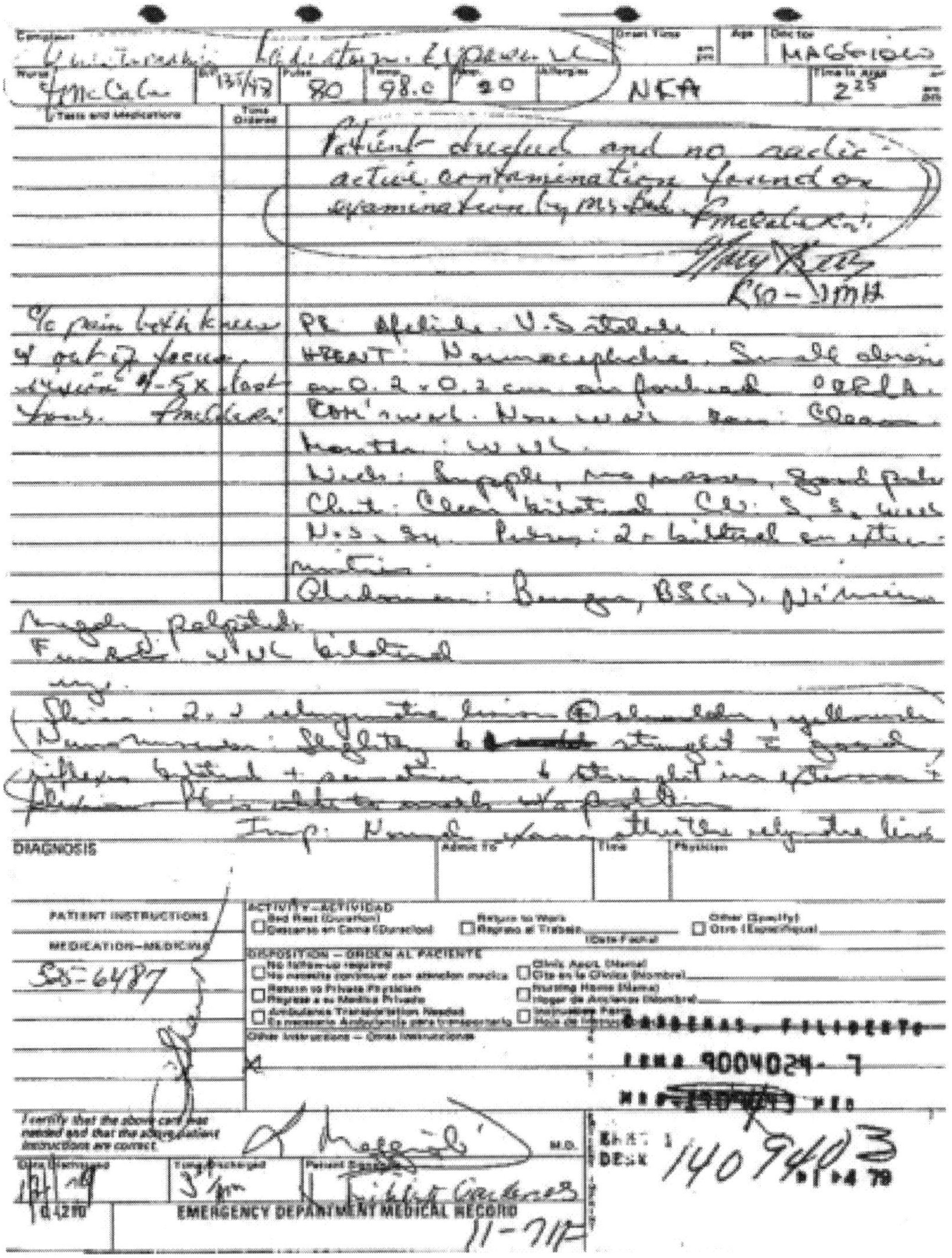

Patient checked and no radio-active contamination found on examination by ms. [illegible]

RSO-JMH

Complaint					Age	Doctor
						MAGGIOLO
Nurse	BP	Pulse	Temp	Resp		Time Is
	131/78	80	98.0	20	NFA	2 25

DIAGNOSIS

PATIENT INSTRUCTIONS

MEDICATION—MEDICINA

58-6487

ACTIVITY—ACTIVIDAD

DISPOSITION — ORDEN AL PACIENTE

Other Instructions — Otras Instrucciones

I certify that the above card was reviewed and that the above patient instructions are correct.

M.D.

CARDENAS, FILIBERTO

9004024-7

EMERGENCY DEPARTMENT MEDICAL RECORD

UFO Abduction From Undersea

CHAPTER 2

Hypnotic Regression

At 5:00 PM on Thursday the 18th of January we received another of the many telephone calls from Filiberto, but this time he urged me to come to his home as soon as possible. Something very strange had happened and he told me that he had with him some other people as witnesses. I hurried to his house as fast as I could.

When I got there he introduced me to a Columbian couple who asked me to keep their real identity confidential. They had been friends of the Cardenas family for several years. They were accustomed to visiting them whenever they came to Miami. As usual they were sitting in the Florida room visiting while Filiberto was on the patio cooking meat on a charcoal brazier for dinner. Iris was in the daughter's room at the hallway near the visitor's position. The Columbian couple, very excited, told me that they had been sitting there talking about personal things when, at a point in their conversation, they raised their sight and saw something like a figure in the middle of the room. This figure was in mid-flight, looked feminine, and disappeared towards the hallway to the bedrooms.

"My wife asked me," said the witness, "Did you see that white figure?", and I said, "Yes, it must be Iris," but she assured me, "No, no that was not Iris." I knew that it could not be Iris by the stature of the figure, but we didn't give it great importance and we laughed. When Iris and Filiberto came to the table where we were sitting, we began to tell them saying, "Don't be afraid but here is what happened..." They replied that they didn't know what we were talking about. So we explained again about seeing the tall figure covered head to foot with a white sheet, that this appeared to us in the room within ten feet of us, made a half leap and disappeared toward the bedrooms. I got up and went to the place where we had seen the aparition, to indicate the place exactly. When I stood there I felt like my hair erected, like the feathers of a rooster. We all then experienced the same sensation by standing in that same place."

Reconstructing the details of the figure we understood that it described a tall aparition with no definite body. It looked like a slender person. It was completely covered from the top of the head to the feet. They could not see the feet and furthermore the feet did not seem to touch the floor. Nevertheless they felt that the aparition had substance and walked softly, like a person without shoes. Each member of the Cardenas family stood in that place and performed the same action as the aparition but the Columbians insisted that it was not any of those. This couple was very serious and enjoyed a good reputation. The husband was a senior officer in an aviation business, a well known business man not given to jokes and trickery.

I must say that this type of manifestation is very difficult to test by scientific methods. My wife, Maria Elena and my associate, Mario Rodriguez, who went there with me, stood in the same place and experienced also the same sensations of cold and erection of the hair.

But, back to the hypnosis. The first hypnotic session was conducted on Saturday the 27th as planned, and took place about 6:00 PM. The hypnotist made several tests to see if Mr. Cardenas would be receptive and commenced the process. This took some 15 minutes during which he made Filiberto raise his arms, balance himself forward and back, and finally making him think he was of rubber. The hypnotist took out a small sewing needle and pricked Filiberto experimentally without getting any reaction. We could see at this point that Mr. Cardenas was completely hypnotized and that he was not responding voluntarily. At this time his memory was like an open book in which we could examine all that had occurred. It gave me great satisfaction to see that Mr. Cardenas could be hypnotized and was a good subject. I had often had my doubts about this and felt that everyone would not be as easy to hypnotize. One necessary condition is that the subject must consent to be hypnotized. Hypnosis is quite effective in cases of amnesia where the subject can not remember any part of his previous life. In cases of extraterrestrial contact, in general, the person has no conscious recall, or they make him forget the experience by creating a temporary amnesia. All people have a conscious and a subconscious mind level. The subconscious is the person's archival level, which can be reached through hypnosis. Here we can find all the information forgotten in amnesia.

The hypnotist begins to talk to Cardenas to see his reaction to hypnosis:

HYPNOTIST - You are very relaxed and serene. All will return to your memory. You are satisfied because you are going to understand and remember what happened.

VIRGILIO SANCHEZ-OCEJO - What do they look like?

FILIBERTO - Seems...like...a...machine..with a figure...a man.

He spoke with a halting voice, almost inaudible, very labored.

VIRGILIO - Do they have names?

FILIBERTO - They say.....this is very strange....

HYPNOTIST - Now when I count to three you will remember all and will tell us...one...two...three...NOW.

VIRGILIO - What did they say to you?

FILIBERTO - My brain is blank....

HYPNOTIST - Now when I count to three, you are going to blot out this order and return to being yourself, completely yourself, with your brain normal. You are going to forget this order that they have given you, and you are going to remember all perfectly...one...two...three....the order is gone and you remember everything.

VIRGILIO - What did they say to you?

FILIBERTO - My brain is blank.

VIRGILIO - But, now you remember everything, is that not so?

FILIBERTO - He told me that I cannot answer.

HYPNOTIST - Now, when I count to three you are going to answer all. You are a free man again, possessor of your will... one...two...three, now...the truth if you can.

FILIBERTO - Yes, but I don't know if they will let me say it.

VIRGILIO - Who will not let you say it? To whom?

FILIBERTO - To no one.

VIRGILIO - And why?

FILIBERTO - Because they told me not to say anything.

VIRGILIO - Is it a grave thing?

FILIBERTO - .... (silence)

VIRGILIO - Can you communicate with them if you want?

FILIBERTO - Yes.

VIRGILIO - How can you communicate with them?

FILIBERTO - It seems like they put something in my head, then they talk to me by means of a sound.

VIRGILIO - How is the sound?

FILIBERTO - Very strange. I feel very humbled in my brain.

VIRGILIO - How do they talk to you?

UFO Abduction From Undersea

FILIBERTO - ....(silence)
HYPNOTIST - You are a free man and you can tell us, also, we are friends with these people.
FILIBERTO - They told me not to say anything.
VIRGILIO - You can ask permission from them to tell us or me alone.
FILIBERTO - They do not want me to tell you.
VIRGILIO - And why?
FILIBERTO - Because, two times I disobeyed them. They ordered me to say something I did not say.
VIRGILIO - What did they tell you to say that you didn't?
FILIBERTO - I do not remember.
HYPNOTIST - But now you are going to remember. When I count to three you will remember...one...two...three. What was it?
FILIBERTO - I am remembering, but I cannot say it.
VIRGILIO - But you can speak about them, true? Where did they take you?
FILIBERTO - One of them was dressed in white, something white, but it was fastened to the body.
VIRGILIO - Was he a human being?
FILIBERTO - I don't know. He seemed like a human being, but as if he was.....like..........
VIRGILIO - Did he speak English or Spanish?
FILIBERTO - At first he spoke as if he were German, but later he changed and spoke some words in English, and I told him "I didn't understand." Then he changed a wave (frequency) with a button.
VIRGILIO - Where did he have this button?
FILIBERTO - Here, on his chest, and then he began to speak as if he were Portuguese, and I understood but not very easily.
VIRGILIO - How many were there?
FILIBERTO - There were three.
VIRGILIO - Where were they?
FILIBERTO - There were three at the time they let me out.
VIRGILIO - To where did they take you?
FILIBERTO - To an ocean. To a part of the sea.
VIRGILIO - Here, on this Earth?
FILIBERTO - Yes, I remember an ocean.
VIRGILIO - Into the sea?
FILIBERTO - Yes. At first, before we went into the sea, we were on the shore of a beach.
VIRGILIO - What happened in the sea?
FILIBERTO - .... (inaudible)
HYPNOTIST - Now you are going to say the same much louder,

tranquil, serene and relaxed.
FILIBERTO - ....(silence)
HYPNOTIST - What is your name?
FILIBERTO - ....(inaudible)
HYPNOTIST - What is it? Speak up, I can not hear you.
FILIBERTO - Filiberto Cardenas.
HYPNOTIST - You are trying to say something and we cannot hear.
FILIBERTO - ....(silence)

Filiberto became restless and began to resist talking. He gave us to believe that something very interesting had happened but that he had been ordered not to discuss it with anybody. He seemed to be fighting internally against the mental block imposed. We decided, for the moment not to insist in this first test. We wanted to move slowly and try to remove the mental block without causing Filiberto any anxiety.

The hypnotist brought Filiberto back to waking consciousness and he opened his eyes and smiled and said, "What happened?" "What did I say?" We looked at him and began to laugh together with him. It was then that we knew that we would come to know the details of his experience.

After this initial test we made no comment pertaining to it in front of Filiberto. We wanted to avoid giving him impressions or to induce him to rationalize the story into a fabricated history. We changed the conversation to different things despite his insistance on knowing what he had said. We thought it better to wait for the arrival of the doctor and Mario Rodriguez. We were worried that something might happen to Filiberto in trance, during the hypnosis, that might require the assistance of a doctor. Also we wanted him to rest for a time so as not to force him in any manner. In any case, we had already prepared him so that when he received the order, he would promptly fall into a state of profound hypnosis.

The doctor and Mario Rodriguez arrived about 8:00 in the evening, almost one behind the other. After greetings and relating our tests up to now, we went back to Filiberto's bedroom and began the second hypnotic session.
HYPNOTIST - What is your name?
FILIBERTO - Filiberto Cardenas.
HYPNOTIST - Louder, I cannot hear.
FILIBERTO - Filiberto Cardenas!
HYPNOTIST - Very good, you will continue sleeping, completely asleep, and you are going to respond to all my questins. What happened on 3 January 1979, just before 10:00 PM? Tell me.

FILIBERTO - ....(silence)
HYPNOTIST - Are you going to tell me?
FILIBERTO - I was with the Police.
HYPNOTIST - Very good, what happened one hour before the police?
FILIBERTO - ....(silence)
HYPNOTIST - You are going to remember all when I count to three...one...two...three. What happened?
FILIBERTO - I cannot tell you.
HYPNOTIST - Why, why can you not tell us?
FILIBERTO - They ordered me not to.
VIRGILIO - Who? Who ordered it?
FILIBERTO - Ka..........
HYPNOTIST - When I count three you will remember perfectly.
FILIBERTO - Kiastro......Kiastro......Kiastro.
VIRGILIO - Who is that?
FILIBERTO - He is the one who was with the people.
VIRGILIO - What people?
FILIBERTO - Two that looked like people but another no. Not the same. They walked and seemed at times like people. They seemed like a group of people that took me.
VIRGILIO - Where did they take you?
FILIBERTO - To a place.
VIRGILIO - In what country?
FILIBERTO - I don't know the country. They said that it was......
VIRGILIO - Where?
FILIBERTO - They told me that it was.....that it ws.... I asked them, Where are we? And then they answered that we were in..... I do not remember.
HYPNOTIST - Now you are going to remember when I count to three...one...two...three. Where?
FILIBERTO - They told me we were in Berin or Berin and another place.
VIRGILIO - What was the other place?
FILIBERTO - I don't remember.
HYPNOTIST - You will remember when I count to three, one... two...three. What was it?
FILIBERTO - .... (silence)
VIRGILIO - What language were they talking?
FILIBERTO - ....(silence)
HYPNOTIST - When I count three tell me. One...two...three.
FILIBERTO - One of them was speaking and he was a man from Earth. He was from no side.
VIRGILIO - In what language did he talk?

FILIBERTO - The same as I, but he seemed like....like....like...
VIRGILIO - Between them what language did they speak?
FILIBERTO - They talked with some sounds, but the one that spoke to me talked like he were Chilean, also something like he might be Argentine.
VIRGILIO - And the others?
FILIBERTO - The others, one was seated in a chair, high, like this, and the chair rotated, and he had some buttons at his feet. He opened the ports with those buttons.
VIRGILIO - What ports did he open?
FILIBERTO - The doors, he opened them with his feet and those buttons.
VIRGILIO - Where?
FILIBERTO - Of the place we were in.
VIRGILIO - That place, what was it? Was it a house?
FILIBERTO - The walls inside looked like a house.
VIRGILIO - What color was it?
FILIBERTO - I can't say what color it was. I have never seen that color before.
HYPNOTIST - Very good. Now let us perform an interesting experiment. When I count to three, see if you can open your mind like a panorama, as if it were a movie, and you will tell us all that happened that 3rd of January after 6:30 in the evening, when you were trying to repair your stalled car. You can tell me all because this is a scene where you can see all that is happening and can remember it. One...two...three. Where are you? Is the car broken? Are you trying to repair it?
FILIBERTO - The car is not broken.
HYPNOTIST - Why doesn't it run?
FILIBERTO - I don't know. Fernando says he cannot understand why it won't run. He is a mechanic, and I am not a good one.
HYPNOTIST - From here go forward and tell everything. What happens?
FILIBERTO - A light appears, making a noise, and I began to look at the light. It hovered over the car and the motor reflected the light. I began to hear the shouts of the woman and her child in the car. Then when I tried to get out of there, I felt like I couldn't move. I was paralyzed. I was very alarmed, and then I felt like I was taken by the shoulder, then by the whole body, and I was being lifted, pulled up.
VIRGILIO - Were you frightened?
FILIBERTO - Yes.
VIRGILIO - And now, do you feel fear in telling me?

FILIBERTO - Yes, because I think it could happen again.
HYPNOTIST - Now, when I count to three the fear will disappear. You are a free man, without fear, without complexes. You are strong and powerful. One...two...three. Do you feel good?
FILIBERTO - Yes, but I cannot move.
VIRGILIO - Continue. Tell me, what is happening?
FILIBERTO - And then I could not move, and I heard them shouting and I could not move.....
HYPNOTIST - Look at the picture. Can you see it all?
FILIBERTO - Yes, I am looking. I can not move, and I am beginning to rise, suspended above the ground, I don't understand..... When the light gets brighter, the sound also gets louder, then I cannot see anything, nothing is happening.
HYPNOTIST - Very Good. Now you are going to illuminate the picture and see everything. Can you see? Here is everything that has happened. Tell me! Describe it!
FILIBERTO - I can not tell you what happened.
HYPNOTIST - Why?
FILIBERTO - Because they don't want me to tell.
HYPNOTIST - And why do they not let you tell? What force do they exercise over you? You have already told us some things and nothing has happened. You are a man, strong and free. You are stronger and more powerful than them.
FILIBERTO - They do not want me to tell.
HYPNOTIST - What not to tell, What?
FILIBERTO - What happened to me there. (sobbing) It is that many people are involved in this. They are many, but until now I do not have a number and they want me to say nothing to nobody. I have to wait three months before I can tell what happened.
HYPNOTIST - Three months? What day?
FILIBERTO - (sobbing) They say three months.
HYPNOTIST - But, what date did they give you?
FILIBERTO - (sobbing) They told me three months. Then they will tell me when to say the things.
HYPNOTIST - How are they going to communicate?
FILIBERTO - With the radio they put in me. (sobbing)
HYPNOTIST - Where did they put this radio?
FILIBERTO - I don't know.......(weeping)
HYPNOTIST - Quiet down, be serene, relax, you feel good. You are quiet, content, very happy and very content because you are now free. Now when I count three you will laugh, laugh good and then you will continue sleeping. One...two...three. You laugh, you are content, very content, content and happy. Continue relating

what you can tell. What else can you tell us?
FILIBERTO - ....(silence)
HYPNOTIST - You don't care to answer any more questions?
FILIBERTO - Yes, I want to answer.
HYPNOTIST - Then tell us all, everything you can say.
FILIBERTO - They.......... (long sigh)
HYPNOTIST - Quickly, tell us all you can say.
FILIBERTO - Well. If they find out then they may do something to me.
HYPNOTIST - What did they do to you? Did they do something to you there?

FILIBERTO - Yes, They did many things to me.
HYPNOTIST - Were they bad?
FILIBERTO - No, I do not think they were bad. But they did many things to me and I watched them, as if I were a strange object.
HYPNOTIST - And why do they want you to say nothing?
FILIBERTO - Until three months, they said.
HYPNOTIST - And you remember everything?
FILIBERTO - Yes, I am seeing it all.
HYPNOTIST - Now you can see it all. You are seeing all that happened?
FILIBERTO - Yes, when they took me.
HYPNOTIST - Now you are going to see everything in a giant picture that you have. You are going to see everything. Are you seeing everything?
FILIBERTO - ....(silence)
HYPNOTIST - Now something very curious is going to happen. As you are looking, all your subconscious will open its doors and leave them open so you can understand when you are awake. Little by little you will remember it all. You will remember little by little when you are awake. Now, what else can you tell us?
FILIBERTO - They put me in front of a wall, that illuminated like a television and I saw many things, such as what was happening. They wanted me to look closely and avoid those things before they happened.
HYPNOTIST - What happened? What thing?
FILIBERTO - They said that we did not have understanding, and that they wanted to help.
HYPNOTIST - Did you not tell them that we would like their knowledge?
FILIBERTO - Yes, I asked them to tell me. Then they told me that they were going to give me knowledge of many things.
HYPNOTIST - Did they tell you?

FILIBERTO - Yes.
HYPNOTIST - What knowledge did they give you?
FILIBERTO - They helped me much with many things.
HYPNOTIST - What knowledge?
FILIBERTO - They told me that until three months I could not report it. Because they wanted to contact other people. That they wanted to contact more people, then would return them. And they have seven that they have had with them for some time.
HYPNOTIST - How did you talk to them?
FILIBERTO - Through the radio.
HYPNOTIST - What radio?
FILIBERTO - They call me.
HYPNOTIST - And where do they have this radio?
FILIBERTO - Inside. They put it inside by the ear.
(Filiberto is referring now to some kind of a transceiver device that the extraterrestrials inserted surgically into his skull above his ears. It was small and was inserted rapidly with some kind of an installation gun. Through this device they are able to override his senses and use them to transmit signals and information, including projection of living scenes.)
HYPNOTIST - For the sound?
FILIBERTO - Yes.
HYPNOTIST - What size is it?
FILIBERTO - Well, I did not see it when they were putting it in. But they told me that "This is for what you are going to hear."
HYPNOTIST - What thing is it that you hear?
FILIBERTO - I continually receive many things, but until three months I cannot say.
HYPNOTIST - What language do they speak?
FILIBERTO - They talked to me as if I were a Portuguese or an Italian who is speaking Spanish.
HYPNOTIST - And you entered the water with them? (Referring to Cardenas report that they took him into the ocean with them.)
FILIBERTO - Yes, but that was afterward.
HYPNOTIST - After what?
FILIBERTO - After they got through making those tests.
HYPNOTIST - But, where did they enter the water?
FILIBERTO - It was in a ship but I couldn't.... It was a thing like this.... I don't know.... I couldn't see behind....what it was that was behind.
HYPNOTIST - And in front?
FILIBERTO - .... (silence)
HYPNOTIST - Did you go in straight or in a curve?
FILIBERTO - Curve. There was a place in which they had to

curve.
HYPNOTIST - What did they have in this place?
FILIBERTO - It was like a tunnel that had to be entered under the water.
HYPNOTIST - And what did you see?
FILIBERTO - Those are things that I cannot reveal.
HYPNOTIST - But some things you have already told us, no?
FILIBERTO - ....(silence)
HYPNOTIST - They did not tell you if you wanted to contact them what you would have to do?
FILIBERTO - Yes, yes if I want to contact them I can do it.
HYPNOTIST - How?
FILIBERTO - But they don't want me to tell you.
HYPNOTIST - But, if you want to communicate with them, you can do so?
FILIBERTO - Yes.
HYPNOTIST - Did they take blood?
FILIBERTO - They put some things in my body.
HYPNOTIST - But, to take blood?
FILIBERTO - And another in my head.
HYPNOTIST - What did they put there? How was it?
FILIBERTO - I felt like they opened me up, like I was open as if breathing in, but I could not see what they were doing.
HYPNOTIST - Who did this to you, men or women?
FILIBERTO - I could not tell if they were men or women because they were covered, enveloped in a very strange garment.
HYPNOTIST - Now, listen well, you're going to continue completely asleep, you will continue responding to all the questions, and you will respond to the questions of other persons that are here with me. You will hear and will respond if you can and will. But you will continue obeying all that I tell you.
VIRGILIO - I would like to question you. Did they tie you up?
FILIBERTO - Once they put me in a chair but I could not move. I was not tied.
VIRGILIO - Well can you describe to me the people, the face?
FILIBERTO - There was the Chilean one. I do not know if he was Chilean but he talked like it. He looked like a Chilean.
VIRGILIO - How was his eyes?
FILIBERTO - Like ours. Like mine.
VIRGILIO - The nose?
FILIBERTO - The nose, as if they had done something to the nose, but he talked and everything, everything was like me, as if he were the same as us.
VIRGILIO - Did he walk or float?

FILIBERTO - The Chilean, well I don't know that he was Chilean, sometimes walked and . . . a thing happened that put me near his hands and . . . I don't know what happened, but it seemed that he had to run and then went up in the air. That was the only time that I saw anything like in the air.
VIRGILIO - When that was under the sea, was it under water or was there air there?
FILIBERTO - What they made me do was when we entered the tunnel . . .
VIRGILIO - Was there air or was there water?
FILIBERTO - No, that was under the water.
VIRGILIO - Could you breathe?
FILIBERTO - Yes, I could there. Every so often they looked at me, then my respiration fouled, I could not breathe well.
VIRGILIO - Did they give you something to eat?
FILIBERTO - No, they asked me if I wanted to eat anything from the Earth, and I said no, that I did not want to eat anything.
HYPNOTIST - And did they eat?
FILIBERTO - They did not eat. I did not see them eat.
HYPNOTIST - How much time have they been there?
FILIBERTO - They said 36 months.
HYPNOTIST - Are they on this plane (of existence)?
FILIBERTO - What plane is that? I don't know.
HYPNOTIST - No, forget the question.
MARIO RODRIGUEZ - I would like to assure you that all you tell us we will not divulge, we will not tell anybody . . .(Uruguayan)

Filiberto at this time interrupted Mario Rodriguez with an emotional voice and shouted: "Thus, thus speaks the man, that is the way he spoke."

HYPNOTIST - But was it him?
FILIBERTO - No, no, but he talked like that, similar.
HYPNOTIST - The voices are similar. Let's see. He will continue talking.
MARIO - Be tranquil because I am not the one who walks with them. I would like to ask you something about what happened if you can tell me? Did you feel heavy? Was your body heavy? Did you feel light?
FILIBERTO - When they put me in the chair, I was fastened to the seat, but later I walked moving my feet, but it was like I was not standing on the floor.
MARIO - Do you remember any object that you saw? Anything in particular that would remind you of something common, something that you see every day?
FILIBERTO - The walls were as if they were panoramas of

television, and they displayed many things of the Earth.
HYPNOTIST - And what did you see in the panoramas?
FILIBERTO - I saw the Earth . . . (sobs)
HYPNOTIST - Very well. Don't tell us until you are ready. Did you see animals?
FILIBERTO - I saw animals . . . great cities . . .
HYPNOTIST - Such as? Were they from Earth or another place?
FILIBERTO - From Earth, yes.
HYPNOTIST - And why were they living there?
FILIBERTO - No, but I didn't see them there. I saw them in the panoramas, the televisions, because they put me in those places that were passing.
HYPNOTIST - And the people were talking with you? Was it of the Earth or another place?
FILIBERTO - When they were putting me there, there was the man, one who seemed like he was the leader of them.
HYPNOTIST - How was that?
FILIBERTO - Sighs . . . I do not understand well, because he was high, so, as in the seat that rotated. He had a cover above.
HYPNOTIST - Did they show you any pyramids?
FILIBERTO - Yes, there is where we were.
HYPNOTIST - Inside the pyramid?
FILIBERTO - Yes.
HYPNOTIST - Where was this pyramid?
FILIBERTO - This pyramid was beneath the ocean.
HYPNOTIST - In what part, At what place?
FILIBERTO - . . . (silence)
HYPNOTIST - Now, when I count to three you will see a picture with the longitude and latitude exactly where this pyramid is located and you will tell me . . . one . . . two . . . three . . . Now.
FILIBERTO - They say that it is between the . . .
HYPNOTIST - Where? Louder!
FILIBERTO - It is near the . . .
HYPNOTIST - You will remember when I say three . . . one . . . two . . . three.
FILIBERTO - It is between . . . Berin and Santiago under the ocean, for there it is. Some four hundred . . .
HYPNOTIST - Degrees of longitude?
FILIBERTO - Four hundred. I don't remember. Only four hundred . . .
HYPNOTIST - Now the degrees of latitude. Did they tell you? Can you remember?
FILIBERTO - There are three pyramids.
HYPNOTIST - And the other two pyramids, where are they?

FILIBERTO - One is on land and the other under the ocean.
HYPNOTIST - In what part?
FILIBERTO - They are signalling me. It is like a light that comes on and makes an arc from one pyramid to another.
HYPNOTIST - And the third?
FILIBERTO - That is the one that is in the Atlantic. The other is on land.
HYPNOTIST - And you, where are you?
FILIBERTO - I am in that which is in . . . in . . . near to Berin.
HYPNOTIST - Quickly answer. one, two, three. One in the Atlantic, one on land, and the other?
FILIBERTO - It is where I am.
HYPNOTIST - But where are you?
FILIBERTO - This is that which is 400 into the sea, but I do not know in what part.
HYPNOTIST - And the one in the Atlantic. Isn't that under water also?
FILIBERTO - Yes, it is in the ocean.
HYPNOTIST - Two under water and one on land?
FILIBERTO - Yes.
HYPNOTIST - How long, would you say, they were there?
FILIBERTO - 36 months.
HYPNOTIST - What do they eat?
FILIBERTO - I don't remember what they eat. I do not know.
HYPNOTIST - Does this estrange you from your family?
FILIBERTO - Yes, but I want to understand all these things because they told me that there are seven (of us) to speak, to prepare for what will come to pass.
HYPNOTIST - Who are these seven?
FILIBERTO - I do not know who the seven are.
HYPNOTIST - They didn't tell you?
FILIBERTO - No. There are seven that they are going to return to Earth.
HYPNOTIST - What else happened?
FILIBERTO - One went in a thing that is going to command and the other six in other places are going to tell what is going to happen.
HYPNOTIST - On what date?
FILIBERTO - After 3 months.
HYPNOTIST - Were there children there?
FILIBERTO - Where this is going to happen?
HYPNOTIST - Where you were
FILIBERTO - There were some small ones there that I could see from a distance, but I don't know if they were children or adults. I

don't know.
HYPNOTIST - How do you know it was 36 months if they were not deceiving. Who told you it was 36 months?
FILIBERTO - They told me that it was 36 months they had been there.
HYPNOTIST - Why did they take you there?
FILIBERTO - Where?
HYPNOTIST - To the place. Where you said you were.
FILIBERTO - Where I was in the air or in the tunnel?
HYPNOTIST - No, in the tunnel.
FILIBERTO - Because that is where they had the controls. They had an information center.
HYPNOTIST - Who operated them?
FILIBERTO - . . . (silence)

At this moment one of the recorders stopped, making a noise.

Filiberto jumped up and began moving and opened his eyes.

HYPNOTIST - Be calm, be serene, be calm, be serene. Close your eyes, close, close, close . . . Sleep soundly, sleep calmly and serene . . . sleep . . . sleep . . . sleep.

Here I made a sign to the hypnotist to terminate this session.

HYPNOTIST - Now a very curious thing is going to happen. When I count three you will wake up laughing because you are very content, very happy and very satisfied, and a strange and interesting thing will occur. Little by little you will remember consciously all these things you have just lived. And you will remember all that you have not told me tonight. You will remember it all little by little, and you will accept it naturally and peacefully. You will continue your life normally and peacefully. Now you will wake up calm and serene and without fear of any kind, fearing nobody because there is nobody to fear. Now you will wake happily.

When Filiberto woke up we let him rest for a few minutes. In a short time I asked him if he could remember anything and he responded affirmatively. The following conversation then took place:

VIRGILIO - Do we have contact with them? (The extraterrestrials)
FILIBERTO - Yes, but they are not yet going to make themselves known to the world. They showed me a place, that gave me the impression that it was another planet.
VIRGILIO - And could you see it well?
FILIBERTO - The first people they showed me were wearing short pants with a loose fit, and they used something like a small cap on the head. I got the impression that they were people from

another planet. But later, continuing to pass as if in a movie, I could see well that those were Chinese communists. Then they must have contact with the people of Communist China. They are carrying out great experiments there. They told me that Communist China would surprise the world shortly. Soon the world will be shaken by the news that is going to come out of there, because the world expects one thing and soon they are going to have another, good, not bad. They have a series of secrets in their hands that they have given to those people. They (the Chinese) are capable of paralyzing great cities, or will be. China has this in her hands at this time.

VIRGILIO - How do you know that this treats of Communist China?

FILIBERTO - Because the thing (panorama) showed it. It showed a place where below a . . . It gave me the impression of the Obelisco de Mariano (in Cuba where Filiberto was raised), but much bigger. Beneath this obalisco there is a tomb of someone, and beneath the tomb is another room, and under that room is the control that can paralyze cities and towns completely.

VIRGILIO - Did the extraterrestrials give this control to the Chinese?

FILIBERTO - They gave them the control, but it is as if they have a power over the minds of them.

VIRGILIO - Of the Chinese?

FILIBERTO - The Chinese.

VIRGILIO - And they control the Chinese?

FILIBERTO - They control them. The thing is that the world will be surprised soon at what the Chinese are going to do. But it is good. It is not bad.

VIRGILIO - When?

FILIBERTO - Soon. Various things have to be done, some before others, but the change is going to be something for which the world cannot wait.

VIRGILIO - And they are going to have control of the Chinese?

FILIBERTO - They have control of the Chinese. There are going to be certain changes, certain things, provoked by the Chinese because there are some negative people, or would be, that in the changes those people disappear.

VIRGILIO - This is what you are saying, you have seen in the panorama like a TV?

FILIBERTO - This I saw later. At first . . .

VIRGILIO - In the picture?

FILIBERTO - It was as if you stood in front of a window.

VIRGILIO - What other interesting thing did you see? Did you see any other part of the world?

FILIBERTO - Yes, there are many places, many things, but I can not define them.

VIRGILIO - What most interested you is the part about the Chinese?

FILIBERTO - Yes, there was another thing that I am remembering. It was about cities. These cities were beautiful.

VIRGILIO - You saw all this in the panorama or through the window?

FILIBERTO - No, no, no . . . The impression that I received was that the panorama thing was not in black and white or TV nor in those colors. It was like it was in natural color, like looking out of a window. But I saw there, through that panorama, many things that passed at the time.

MARIO - Did you see any disaster, any negative scene?

FILIBERTO - I have the idea that there is going to be a great disaster. But great, great . . .

VIRGILIO - Disaster natural or a product of wars?

FILIBERTO - No, no, it wasn't from wars.

VIRGILIO - Then?

FILIBERTO - I have an impression of having seen at one time hundreds of miles of people running disoriented along the roads everywhere.

VIRGILIO - Is there any kind of prevention that we can undertake to avoid this?

FILIBERTO - They were showing me something about those things.

VIRGILIO - Changing the subject, do you remember where they left you?

FILIBERTO - I don't know . . . I can't . . . (He began to sweat, became nervous and agitated)

Then we decided that we must know the exact place where Filiberto was left when he was put out of the ship. We knew from the official police report that Filiberto was found on the Tamiami Trail at 137th Avenue. But nobody knew exactly where the ship let him out. The following day, the 28th of January, we were again together at Filiberto's house. We departed in two automobiles in the direction of the Tamiami Trail. With me was the hypnotist and in the other car, following us, were Filiberto and Mario Rodriguez.

Previously, in the house, the hypnotist had put Filiberto in trance and suggested that he remember the exact location. He was awake but under the suggestion given when we left the house. On the Tamiami Trail, at 137th Avenue, Filiberto sig-

UFO Abduction From Undersea

This was the first familiar sight upon Cardenas' return to Earth. Ironically it was a black automatic pistol on an orange-buff colored background on a big sign alongside the road that was illuminated by the approaching cars as he stumbled up onto the highway. This sign was only a little over a hundred feet from where Cardenas came out of the swanpy grass of his debarkation point from the spacecraft. This sign helped definitely fix the location later.

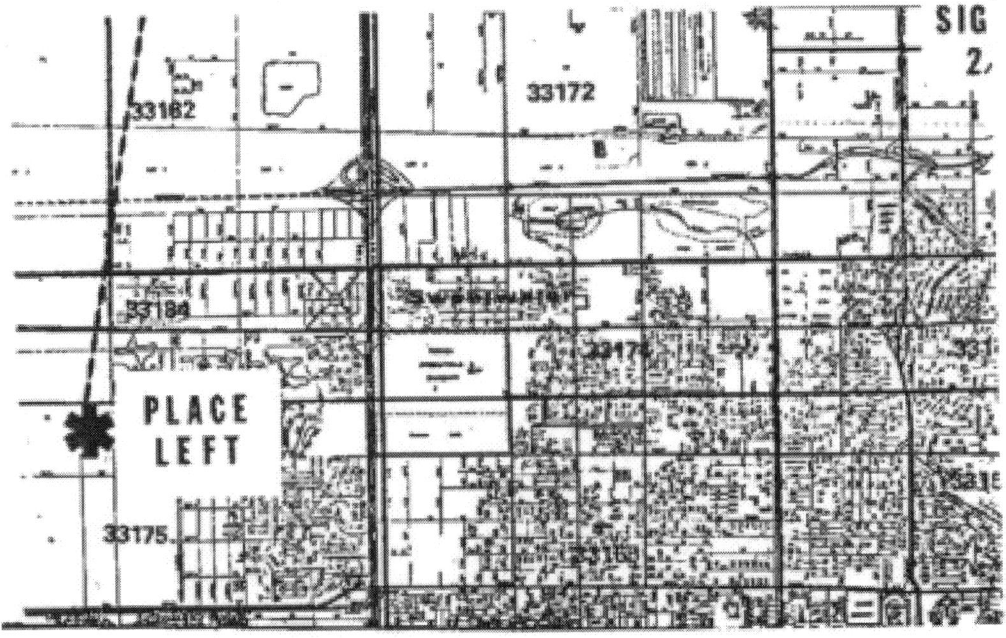

naled us to continue more slowly. We stopped at the entrance to a small lateral side road (more a two lane trail). There we got out and the hypnotist began to ask Filiberto to concentrate, to remember the place. "You know where it is. You are going to find it. You will guide us to it. Look around you. You know where it is." Filiberto, without saying a word, began to walk along the road. We followed quietly. We had walked about 100 meters when he turned and said, "It is about here, I am sure."

Now he walked a little faster. We followed close by. Soon he stopped and turned, and said to us "It is not here, we have passed it." We returned a short distance and he stopped again and said, "It is about here, I remember, from here I could first see the lights of the cars coming on the Tamiami Trail. I remember that I fell down. I could not support myself on my feet. I felt very bad. I headed toward the headlights." The hypnotist said to Filiberto, "Fix it good, you know that you were here. You will remember the place. You will remember all. Look around you. You know where you are. We are going to remember where they left you. You know. Where was it? The exact place?"

Filiberto answered, "Yes, I am remembering . . . it was about here . . . I stopped here . . . ," and he commenced to go into a place to the east of the trail. It was a meadow, a little swampy. The grass came up to his knees. I followed him. The hypnotist and Mario waited at the side of the trail. This place could be infested with vipers and snakes. Filiberto was not walking now, but was running now through that meadow shouting, "It was here. Now I remember. I am remembering." Tears came to his eyes. Sometimes he stopped, looked around him and then continued to run. I followed close behind him. We moved this way until we came near a wide-branched tree. Filiberto stopped, turned toward me and with a face full of tears shouted, "It was here! I am sure. The ship was here. This is where they let me out . . . I remember that I was stopped by the tree. Beyond it is a lake." We headed toward that. After passing between the trees we came upon a small lake. "I remember that I received a stroke on the head from a branch. I saw the moon reflected in the water. I was like I was completely disoriented, then I went in the other direction, until I came upon that trail. I saw the lights and I headed toward the highway. There they found me." We remained there a time in that place trying to discover some evidence or mark. Three weeks had passed, and the rain and time had had its effect. Nevertheless we could see some branches scraped and broken in that place. The vegetation had grown some, according to Filiberto. Now he remembered that the mark on his forehead was produced by his

UFO Abduction From Undersea

This is the sign marking the intersection of the small dirt road with the Tamiami Trail at 142nd Avenue SW, Miami, Florida.

running into the branch of the tree. We walked back to the trail informing Mario and the hypnotist about what had occurred. Filiberto continued to be emotional and agitated. We had to quiet him. We decided to terminate the investigation for the day.

The sudden revelation of devices installed in Mr. Cardenas' head during the physical examination aboard the alien spacecraft excited us and we immediately arranged for radiographic X-ray pictures of the witness' skull to find them.

Pictures were made from the left and front sides of the head and a careful examination of the area above the ear was made. Nothing unusual was detected and we were disappointed. The technician explained, however, that it was still possible that devices were there but that they were simply transparent to X-rays of the type produced by his machine. We proceeded with other less discouraging developments in this remarkable case.

EDITOR'S NOTE:

In an attempt to further establish the underwater "tunnel" mentioned by the witness, it was learned that this "tunnel" was not of solid rock as we think of a tunnel, and it did not have any projecting stalactites or stalagmites as already mentioned by the witness. He could not describe its entrance opening in any frame of reference known to him, and he had difficulty describing the walls. They were not of solid finished material like brick or stone, but were translucent and flowing LIKE FIRMED WATER. The ships flew in an "airspace" that opened in front of the craft as they proceeded, and may have closed again behind it, and no water or anything else actually touched the surfaces of the vehicle itself. The swiftly flowing "water" was close but did not touch the crystal (windshield) in front of the witness' face.

It appears to us that the witness is describing a ship-generated force-field of some kind which separated the mass of the material ahead of it and produced a capsule of "space" around it in which the craft flew. The curve in the tunnel mentioned may have been simply a re-directing of the force-field for a change of vector that was controlled by the extraterrestrial pilot sitting to the right of the witness in this small vehicle. This rush of water not touching the ship has been described by another UFO abductee who was taken in a spacecraft to an underwater base.

UFO Abduction From Undersea

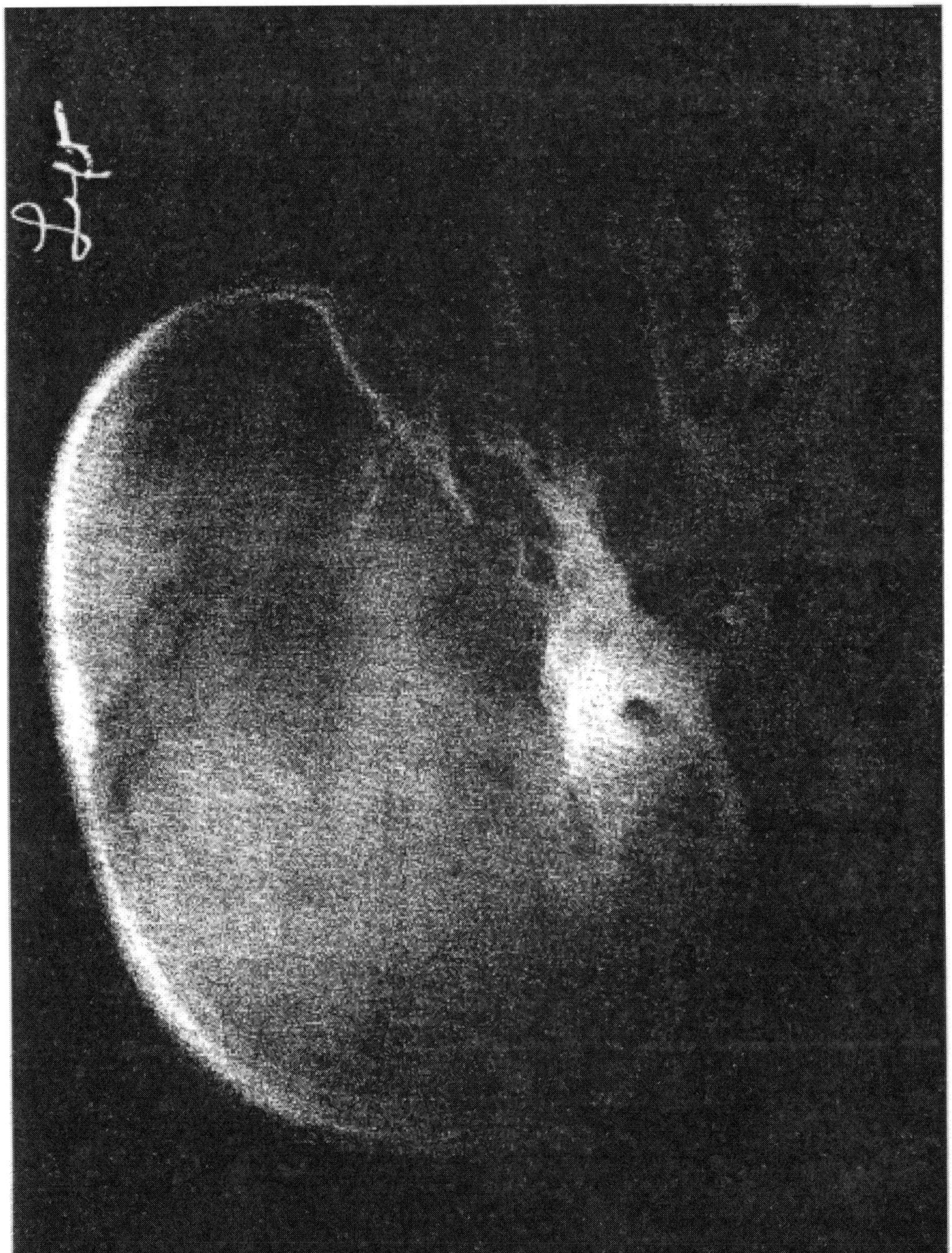

UFO Abduction From Undersea

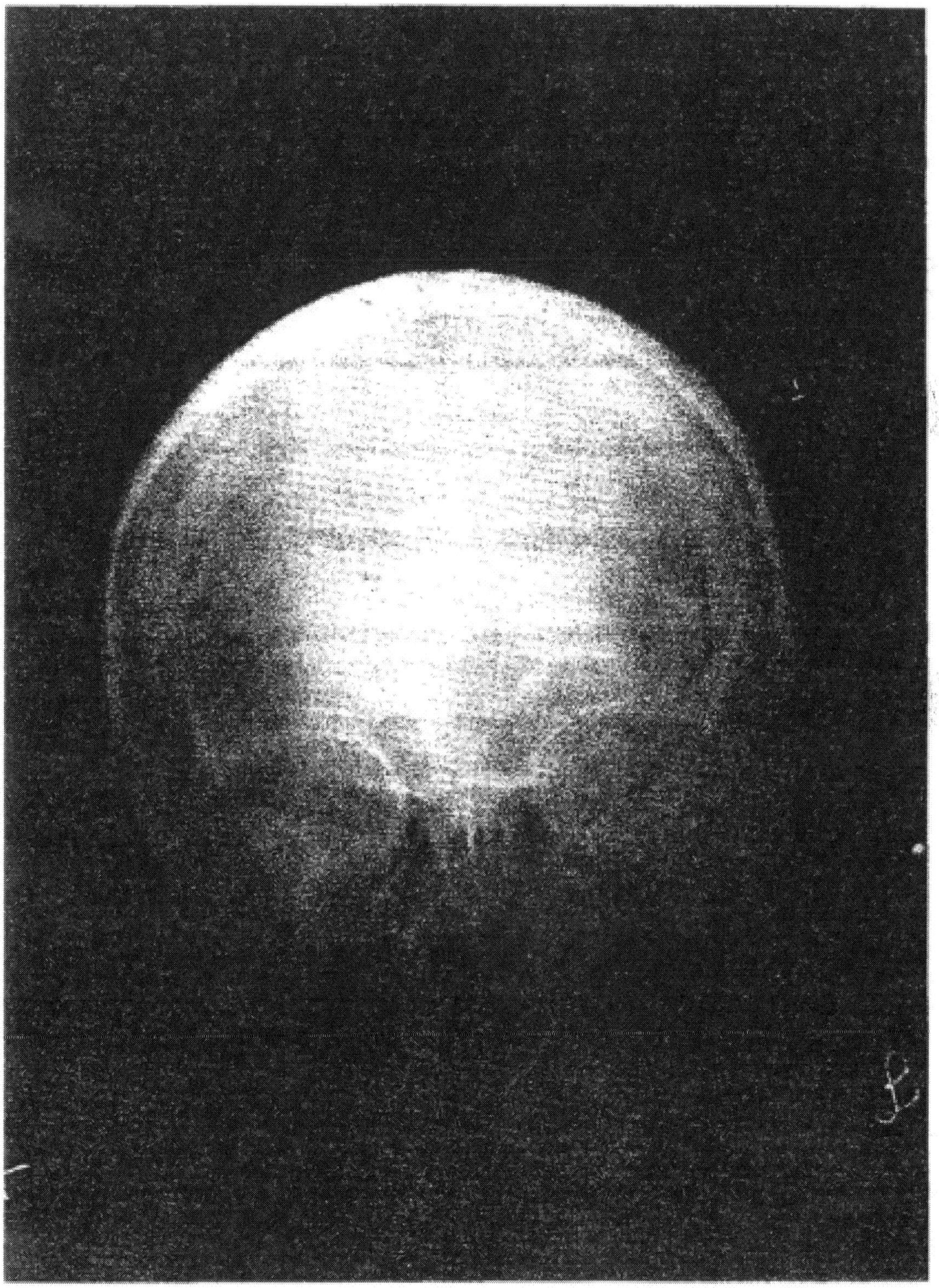

Above—Dr. Virgilio Sanchez-Ocejo in his study in his home in West Miami. Below—Dr. Sanchez-Ocejo and Filiberto Cardenas at the Miami International Airport.

UFO Abduction From Undersea

CHAPTER 3

Third Hypnotic Session

The third hypnotic session was conducted in the Cardenas home on 31 January 1979 at 8:30 in the evening. After placing Filiberto in a deep hypnotic trance we commenced questioning him:

HYPNOTIST - What is your name?

FILIBERTO - Filiberto Cardenas.

HYPNOTIST - What happened on the 3rd of January?

FILIBERTO - A light put me . . . seems like the light paralyzes . . . Then someone put something behind me that hauled me up. After that I was pulled as if I was on air and then I felt like I was rising. They took me, and I went in, in a thing and one of them took me by the arm and they seated me on something like a bench and then they put something in front of me so that I would not fall forward. And then they asked of me if I wanted to stay, or if I would like to go with them. I asked them, "Where are we going to go?" They said, "Yonder to another place, but we will return quickly.

HYPNOTIST - In what language did they speak?

FILIBERTO - They began with another language, then they spoke as if they were Spanish, but very strange. I did not understand well what they were saying. Then they took me far away. I saw something like stars, as if they were passing on the side, but at great speed. Then they took me to a place that when we were arriving looked like the Earth.

HYPNOTIST - What else?

FILIBERTO - Then they told me that I should look well because our globe is not the only one there is. Look, 10,000 years before your time, this other place was created here where people live. We are 60 times your size, and we are more powerful than you because we are more advanced than you. Then they told me that we have not wanted to be helped. There has been some 4,000 years since they began to have contact. When they gave us messages the people misinterpreted them badly. That every time

they have come to a particular place, they said, the people adore them as if they were gods. And they are beings superior to us, but they are still far from the gods that we speak of. Some that they have are advanced, others are very much advanced. They have much technical science, but they are not saints though people adore them as saints. They are preparing now, the things that are necessary so that we do not give them the reception we did in other times. It has been thousands of years since they descended last. The people then adored them and said that they were saints come to Earth.
HYPNOTIST - Continue.
FILIBERTO - There they demonstrated much technical science. They told me, "Look what is going to happen there. We have no intentions undesirable with you, but we want to help you and you will become more advanced. But when we have given instructions to anyone and we have made contact with them to give them knowledge of these things, they do not believe it. That in general they say that we are of forms very distracting, and that has been the drawback of the terrestrains. Because we do not prefer the ones over the others and in each part of the world are distinctly different races, they each seek superiority and believe us more knowledgeable (and seek to use us). They said that they have classes also, but that of the classes, those with the lesser intelligence or less scientific technology, could still be masters to teach thousands of years more knowledge than those of Earth.
HYPNOTIST - Continue.
FILIBERTO - They showed me and said, "Look at what I have here in front of me," and they had kind of a stone. That stone was activated by means of a reflection of light. That mirror of light was capable of burning whole cities and great territories. They said the forces of Earth could have vast arms, but only one ship of theirs was capable of destroying them all. But they do not intend to cause harm because they do not want us to fear them. If we don't move forward, they will use more forceful demonstrations. But they are going to have to give a lesson to humanity to be able to save the rest of the world. They cannot advise us on great catastrophes or great things that are going to happen. They also have special equipment, or something like that, they told me, that is like an electric battery, like a light that they call... I do not remember... but they said that it is the fourth ascendency above laser rays, that they used thousands of years ago, on Earth, laser rays and that they want to have now an access before we finalize this stage, this lap that we are now beginning, a stage that I interpreted as if it were years. In a short time they intend to

have important demonstrations. They told me that the distinct forms of religions, that we use, for a great part are dominated by people who seek aggrandizement, that develop into personality cults and gain power and abundancies of many things. They say that we terrestrians need a religion, but a distinct religion (personal), not in groups and the things that they are doing, and that each one within themselves symbolize the same God. They say that the head, in these moments can perform good works, but he has around him men of lesser intentions that apparently come from the intelligence of cosmic space, or as we call it, God. But that all these things are with a tendency to aggrandize which is definitely a bad system. I interpreted what they wanted to call bad as the devil. And that the head is trying to accomplish certain things, is trying to come down, is trying to humble itself but is trying to clean up the things that it has around it. I interpreted the head to be the Pope of the Catholic Church. They reprehended me strongly because I did not complete with them, the mission that they gave me. I told them that I had tried to complete in part the mission but that the people would not believe me. Then they told me that for those ones they have prepared this, so that the people will believe. And the people will believe. Because they have to believe. They don't want to take hard measures with anybody, but they are going to do what they have to do. After much time . . . (inaudible).

HYPNOTIST - Sleep soundly and continue talking loud and clear.

FILIBERTO - They told me, more than 8 months ago, what was going to happen and the people did not believe me.

HYPNOTIST - What happens?

FILIBERTO - They told me that the leadership of the Catholic Church will be without its head (the Pope) and that later another will come.

HYPNOTIST - What day is today for you?

FILIBERTO - Eight months from the last year (or the last of this year).

HYPNOTIST - Why do you say that it will be from the last year?

FILIBERTO - This is the last year that they are going to be trying the thing because, except for them they would act differently.

HYPNOTIST - Continue sleeping profoundly and continue narrating loud and clear.

FILIBERTO - They told me that if now I do not complete the third mission before the beginning of another year they are going to separate from me and also to withdraw from many others who also have done nothing. I told them that if they gave me the power so that the other people would believe what I say, on their behalf, and then told me what they want, as I have said here, at least some part would come to believe and it would be a preparation for others also to speak messages and the beliefs of those they call scientists, if they want to be scientists, increasing the faith in other things, and there will come great things and actions of another kind. There are many ungodly men here on this planet, in this year and before, that will be made into ashes. Another turned me around in reprimand and he had a great book in his hands where he had annotated the inscriptions when he spoke to me about the head of the church. I tried to explain these things to several acquaintances of mine and also to many other people. I tried to tell some that were doctors and some artists and other people of certain prestige, but they don't believe me. They told me that I possibly have bad nerves. These things are harmful to me because I experienced something similar when I was a child with my family. When I told them these things they also said that I had bad nerves. That was the first time, then the second, and now the third. But now they said that is not the manner to proceed, because now they are not tempting me. But they have their plans, and the plan is: Live for a time here and transform the system in all its aspects.

They spoke to me as I have related, and all that they told me and showed me I have stated, exactly as I told you happened. I asked them if they had killed. They said no, but they understood that it could appear so because they could understand the future.

The pope dies, and then shortly after that the second pope also dies. There is a struggle to designate one who is not a Roman and then they told me that it would endure for a little time, but that there is a conspiracy against him. After that will come one who is not born on that place (Italy). He is going to discover the New World. He is going to come to preach to the New World in our own language. And so they accounted to me. I have told about 86 people about this, including newsmen and artists.

On February 6th of 1973, I was given a message of importance that that also was received from them, but without them presenting it to me. I saw it as if it were in a television. I saw it giving me instructions. That time I was not where there were many newspaper reporters nor did I make any effort to report it to them. The Security Intelligence Services of this nation (The United States) did not believe me though they interrogated me for 15 days over what I told them what could happen, and finally determined that I was suffering from nervous alterations because I had dreamed it. Some time later, having taken no measures concerning what I had reported, and I had reported all that they had transmitted to me, that they (the extraterrestrials) had shown, everything came to pass exactly as said. It pertained to a conspiracy to withhold on the part of President Nixon and Vice-President Agnew of the United States, but they didn't believe me. They had 3,000 feet of recordings. There were four distinct bodies of security of this country. It pertained to an atrocity in the plans they had for Earth, for the inescapable changes that are coming. They do not want me now to reveal anything about this because they say the end of the plan is approaching. I can only say that I am going to be one of those that will be announcing the things that come to pass in this world.

HYPNOTIST - Continue sleeping and continue to describe loudly and clearly. Tell us what is going to happen.

FILIBERTO - Many things will happen now, but not because they are going to make it happen, but they want to announce it and prepare us so that nobody disappears.

HYPNOTIST - Do you understand it?

FILIBERTO - Yes. They want that someone they designate take the information to the public media so that we can take the measures necessary, or on the contrary, refuse to accept the information as they choose.

HYPNOTIST - What are you going to do?

FILIBERTO - If you will accept the information I will tell you.

VIRGILIO - Who are you?

FILIBERTO - I am . . .

HYPNOTIST - Your name? When I count three . . .

FILIBERTO - I am Filiberto Cardenas now.

VIRGILIO - And before?

FILIBERTO - Well, before it was them that were doing the talking.

HYPNOTIST - Now I am going to count again to three and you will continue speaking loud and clear . . . one . . . two . . . three. Now.

FILIBERTO - Two nights ago, I received a message. I have been receiving messages from them and they know all that you are doing with me. They are satisfied at what you are doing with me. There are two of all the personnel that are interested in this thing about trying to investigate what in reality is going on here, what is the message. Two of those are going to have direct proofs. Then they will speak, because it will also bring them to turn around (in their thinking). They are a man and a woman. It will happen to them. It will not last long. In a brief time they are going to pick them up . . . Later, following what is to come, they will receive a type of communication of a manner that is not

normal for them. But they are going to have the opportunity, then they are going to be able to say that this was no experience of another person, but was lived by them.
HYPNOTIST - Sleep soundly. Continue loudly and clearly.
FILIBERTO - I was 7 years old when they presented themselves to me the first time, but I could not understand. It frightened me much and I thought it was an older brother of mine that had a big lantern. It transformed me. I remember that I had power to cure at that time, and I saw many things. They announced some things (then). My father and mother and my brother took me to a doctor who was a psychiatrist but he always said I was not going crazy.
HYPNOTIST - How old were you?
FILIBERTO - That began when I was 7 years old.
HYPNOTIST - At that time, could you levitate from the floor?
FILIBERTO - One time, in a fire, I rose above the house.
HYPNOTIST - Can you do it now?
FILIBERTO - Right now I can not tell you what I can do, only I . . .
HYPNOTIST - Continue narrating loud and clear, rapidly.
FILIBERTO - I can do many things, but I can not tell you. Some of you will have experiences with this and then you will understand what others can do, those who already have had experiences.
HYPNOTIST - Continue speaking clearly and loudly. Be calm, relax. (Then the hypnotist produced a needle and pricked Cardenas' arm. I saw it make a mark but Filiberto showed no reaction.)
HYPNOTIST - Do you hear me?
FILIBERTO - Yes.
HYPNOTIST - Filiberto, can you speak in another language? Can you speak in English? Continue speaking in English, if you can.
FILIBERTO - I can say nothing in English now.
HYPNOTIST - Can not or will not?
FILIBERTO - I can speak, but later.
HYPNOTIST - Do you know what they are going to do?
FILIBERTO - I don't know.
HYPNOTIST - Continue your narration speaking loud and clear.
FILIBERTO - For 22 months, I have been having experiences with someone whose name they have not told me.
HYPNOTIST - They did not tell you?
FILIBERTO - No.
HYPNOTIST - Was it here on Earth or away from here?
FILIBERTO - It was very far.
HYPNOTIST - Continue narrating loud and clear.

UFO Abduction From Undersea

FILIBERTO - They showed me important things. Things that they can make appear and disappear in front of one's eyes, that not only their ships can do this...(illegible). They informed me also that we have to be careful because other places that do not pursue the same objectives, are making themselves as angels. They are not as advanced as the good ones but they are much advanced and are very important and they told me, if those pursue bad objectives against us, they could do two things. They could destroy this planet with the same arms that this planet has, without using any of theirs, or on the contrary, transport away our great armaments in one operation, that for us terrestrians would take no more than 20 minutes of our time. They could make us disappear into pieces in 20 minutes, or in the same 20 minutes leave us with no armaments capable of destroying anything because they can be visible or invisible as they choose.
HYPNOTIST - What combustible do they use for this?
FILIBERTO - They did not tell me.
HYPNOTIST - Speak loudly and clearly.
FILIBERTO - They could appear, being at our side and we didn't see them, but if they like, they can leave us at once. They have around the world, or better, of our planet, at this time, since some years ago having conducted experiments, 81 begotten beings (half extraterrestrial and half terrestrial) living on Earth. Most of them have completed missions while others are still little. But there are many of them who have completed missions of great importance.
HYPNOTIST - And why did they tell you all these things? For whom did they tell you?
FILIBERTO - Precisely for my test, to see if I was a proper messenger for when things begin to happen. Because others will come who will also make the announcements but the people will not believe them. To help make them believe the others when they appear.
HYPNOTIST - On this occasion did they mention what things are going to happen?
FILIBERTO - I asked them about that, for some things.
HYPNOTIST - And what did they say?
FILIBERTO - Among other things, there will disappear, here precisely on Earth, great portions of land and whole cities
VIRGILIO - When?
FILIBERTO - They said in a short time. It is not that they are going to do anything, but to see if they could prevent, at least, a little and save some numbered millions of people.
VIRGILIO - Two or three months?

FILIBERTO - No, they said a brief time, but exactly they didn't say, then they let me see a "televisor" of the terrestrians that are going to disappear.
HYPNOTIST - Who are they?
FILIBERTO - When you asked me "who are they?" why do you want to know? You. Is it in your power or disposition to prevent the damage that all these people are going to suffer?
HYPNOTIST - Me, no. But why did they tell you then?
FILIBERTO - For what do you want to know?
HYPNOTIST - For the same reason they have told it to you.
FILIBERTO - They told it to me so that I can give the message to humanity and humanity can believe and save themselves.
HYPNOTIST - Why don't you give it then?
FILIBERTO - Because you cannot mount a capability to do anything to avoid it.
HYPNOTIST - Who are you going to tell that has such capability?
FILIBERTO - People are coming that are capable, by means of the media of communications, to spread the message that can save those who believe it.
HYPNOTIST - What is your name? What do they call you?
FILIBERTO - I am not going to tell you what they call me. It seems like you do not believe these things. It might be possible to give you a test to help you believe this. (At this time we started speaking to him in English.)
HYPNOTIST - What are you talking about? (in English) Do you understand me? Why don't you answer me now?
FILIBERTO - . . . (silence)
HYPNOTIST - What? About what? (in English)
FILIBERTO - I don't know . . . (in Spanish)
HYPNOTIST - You don't know what? (in English)
FILIBERTO - Nothing.
HYPNOTIST - Now a doctor is going to talk to you about something very important. (in English)
DOCTOR - What kind of illnesses do you have there? Do you have much illness? Are they the same as ours? (in English)
FILIBERTO - . . . (silence)
DOCTOR - Can you give us any of the knowledges that they have?
HYPNOTIST - Speak, relax and speak. (in English)
DOCTOR - It is very important for us to know cures for the illnesses of men. Do you know anything about this . . . ? Why won't you help? Why don't you talk? (in English)
FILIBERTO - . . . (silence)
HYPNOTIST - When I count to three you will talk, one . . . two . . . three. Speak.

UFO Abduction From Undersea

FILIBERTO - . . . (silence)
DOCTOR - Why won't you help us with our illnesses? (in English)
FILIBERTO - . . . (He becomes restless. We returned to speaking to him in Spanish.)
HYPNOTIST - Relax, rest, sleep soundly. Now, continue narrating everything loud and clear.
FILIBERTO - They say, if you want, they can tell many things. If you want to give them tests or prove them for mediation by me they say they are going to talk in any language that is spoken by us. Whatever you select. What they are doing with me is no simple pastime, but something that is playing with the happiness and the joy, the peace and the life of millions of beings.
HYPNOTIST - Why should we believe in them if they don't believe in us? If they are so powerful, why don't they give proofs immediately?
FILIBERTO - One of the proofs you already have.
VIRGILIO - What is that?
FILIBERTO - They already have given, they are giving, and they continue giving.
HYPNOTIST - What is it?
FILIBERTO - All of the things that we have been saying, and all the things that are to come soon.
HYPNOTIST - Continue sleeping soundly but you will continue relating rapidly and strongly all that has passed since when your car broke down, that was where we began . . . Continue rapidly.
FILIBERTO - That part I have already told to you.
HYPNOTIST - Have you already regresses, or have you not regressed?
FILIBERTO - I still am where I was presenting something (seen) in an apparatus that looks like a television from here, from Earth. Those terrestrians who are going to be destroyed, or better, that are going to become great or immense lakes or parts of the sea. There is another city very distant which will also become ocean or a lake of importance.
HYPNOTIST - In America or in Europe?
FILIBERTO - The city is called . . . the capital of Mexico!
HYPNOTIST - Very soon?
FILIBERTO - This will happen in a little time. They are not going to do this. They always say with emphasis, "We didn't do this, we want to prevent these happenings." When I asked them if they could do something they said no, that the inhabitants of those places have been abandoned. Because there is something, there is something that is . . . (silence) . . . I asked them if this was

punishment for something. But it is not, rather it is something natural and they told me in a form that I cannot see or analyze. I don't remember exactly what they said but that this must come to pass, and it will come to pass. The means of salvation of the people or inhabitants, that are millions, in those distinct places, is to abandon those places.

HYPNOTIST - What is the capital of Mexico?

FILIBERTO - The capital of Mexico is one.

HYPNOTIST - What are the others?

FILIBERTO - All, almost all the great population centers of California, all will go into the sea . . . (inaudible)

HYPNOTIST - You will continue sleeping, narrating all. Someone else is going to ask questions for your response.

MARIO - Will all this come to pass after the three months that you mentioned in the beginning?

FILIBERTO - This that is going to happen?

MARIO - Yes.

FILIBERTO - No.

MARIO - What will happen after the three months?

FILIBERTO - After the three months will come distinct messengers to give evidence, to give messages and each day they will be giving more (people) those messages, and each day the people will believe more in these things that they have been believing for five years.

MARIO - How many messengers are they going to bring?

FILIBERTO - Six or more.

MARIO - Will they come together?

FILIBERTO - To distinct places.

HYPNOTIST - Do any come in anything?

FILIBERTO - All are coming in ships (spacecraft).

VIRGILIO - Are they from Earth or from that other place?

FILIBERTO - The six that are coming are from this Earth, that some time ago were carried away (in spacecraft). They are being prepared.

VIRGILIO - Have you seen them?

FILIBERTO - I did not see them.

HYPNOTIST - Will they say the same thing?

FILIBERTO - I asked them a question, "Is the 'Chilean' one of those?" and they replied that at this time that was not in their plans, but it could be.

HYPNOTIST - These seven, do they come after the three months?

FILIBERTO - In three months, into distinct parts of the world. They are going to do something. Exactly what they are going to do I do not know.

UFO Abduction From Undersea

HYPNOTIST - And this of Mexico, will it happen this year?
FILIBERTO - I do not believe it is this year. They said soon but that is not going to be within this year. For Mexico they told me other news.
VIRGILIO - Which?
FILIBERTO - In the order sentimental to me, or being an impression personal. There will be happenings in Mexico where, I see . . . there is a demonstration as if it is a movie of what is going to happen. I see several Mexican artists together with some other people that are dead. They are famous people. They told me all these things so as not to detract from anybody but also so that I would not take it for a dream. The things that I have been shown are distinct proofs that they are giving me not to detract from my mission (to in fact emphasize it and make it credible to the witness). That I have had also, they told me, another . . . (inaudible.)
HYPNOTIST - What artists are those? Do you remember?
FILIBERTO - Yes, I remember, but that no . . . good, one of them is well known, they are all well known and some of them are people of television and movies. One of them is the comic known as . . . Cantinflas, and another is . . . Velazco, these are the ones most seen . . .
HYPNOTIST - When will this happen?
FILIBERTO - This could be during the year. One will have, will disappear and the others will have grave dangers. There are a number. Here in the United States we will have an illness, there is a woman (actress) with very attractive eyes whose name is . . . I don't remember what . . . is going to have an illness, and the illness she has is going to be published throughout the whole world. She is an artist who is very famous. Also I was shown much about her politics in the United States. If it were not for this illness she could become the first lady of the United States. In politics her husband could come to be the president of the United States.
HYPNOTIST - Rest, be calm, sleep soundly. Relax but you will answer the questions that we are going to ask now.
VIRGILIO - Why don't they communicate directly with the Chiefs of State?
FILIBERTO - I can not answer exactly. I do not have the information exactly, but they speak of the vanity of man who thinks himself wise and believes himself powerful and important, and that they are very difficult. They mentioned as examples the government of kings of antiquity as well as those in the modern epoch.

VIRGILIO - Why don't they select figures like the Pope?
FILIBERTO - The Pope is one of those selected at this time, only there is a series of questions and some interferences that they do not want to go into in clarifications with me.
VIRGILIO - Is there any way that we can communicate with them if one wanted to?
FILIBERTO - They can communicate through me.
MARIO - When you want to communicate with them, can you do it?
FILIBERTO - It is possible that I could do it, but not from this position.
HYPNOTIST - If you tried, would they know?
FILIBERTO - By going to other points.
VIRGILIO - Other points of the Earth?
FILIBERTO - By going to other points of the Earth together with some from the groups who have helped me they would have an experience together with me so that upon their return . . .
VIRGILIO - Where are those points?
FILIBERTO - I cannot tell you now. You are going to know when we have the experience.
HYPNOTIST - You were speaking, when you told us of the artists, of a thing that they were going to say. Now can you continue relating?
FILIBERTO - There is another message they gave me about a person of considerable importance in the world but they want to avoid the catastrophe of wars.
HYPNOTIST - Keep talking loud and clear.
FILIBERTO - I know what you are trying to do with me, and they know also, and so they are telling me to take care about what I am saying. But nevertheless, though I cannot tell you directly, it is possible for you to guess the person. I am going to mention two. One is the ruler of Egypt. The government of Egypt, in a short time will lose its leader. It will also lose its government and there will be great disasters throughout its territories. It could put this whole planet in peril of being disintegrated by a war of great consequences.
HYPNOTIST - This could occur before the end of 1981. They want to avoid all this. In this year there is a great conspiracy against the government of Egypt, but there is also against the government of Israel. At the same time there is a great conspiracy between the people that control energy, in Kuwait and also in Arabia where they have petroleum energy. All those governments will disappear.
HYPNOTIST - They didn't tell you anything about Cuba?

UFO Abduction From Undersea

FILIBERTO - They said something about a relationship that they are making. They are making a relationship among all these places, but they are making a special relationship here in the Americas. They said that Cuba, at this time . . . well they did not say exactly Cuba, but I interpreted it that way...is the goad that could cleave to make possible the exploitation of the...the... (inaudible)...and that it could make explosion of the explosives.
HYPNOTIST - Where?
FILIBERTO - Well, they did not clear that up, but it is of much importance. This man, who is in Cuba, said he had contact one time, but was cut off. I also was diverted and they are not obliged to any person to tell what the cosmic intelligence of space has in store for this whole world, of free will. They are lesser and can not remove the free will of the people. They can not oblige us to follow a course that they may consider better. This is what happened to that person that was on that island, which I interpreted to be Cuba.
HYPNOTIST - Good, continue talking loud and clear. Now we are going to ask a question. Respond to it.
MARIO - The new relations between the United States and Communist China, is it beneficial? Is it in response to any kind of intervention by you?
FILIBERTO - . . . (silence)
HYPNOTIST - Quickly, answer, one . . . two . . . three.
FILIBERTO - I have not had an opportunity to see anything about those relations. When you say you, to whom are you referring?
MARIO - To whoever has been intervening in what has been described.
FILIBERTO - Are you referring to those people who took me?
MARIO - Yes.
FILIBERTO - They showed me a relationship that existed. In China, at this time they have not developed great armaments, but with the one it is sufficient to paralyze great extensions of the world. There are only a few who have this secret. The whole government does not have the secret. They have been undergoing a transformation because this is the way they are forced to go . . . What they were before the transformation, they say they are now the total opposite. They showed me an example with one who was afoot and they said, "This was their inclination," then the person reversed his position front to back and they said, "So is going to go to China."
HYPNOTIST - They are going to ask another question. Respond loud and clear.

UFO Abduction From Undersea

VIRGILIO - I s it true that they have controls under the monument in China?
FILIBERTO - They have them.
VIRGILIO - Do they control the manner of thinking of governments?
FILIBERTO - They can do this. Those who have the controls are not precisely the higher government. They have power, including killing from a distance, for that which disturbs their plans for what they are going to do. They don't want to say so, but if their plans are hindered it seems that they might be disposed to use them to avoid other greater events disturbing the established plans.
VIRGILIO - What interest do the extraterrestrians have in us?
FILIBERTO - They need to expand to other places and they want to make certain scientific tests. They have good missions because they have a universal love and they understand what has come to pass here. They are also coming from other places where life (like ours) exists. It is only a mission. They say that they still have in them some vanity, but not as much as we.
HYPNOTIST - Sleep profoundly, peacefully, relaxed, tranquil...
VIRGILIO - Did they say anything about the pyramids?
FILIBERTO - They began to speak about the pyramids. Then it was when we descended.
VIRGILIO - Of which pyramids did they speak?
FILIBERTO - They began by speaking of the pyramids that control the Earth globe.
HYPNOTIST - Which are they? Give us their names.
FILIBERTO - Then they said to me we are now going to the greater.
HYPNOTIST - Which was it?
FILIBERTO - That which contains the special controls.
VIRGILIO - They have controls?
FILIBERTO - They have special controls in a mountain that is at the edge of a beach.
HYPNOTIST - Where is that?
FILIBERTO - I don't know exactly, but it was near Berin.
HYPNOTIST - The Bearing Straight?
FILIBERTO - Yes, near there, and another village.
HYPNOTIST - What country, or what city, is near there. What did you pass?
FILIBERTO - I didn't pass by any city, we descended directly to the edge of the beach and there they worked a combination on a rock that was there and they opened like a tunnel that went out toward the sea. Other ships that were there came out and they

followed behind us and we all went into the sea at great velocity.
VIRGILIO - In the Atlantic, or the Pacific?
FILIBERTO - It is between Berin, and they said Berin, and I understood Santiago. These are the reference points, and then 400 into the sea, but I do not know what is 400 into the sea. They went at a speed, a speed such that I could see nothing ahead. It was a fantastic velocity for under water.
HYPNOTIST - Did they tell you many more things?
FILIBERTO - They spoke of and there they showed me the other pyramids that are around the world.
HYPNOTIST - Which were they?
FILIBERTO - Another that is in the center of the land, another that is . . .
VIRGILIO - Under the water?
FILIBERTO - In the water, but in the Atlantic.
VIRGILIO - And the one in the center of the land?
FILIBERTO - That one I cannot say where until after the 3 months.
VIRGILIO - Is it in the center of this Earth?
FILIBERTO - Seems like I cannot say, seems like that is in the mission for another person. They showed me but they did not say clearly where it could be found.
HYPNOTIST - And why do you have such fear of talking on other occasions?
FILIBERTO - On other occasions? With whom?
HYPNOTIST - Who are you?
FILIBERTO - . . . (silence)
HYPNOTIST - Be calm, serene, relaxed, sleep profoundly . . .
HYPNOTIST - What did they do to your hands?
FILIBERTO - They made many tests on me, and there were 108 marks which I had all over my body, and it seemed like it was necessary to make the number 108. They took many tests of all the things. They said also that I, as well as many others, am going to have proofs of superior energy, which is what they called it, superior energy of the reproductive organs, sexually, to make tests, to see the results they are going to have, because the results they have had here on Earth already are conclusive and they are continuing the experiments.
HYPNOTIST - Did they tell you why they selected you when you were a child?
FILIBERTO - I asked them this question and they told me that it would be disputed, but after other things have come to pass that no . . . (disturbed)
HYPNOTIST - Be calm, serene, relaxed, sleep soundly . . .

UFO Abduction From Undersea

Filiberto began to show tiredness in his voice and for this reason we decided to discontinue and postpone further hypnosis to another day. Then the hypnotist proceeded to awaken Filiberto, always suggesting that he would be able to remember everything and all that happened and that it would not cause any emotional problems.

After the hypnotic session we passed to the living room of his house to make our commentaries and prepare for the next session, leaving the doctor time to make a quick examination of the witness's physical state. We spent nearly an hour talking of other things of lesser importance, when suddenly Mario Rodriguez and my wife Maria Elena raised both their hands to their ears and covered them. Their faces became disfigured with pain and they were rocking back and forth in their seats, almost bumping their heads on their knees. And then they both began to shout at once AY! AY! AY! . . . The rest of us looked at each other in surprise. And then we began to ask, what happened, what is going on? A few seconds passed, which seemed like eternities, and then both began to raise their heads again. Their faces no longer showed the pain but surprise at what had happened to them. Maria Elena was the first to speak. "It has passed." We insisted, "But what was it that passed? Tell us." After a few minutes of guarded silence they commenced to explain that it felt like a whistling noise in their ears, that it was increasing and pulsating until they began to feel an intense pain in the ears, and that their reactions were uncontrollable. We looked at each other without words and suddenly understood that they were the persons mentioned in the hypnotic session, "Two of those are *going to have direct proofs*. Then they will speak, because it will also bring them to turn around. They are *a man and a woman*. It will happen to them."

From that moment Maria Elena as well as Mario began to involve themselves in this case in such a manner that today, as I write these lines, she assures me that "This is not only an experience of other people, because we have lived it for ourselves." Both of them have continued developing their psychic faculties in a surprising manner, especially Maria Elena.

That same night, as we were coming home from the Cardenas' residence to our place, in a surprising manner she said to me that she would like to go to the place where Filiberto appeared (when he came back from the first abduction). I looked at her a little strangely but acceded. It was already 11:30 P.M. when we headed out in that direction. It was intensely cold for which we remained in the car with the heater running. The night was dark and when I turned out the lights we could not see anything. Only the cars that came by once in a while. We stayed like that for nearly an hour until we decided to return. At home, only a few minutes had passed before we heard the telephone ring. It was Filiberto, and without any preamble he asked, "Where were you? What did you do in the place where they found me?" Before we come out of our surprise, he said that he knew that we had gone there. He was very sure and he had called us to prove it.

Things similar to this have happened repeatedly, sometimes with us and other times with Mario, forming a contact triangle. For me, the result was easy verification of all these things. For example, Maria Elena woke me one morning and said that she could hear the sound in her ears. Another day, in the morning, Mario and Filiberto both called to inform that they had heard the sound in their ears the night before. And it always happened at the same time!

This kind of telepathy developed among those three until we began to wonder what was going to happen. On various occasions Maria Elena received messages after hearing the sound. These messages ordered her to go to certain places. Almost always Filiberto would be there. We went every time this happened but nothing else resulted. Nothing in particular happened that would make one think that this was motivated by the extraterrestrials. We always came back disheartened because we always went thinking we would return with some new proof. Perhaps a contact with them, the extraterrestrials, would take place. We continued going with the same hope every time that Maria Elena heard the sound in her ears, or they seemed to desire, or to order, us to go to that place. I still have hope that something will happen in some coming day.

CHAPTER 4

Fourth Hypnotic Session

The fourth,and last hypnotic regression was also conducted in the Cardenas home in Hialeah. This took place on 10 February 1979 at 7:00 P.M. After having put Filiberto into a hypnotic sleep we commenced to question him further.

HYPNOTIST - What is your name?
FILIBERTO - Filiberto Cardenas.
HYPNOTIST - Very good. Speak loudly and good and clear so that we can hear you. What day is today?
FILIBERTO - Saturday . . . Saturday . . .
HYPNOTIST - Saturday, what?
FILIBERTO - No, I don't know what day today is.
HYPNOTIST - Today is Saturday the 10th of February 1979. Sleep soundly. Every minute, every second that passes you will sleep more profoundly. Now when I count to three, we are going to travel rapidly in time. We are going to go back to Saturday the 3rd of February. One . . . two . . . three. What day is today?
FILIBERTO - Saturday.
HYPNOTIST - What Saturday? . . . Quickly.
FILIBERTO - Saturday 3 and 10 . . . 3 and 10 . . .
HYPNOTIST - That is the hour, very good. Give me the day?
FILIBERTO - Saturday the third.
HYPNOTIST - What hour is it?
FILIBERTO - About seven . . .
HYPNOTIST - Where are you?
FILIBERTO - . . . (silence).
HYPNOTIST - Answer . . . rapidly . . . When I count to three . . .
FILIBERTO - Seven twenty eight.
HYPNOTIST - Where are you?
FILIBERTO - Where am I now?
HYPNOTIST - Yes.
FILIBERTO - Now, I have just arrived at my house.
HYPNOTIST - Very good. Now, when I count to three, let us continue traveling in time, and let us go back to the 10th of

January . . . one . . . two . . . three. Now. What day is today?
FILIBERTO - Tenth of January, no?
HYPNOTIST - What time is it?
FILIBERTO - It is five twenty.
HYPNOTIST - Where are you?
FILIBERTO - I am in my house. I see that it is five twenty on my watch and the other clock reads five forty-two.
HYPNOTIST - Very good. Now, when I count to three we will go back to 3 January . . . one . . . two . . . three. Now. What day is it?
FILIBERTO - Three January.
HYPNOTIST - What time is it?
FILIBERTO - It is 8:29.
HYPNOTIST - Where are you?
FILIBERTO - I don't know, because there are people surrounding me and they look like police or similar.
HYPNOTIST - Very good. Are they police?
FILIBERTO - Yes, some are police and others are not.
HYPNOTIST - Very good. Now, let us go back in time one hour. What time is it?
FILIBERTO - . . . (silence)
HYPNOTIST - Quickly, what time is it?
FILIBERTO - Do you mean the time on my watch?
HYPNOTIST - Yes.
FILIBERTO - It is 7:28.
HYPNOTIST - Where are you?
FILIBERTO - I am in a place where they took me . . . I don't know where this is. I am here . . . Well, I can not see outside because of the walls that are here and the people that are here.
HYPNOTIST - How are the people?
FILIBERTO - Well, there is one who is seated in a big seat.
HYPNOTIST - How is he?
FILIBERTO - He has a cape . . . He has a cape . . .
HYPNOTIST - What color?
FILIBERTO - It is of distinct . . . as if it were of other colors, and I don't know well, because there is a light behind him as if it were an enormous sun . . . I can not see well.
HYPNOTIST - How many are there?
FILIBERTO - On my right is another that looks like a doll, that of . . . looks like people, in the form of people, but they don't look like people.
HYPNOTIST - Can you see their faces?
FILIBERTO - Yes, the face is square as if it were a robot. A robot!
HYPNOTIST - Can they talk to you?
FILIBERTO - Yes, he is talking, but he talks as if he were a doll.

Like if he was a machine of theirs that talks.
HYPNOTIST - And what does he say?
FILIBERTO - Well, he says each thing like, now ... you ... go like ... I don't know, but like I know they are not going to let me return or anything ... I go already ... in any case ...
HYPNOTIST - In what language does he talk?
FILIBERTO - They talk to me as if they were so . . . a . . . they talk to me as if they were trying to imitate Spanish. I often understand but often can not understand well but, as if it were a Portuguese or an Italian talking like that in Spanish.
HYPNOTIST - What does he say?
FILIBERTO - Well, I don't know, but they seem sincere, but now it seems that they are not going to let me return there, but he is looking so . . . He is like signaling so . . . I don't know but . . . it is me they are looking at . . . and that other that is to the left as if . . . as if it were a door that opens so . . . and then they are making a series of figures and like possessions such as things that they are making here.
HYPNOTIST - Look around and describe what you see. Are you standing or seated?
FILIBERTO - Well, now the other is indicating to me that we will go there, where he is.
HYPNOTIST - And what does he say?
FILIBERTO - Him on the left, him on the left . . .
HYPNOTIST - Are you seated or afoot?
FILIBERTO - Now I am standing. I am walking toward there . . .
HYPNOTIST - What things do you see around you?
FILIBERTO - But he is talking to me, then when you speak I can not hear.
HYPNOTIST - Well, tell me what he says.
FILIBERTO - He is telling me a series of things. Then he is showing me like a book that has ancient writing.
HYPNOTIST - What does the book say?
FILIBERTO - Let me see ... let me see ...
HYPNOTIST - In what language is the book written? Do you understand it?
FILIBERTO - It has many photographs of many places.
HYPNOTIST - Of where?
FILIBERTO - They are asking me if I know that place.
HYPNOTIST - Do you know it?
FILIBERTO - Well, that place, it seems as if I have seen it in some magazine or something like that, or a newspaper, because it seems as if it were the Valley Vinales (in Cuba).
HYPNOTIST - What do they want to know about that?

UFO Abduction From Undersea

FILIBERTO - They are showing me the photograph.
HYPNOTIST - And what does the writing say?
FILIBERTO - No writing, nothing written, I do not see any writing.
HYPNOTIST - Change the page and see if there is any other photos.
FILIBERTO - ... (silence)
HYPNOTIST - What else is there?
FILIBERTO - . . . (silence)
HYPNOTIST - Answer, tell me, what is there?
FILIBERTO - There is another photograph of . . . it is as if coming out through the front of the . . .
HYPNOTIST - Of where?
FILIBERTO - Of Matanzas (in Cuba), there outside . . . but as if it was an island. There is a photograph that shows it as an island!
HYPNOTIST - Where? In Cuba?
FILIBERTO - Yes, in Cuba.
HYPNOTIST - And what do they say?
FILIBERTO - Nothing, they are showing me.
HYPNOTIST - What else have they said? What else have they showed you?
FILIBERTO - Now they are showing me that . . . They are showing . . . look, they are indicating with their finger the things.
HYPNOTIST - What are they indicating?
FILIBERTO - But, this one does not speak, he doesn't say anything.
HYPNOTIST - Ask them something to see if they reply.
FILIBERTO - The other is, now he is speaking of the . . .
HYPNOTIST - Of what?
FILIBERTO - They say that they know all that we are doing, that I can not . . . go, that if I . . . what do you call it . . . lose the time if I answer you. (The next part is apparently addressed to the aliens that he is with at the time.) If you make me say that things are such, and you tell me a lie, we will know if it is a lie or whether it is the truth. You understand? If it is a lie or if it is the truth then, why did you bring me here? I have a young daughter, and I have two children in Cuba, and I have a wife and two brothers and my whole family, then why did you bring me here?
HYPNOTIST - What does he sav?
FILIBERTO - He sort of smiles, and I can see there what he is transmitting, and I have confidence that now he will return me. He says that there is to be given another trip to the other side first.
HYPNOTIST - And did you go to a place with them?

UFO Abduction From Undersea

FILIBERTO - Well, they brought me there to that place. I don't know what this place is here.
HYPNOTIST - How is the place? Look around you to see what you can see.
FILIBERTO - It gives me the impression as if I were a . . . as if I am inside of something that they are moving.
HYPNOTIST - Do you have your watch on?
FILIBERTO - Yes.
HYPNOTIST - What time is it? Look at your watch and see what time it is.
FILIBERTO - My watch says 7:36 now.
HYPNOTIST - And how long have you been there in that place?
FILIBERTO - First we went by another place, and later we passed another. At first they showed me some things, and they came to me with a mask. It was by means of that that they put in my head a series of things there. Then, I don't remember what happened, because, I don't know, they did something to me that . . .
HYPNOTIST - Did this take much time?
FILIBERTO - Well, it seemed to me to be a little time but my watch marked an hour which is more time for that which they did to me.
HYPNOTIST - And they didn't tell you anything?
FILIBERTO - They talked, but it was as if . . . they talked to me, this other talked also but more as if with his eyes, I don't know . . .
HYPNOTIST - Did you understand?
FILIBERTO - Yes, I understood, and I heard this as if it were a voice but it is that they are people that ... I ... no ... they are strange people, those ones.
HYPNOTIST - What were their eyes like?
FILIBERTO - Well, the one that I understood best was the one who was seated in the chair, who seemed to be their chief or something like that, because he had three eyes.
HYPNOTIST - Three eyes, equal, that were normal?
FILIBERTO - No, they were only a little such, longer toward the sides, and he had one in the middle, but the one in the middle I don't know, it was as if it were artificial, as if it were a magic eye.
HYPNOTIST - Did they have any symbol, a flag or something?
FILIBERTO - They have a symbol that is like it can move with the . . . it is like a chain, they had something like a chain on their collar, and then around that a thing in the form of a triangle, and it was like as if it were a stone that shined much.
HYPNOTIST - The point of the triangle, was it up or down?
FILIBERTO - The triangle had the point down and a point up. I

don't know how that thing is, because when they do something it moves. Sometimes it has the point up and sometimes down.
HYPNOTIST - They didn't tell you, or say anything to you in the course of the trip?
FILIBERTO - Yes, but it is like they have told me very many things.
HYPNOTIST - Tell me what you remember.
FILIBERTO - They told me . . . Well, that which I most remember, they told me, "We will bring you here 18 months," and then . . . "Look, we are going to pass to the other side because you have to do other things here." And then I asked them, how was it that . . . and then they told me that my watch was running behind, or that my watch functioned slowly. But that already 18 months of theirs had passed.
HYPNOTIST - Have you eaten?
FILIBERTO - Well, they gave me some things, I don't know what . . . It was not any food like I eat there with my family.
HYPNOTIST - What was it?
FILIBERTO - It was a thing, like it was some tablets, something like that but much better, I can not explain how it was . . .
HYPNOTIST - What did you understand?
FILIBERTO - Because they were showing me some things, and then it was like an . . . interference . . . My head hurts badly now.
HYPNOTIST - What time is it? Look at your watch.
FILIBERTO - Why do I have to look at so much?
HYPNOTIST - What do you see? What do you see?
FILIBERTO - There are distinct, what do you call them, the walls here are like they were various televisions that are showing various parts . . .
HYPNOTIST - What do you see in the televisors?
FILIBERTO - A series of images, and things of a ship, of mountains, of mount, the mountain . . . of an airplane, very speedy, such that it was like . . . you see an airplane . . .
HYPNOTIST - What is? Louder, I can't hear you.
FILIBERTO - That airplane, that I am looking at in the televisor now seems that it . . . How do you call it? . . . I have seen in a magazine that is . . . I don't know what you call it but it is French that is very big . . .
HYPNOTIST - The Concorde?
FILIBERTO - That, I think it is that that they are showing. Then there is like a round apparatus flying circles around it as though observing and taking pictures of it . . . Yes, they say this is their first flight that they have made, and they are observing when this first flight is made, because they want to know about the

advancements being made by Earth.
HYPNOTIST - Are they more advanced than us?
FILIBERTO - Well, they told me, this that is as if it were a machine, a robot, said that they were thousands of years more advanced than we are, but it didn't tell me how many thousands. But I am thinking that they said that I had 18 months, as they told me the last time, that I have 18 months here, but I am seeing that my watch does not run . . .
HYPNOTIST - What time is on your watch?
FILIBERTO - It is 7:37 and some seconds, but it is that I am seeing so many things that it is . . . but is . . . is the most important that I am seeing now.
FILIBERTO - The thing about China, the thing that the Chinese are doing, they are showing another time.
HYPNOTIST - What thing are they showing?
FILIBERTO - It is about an obelisk, then they are showing the things that are under the obelisk.
HYPNOTIST - What things are under the obelisk?
FILIBERTO - Under the obelisk . . . it is like a monument, like the obelisk of Columbia in Cuba but much greater, very much bigger, and then there below there is like as if it were a tomb, and under the tomb there is something like controls that the Chinese can use from there. But it seems that they are keeping this a secret, or it seems like in the whole world there is no other control like this.
HYPNOTIST - Can you speak to them? Will they respond?
FILIBERTO - They are speaking to me.
HYPNOTIST - And can you ask them some things?
FILIBERTO - Well, when they communicate with me. Other times . . . but there are times when I can ask and other times when I can not ask.
HYPNOTIST - Are they tall or very little?
FILIBERTO - The chief, the one who is seated, I have not seen him standing, but from what I can see he seems to be about my size. But he looks like he is very strong.
HYPNOTIST - Is he wearing shoes or boots?
FILIBERTO - It is like I can not make out good, because, it is like one piece suit.
HYPNOTIST - And the others, the rest?
FILIBERTO - The other, it is like he is showing me a book, the one that wears the suit that tightly fits his body, it is like the women who wear *spandex* in Cuba. That is what comes to my mind, closely fitted to the body.
HYPNOTIST - Do they have hair?

FILIBERTO - He has like, like such hair, but it looks like the hair that they put on dolls, blond. Looks like false hair.
HYPNOTIST - Why do they pick you up?
FILIBERTO - They have not yet told me. They say they have to make many contacts, many things, that they are doing with many thousands of contact people.
HYPNOTIST - Have they made any tests on you?
FILIBERTO - When this began, what I saw in this place where I was I don't know. I had fainted.
HYPNOTIST - Was it much time before you regained consciousness?
FILIBERTO - Yes it was, well the last time that they talked to me they said after 18 months. Now I don't know how much time has passed.
HYPNOTIST - Toward where are they going now? Do you know? Have they told you?
FILIBERTO - They say we have to finish the trip before they can return me to Earth.
HYPNOTIST - A trip where?
FILIBERTO - They didn't tell me. They said they have to make another trip.
HYPNOTIST - Did they tell you where?
FILIBERTO - Well, they were talking there of a series of things to . . . good, I was resting and I felt sure that they would bring me down but . . .
HYPNOTIST - Did you ask then if they were from Earth, or another planet, or where did they come from?
FILIBERTO - No, they were from another planet. I had the feeling that I was not on the Earth. Now I am not on the Earth.
HYPNOTIST - Why didn't you ask them what planet they were from? Couldn't you ask them?
FILIBERTO - It was like there was an interference. You were asking me a question about something, they were talking to me about something else, then . . .
HYPNOTIST - Tell me what they were saying. What were they saying?
FILIBERTO - Now they are taking me to another place.
HYPNOTIST - Where is that place?
FILIBERTO - It is an opening, then I am mounting like . . . They are putting me in a . . . as if it were the first seat in which they had put me, I don't know. It was like I was fastened to the seat!
HYPNOTIST - In the same place?
FILIBERTO - No, now it is another place.
HYPNOTIST - Did you disembark from the ship you had?

FILIBERTO - No, no, we are in the same ship.
HYPNOTIST - What are you doing now?
FILIBERTO - I don't know, it is like I was fastened . . . Like . . .
HYPNOTIST - Look around you.
FILIBERTO - ... (silence)
HYPNOTIST - Can you tell me, what do they call it?
FILIBERTO - This one, this one with me no ... say nothing.
HYPNOTIST - The other, doesn't he say what it is called?
FILIBERTO - I have the sensation that around me are many people, but I only see the one.
HYPNOTIST - Nobody has told you their name?
FILIBERTO - They speak . . . so that I, they communicate as if . . . I don't know what systems they have.
HYPNOTIST - Look around you. What do you see around you?
FILIBERTO - I am looking at what is here.
HYPNOTIST - What is there?
FILIBERTO - Well, there is a wall narrow, a very narrow place and then a . . . as if it is reduced now, I don't know how it was.
HYPNOTIST - What color is it?
FILIBERTO - It is a color . . . Well, I only see a little, so, of the front. I can't see the sides because they have me so, as if it were . . .
HYPNOTIST - What does the front have?
FILIBERTO - The front is like a wall. Like a . . .
HYPNOTIST - The televisors, can you see them now?
FILIBERTO - No, here where they have put me now, there is no televisor.
HYPNOTIST - Look at your watch to see what time it is.
FILIBERTO - No, I can not see it because they have my hands held down for what they are doing now.
HYPNOTIST - Are you sitting or standing?
FILIBERTO - No, they have me seated, I am sitting.
HYPNOTIST - Have you asked them anything?
FILIBERTO - Yes, how much time will we be here?
HYPNOTIST - Have they responded to your questions?
FILIBERTO - They always tell me, "Look, we ask you the questions." Then it is as if they are lecturing me, or as if there are things . . . Then they did something to me like, they passed . . . Well, one of the first passed a . . . as if it were a machine . . . I thought they were going to electrocute me, or something. Later I saw in another part . . . Then they made me . . . I don't know . . . they each made me do something different.
HYPNOTIST - Now, what are they doing?
FILIBERTO - Now they are opening the port in front.
HYPNOTIST - What is happening? Are they still holding your

hands down?

FILIBERTO - Yes, I am here.

HYPNOTIST - Who opened? Who went out the door?

FILIBERTO - I saw as if it were a thing . . . as if it were a smoke . . . as if it was like, a thing . . . and a very strange cold.

HYPNOTIST - Are there people there?

FILIBERTO - Now it is as if it came detached from the other part.

HYPNOTIST - And where are you going now?

FILIBERTO - I don't know where we are going.

HYPNOTIST - Can you see outside?

FILIBERTO - Forward I can see as if . . . (Filiberto at this moment began to change. He moved restlessly in the seat.)

HYPNOTIST - Be calm, be serene, relaxed, very sleepy. When I count to three you will continue sleeping soundly, very calm, well relaxed. Your eyes are closed, you are sleeping soundly. Nothing or nobody can wake you except me, sleep profoundly, quietly . . . You said there was a door that they opened and there was a kind of smoke. What was that?

FILIBERTO - It was as if the aft part where I am now, separated from the other.

HYPNOTIST - Can you see outside?

FILIBERTO - I can't see anything outside. I see what looks like smoke, something, and it gives me a sensation as if my body is pressed ahead, and toward the rear I don't know what the thing is.

HYPNOTIST - Are you jettisoned? (Separated from the other part)

FILIBERTO - No, I am still here.

HYPNOTIST - Are you still sitting in the seat?

FILIBERTO - I am in the same place, yes.

HYPNOTIST - What time has passed there?

FILIBERTO - I don't know what time has passed.

HYPNOTIST - Let us wait a few minutes in time to see what happens. . . . What has happened now?

FILIBERTO - Toward the front I can not see anything. This one does not say anything.

HYPNOTIST - Is there someone there with you?

FILIBERTO - Yes, the one that went behind.

HYPNOTIST - And, he won't let you talk?

FILIBERTO - I try, but it is as though he does not hear me, I don't . .

HYPNOTIST - What time is it now? Can't you see your watch?

FILIBERTO - I can not see it because I am like as if I am paralyzed in this thing here.

HYPNOTIST - Did he not talk with you before?

UFO Abduction From Undersea

FILIBERTO - All those days he talked with me.

At this point some of the previous confusion began to make a little more sense. The time is different. He has the distinct impression of having spent days of time with them and of having traveled extensively, to many places, and even away from the planet and back, and he is still within the two hours he was absent from Hialeah. They seem to have passed many days of time in the continuum he is now in.

HYPNOTIST - What did he say?

FILIBERTO - They have shown me distinct things, they have put me in distinct conditions, and they also took me to one of their fiestas, some time ago.

HYPNOTIST - How was the fiesta?

FILIBERTO - But that was much time ago.

HYPNOTIST - Have you slept much since then?

FILIBERTO - Well, I don't know, seems like I have . . . I didn't see him and suddenly someone is standing at my side, then he asks if I am rested, if I am sleepy, and I don't know what trouble. It seems like they want to drive me crazy.

HYPNOTIST - How did you sleep?

FILIBERTO - Well . . . At times it was as if I were walking and then I was still here paralyzed. Well, yes, I rested already. What they want to do is make me crazy and then to see . . . I don't know.

HYPNOTIST - And the fiesta there, how was it?

FILIBERTO - They did a . . . thing very strange there.

HYPNOTIST - What was it?

FILIBERTO - There was a person much smaller, and others much bigger and . . .

HYPNOTIST - What size were the smaller ones?

FILIBERTO - There are smaller ones that are only a little more than my child (about five years old).

HYPNOTIST - But were they children?

FILIBERTO - There was one who had what looked like breasts, but they wanted to drive me crazy. I think they were putting the . . . the . . . What do you call it? Look, now we are arriving here. Look, I am seeing the Earth here!

HYPNOTIST - From where?

FILIBERTO - We are here . . . (muttering)!

HYPNOTIST - Where this time? Where is the Earth?

FILIBERTO - It is a part of the Earth at the shore of a sea.

HYPNOTIST - Do you see people?

FILIBERTO - No, here I see no people. What I see over there is like a baby horse, very little. But now we are coming down. It is a strange little horse. It is not a horse like those here (later we were

able to figure out that what Filiberto saw was a llama).
HYPNOTIST - But, are you on Earth?
FILIBERTO - Yes, we are at the edge of water. It is like we are a helicopter where I go, but . . . with a strange sound.
HYPNOTIST - And are there people there inside?
FILIBERTO - The guy I saw there.
HYPNOTIST - In front of you?
FILIBERTO - Yes.
HYPNOTIST - Have you arrived?
FILIBERTO - Yes. Right now I do not feel like I am in my body. The things are still in front of me and behind me (evidently braces, supports or something to keep him in place). It is like it is united with my body in front and behind.
HYPNOTIST - Are you loose (released from immobilization)?
FILIBERTO - No, they still have me here.
HYPNOTIST - Pressed in position (with hands down)?
FILIBERTO - Yes.
HYPNOTIST - You can not see your watch?
FILIBERTO - I still can't see it.
HYPNOTIST - And now, what is happening?
FILIBERTO - I can see everything in front of me. I see a . . . like as if it is a mountain. I see like it is a shore of a sea and the edge of a mountain.
HYPNOTIST - Are you still in the air?
FILIBERTO - No. I am like as if I were hovering in a helicopter here. I don't know, seems like it is a helicopter, but it is very fast.
HYPNOTIST - And the people do not move?
FILIBERTO - This moves, this descends.
HYPNOTIST - Are there people outside?
FILIBERTO - I do not know because I can no longer see the view ahead. I am seeing very bad because I have my eyes very . . . I want to wipe them but they won't let me . . . like very dangerous.
HYPNOTIST - Tell me when someone arrives there?
FILIBERTO - Ha . . . Ha . . . Yes . . . (inaudible)
HYPNOTIST - What is happening now?
FILIBERTO - (Whispers . . .)
HYPNOTIST - What? Louder, I can not hear, louder, louder.
FILIBERTO - If I am good here, why are you going to put me there?
HYPNOTIST - What do they want to do?
FILIBERTO - They are putting me down below.
HYPNOTIST - Who is putting you below?
FILIBERTO - The other . . . (inaudible)
HYPNOTIST - Louder, louder. I can't hear.

UFO Abduction From Undersea

FILIBERTO - . . . (inaudible)
HYPNOTIST - How? Speak louder. I can not hear.
FILIBERTO - Because there is this type here . . . but why no . . . Who are you?
HYPNOTIST - Are you asking the type?
FILIBERTO - Who are you? Because I am speaking with the type here and he is saying to me . . .
HYPNOTIST - What does that type say to you?
FILIBERTO - The type is making a signal. He takes out an apparatus and fires it, as if it were, I don't know . . . like a shot. But I didn't hear anything. Toward the mountain, and now I am looking at the mountain from above and I can see vegetation, there above and everywhere. Now I am at the shoulders of the sea that I saw shortly before. I am in front of the mountain. They rotate the whole machine. Rotate it but with me inside. I can not move and remain nailed here.
HYPNOTIST - Is there much vegetation? Green plants?
FILIBERTO - No. Primarily it is like it is rocks. At the edge of the sea also. There above I can see plants.
HYPNOTIST - Is the sun out?
FILIBERTO - No, no. the sun is not . . . I can see clearly, but the sun is not out. It looks more like moonlight.
HYPNOTIST - Are you still alone?
FILIBERTO - Still nobody here.
HYPNOTIST - See if you can move.
FILIBERTO - No, no, I can not.
HYPNOTIST - Nor can you see your watch?
FILIBERTO - This is moving now.
HYPNOTIST - Did it start up again?
FILIBERTO - Now I can not see the mountain. What I now see is the sea. And this type is looking at me from the side, but he does not say anything.
HYPNOTIST - The one that is controlling the apparatus?
FILIBERTO - Yes. It is moving.
HYPNOTIST - But he, is it he who operates the controls?
FILIBERTO - I don't know if it is the controls or not, because now they have put a crystal in front, and the only thing I can see is the crystal.
HYPNOTIST - What is with the crystal?
FILIBERTO - No. It is a crystal in front. I see it from behind. I am seeing the sea from here. Now we are slowing down.
HYPNOTIST - Of what color do you see the sea?
FILIBERTO - The sea is like . . . well, like a sea, but it is a sea that is not very blue such as that of Cuba, or as in Miami. It is a gray

color.
HYPNOTIST - Does it have many waves?
FILIBERTO - Yes, it has, but I don't know, can't see, because already we are into the sea! This went in and under the water!
HYPNOTIST - How did it enter the water? Did it go under the sea?
FILIBERTO - Yes, that I could see from behind. It is like it was . . . I have the impression that it ate (dissolved or disintegrated) much of the water in the crystal in front of me. I did not see anything. It was like a cloud in front of me.
HYPNOTIST - Continue. Where did they take you? Couldn't you ask them where they were taking you?
FILIBERTO - Wait, I am afraid. Because what if there comes an animal here, or anything else. I believe what they are making is a test . . . these people . . . Man! What thing is bigger!
HYPNOTIST - Can you see clearly, or is everything still dark?
FILIBERTO - I can see nothing in front.
HYPNOTIST - And do you go rapidly?
FILIBERTO - Seems like much velocity.
HYPNOTIST - Are you alone?
FILIBERTO - Not now.
HYPNOTIST - Can you see your watch? See if you can see.
FILIBERTO - No, I can not. I still can not move . . . there is a turn, the curve is such . . . a slight curve there, what is there?
HYPNOTIST - What is ahead of the curve?
FILIBERTO - We are entering into a tunnel, or as if it were such a thing there.
HYPNOTIST - Is it of stone?
FILIBERTO - No, like as if it were a tunnel, such . . .
HYPNOTIST - Is the tunnel of stone?
FILIBERTO - I don't know. It is like a cavity (cave) but I don't know . . . of water, . . . I cannot define well what it is.
HYPNOTIST - They have not stopped yet?
FILIBERTO - No, not yet.
HYPNOTIST - Are you under the water?
FILIBERTO - We are coming up.
HYPNOTIST - Have you arrived?
FILIBERTO - Yes, now I can see better ahead. It seems like we are now no longer moving.
HYPNOTIST - What do you see in front?
FILIBERTO - It is like it is a . . . good, it is like I can not explain what I see.
HYPNOTIST - Never mind. Tell me more or less.
FILIBERTO - One time I went to the caves of Matanzas (in

Cuba), but what this lacks is the stalagmites. This does not have them. But it looks like a cave.
HYPNOTIST - Do you see people there?
FILIBERTO - No, I still do not see anybody here.
HYPNOTIST - Vegetation?
FILIBERTO - No.
HYPNOTIST - Houses? Things? Do you see? Look.
FILIBERTO - I can't. I can't see anything.
HYPNOTIST - Is it light or dark there?
FILIBERTO - This has a kind of light, as if it comes from the same walls. Something like that.
HYPNOTIST - And the people that are there . . . What are they doing?
FILIBERTO - No . . . I still don't see people. I am still here with the crystal in front. (Apparently still restrained)
HYPNOTIST - And the one that was with you. He is not with you?
FILIBERTO - I don't see anybody.
HYPNOTIST - Are you alone? Did they put you out?
FILIBERTO - No. They still have me here.
HYPNOTIST - What is happening? Tell me?
FILIBERTO - . . . (silence)
HYPNOTIST - Let us continue advancing in time, and when I count to three, five minutes will pass. One . . . two . . . three. Now. Are you out?
FILIBERTO - No. They still have me here.
HYPNOTIST - What do you see there?
FILIBERTO - I am looking at the cave here and like as if it is a form of . . .
HYPNOTIST - Of what?
FILIBERTO - It looks like a pole stuck in the floor. But it has the form of a serpent . . .
HYPNOTIST - Where? Inside the apparatus or outside?
FILIBERTO - No. Outside, outside . . . in front. From inside the apparatus I could not see it. I believe there is another apparatus behind me, the same as the one I came in . . .
HYPNOTIST - Is it a symbol, that serpent?
FILIBERTO - It is big, like a light pole. But then it is in the form of a serpent. There above, a door is opening up there now. In the wall . . .
HYPNOTIST - Continue, continue.
FILIBERTO - . . . (silence)
HYPNOTIST - What are they doing? What is happening now?
FILIBERTO - . . . (silence)

UFO Abduction From Undersea

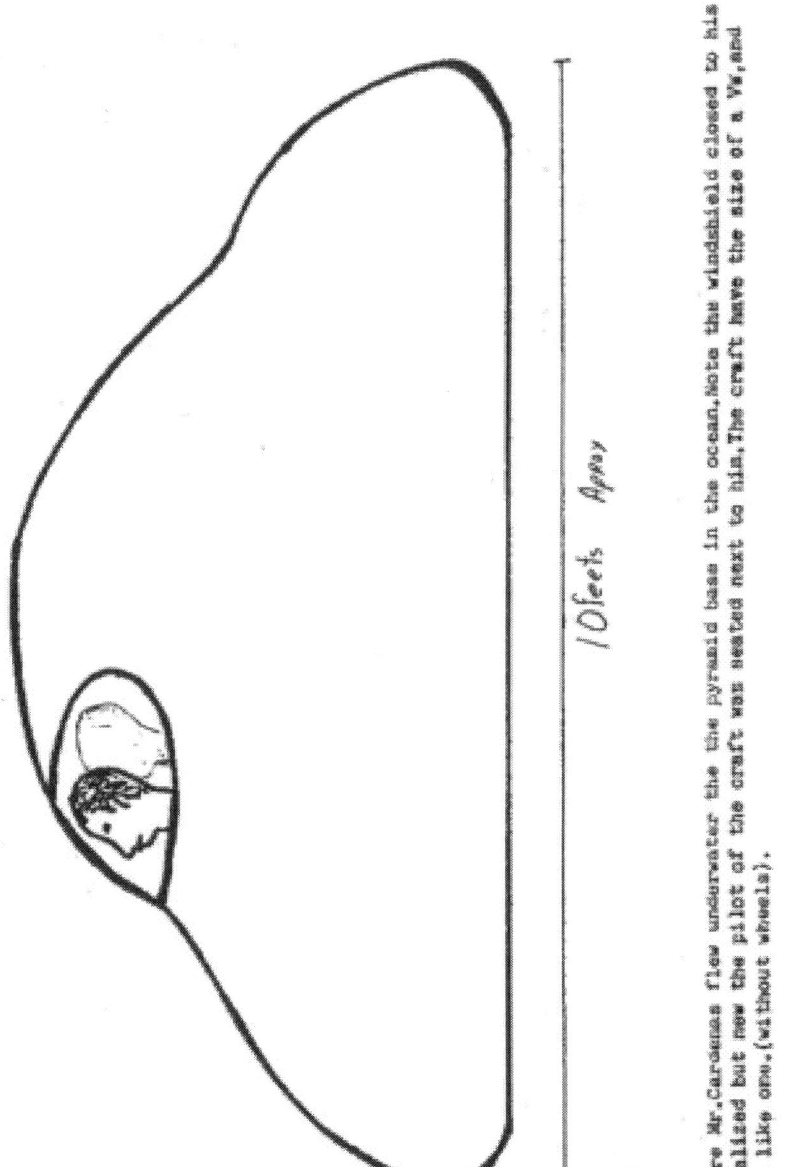
10feets Appx
5 feet Approx.
Small craft where Mr.Cardenas flew underwater the the pyramid base in the ocean.Note the windshield closed to his face.He was paralized but new the pilot of the craft was seated next to him.The craft have the size of a Vw,and its shape looks like one.(without wheels).

This is the sketch of the small craft that the extraterrestrials put Cardenas in for the trip underwater. The crystal mentioned is nothing more than the windshield of the ship, called crystal in Spanish. Cardenas was completely immobilized by some unseen force the whole time he was in this craft.

UFO Abduction From Undersea

HIALEAH, FLORIDA

3 January 1979

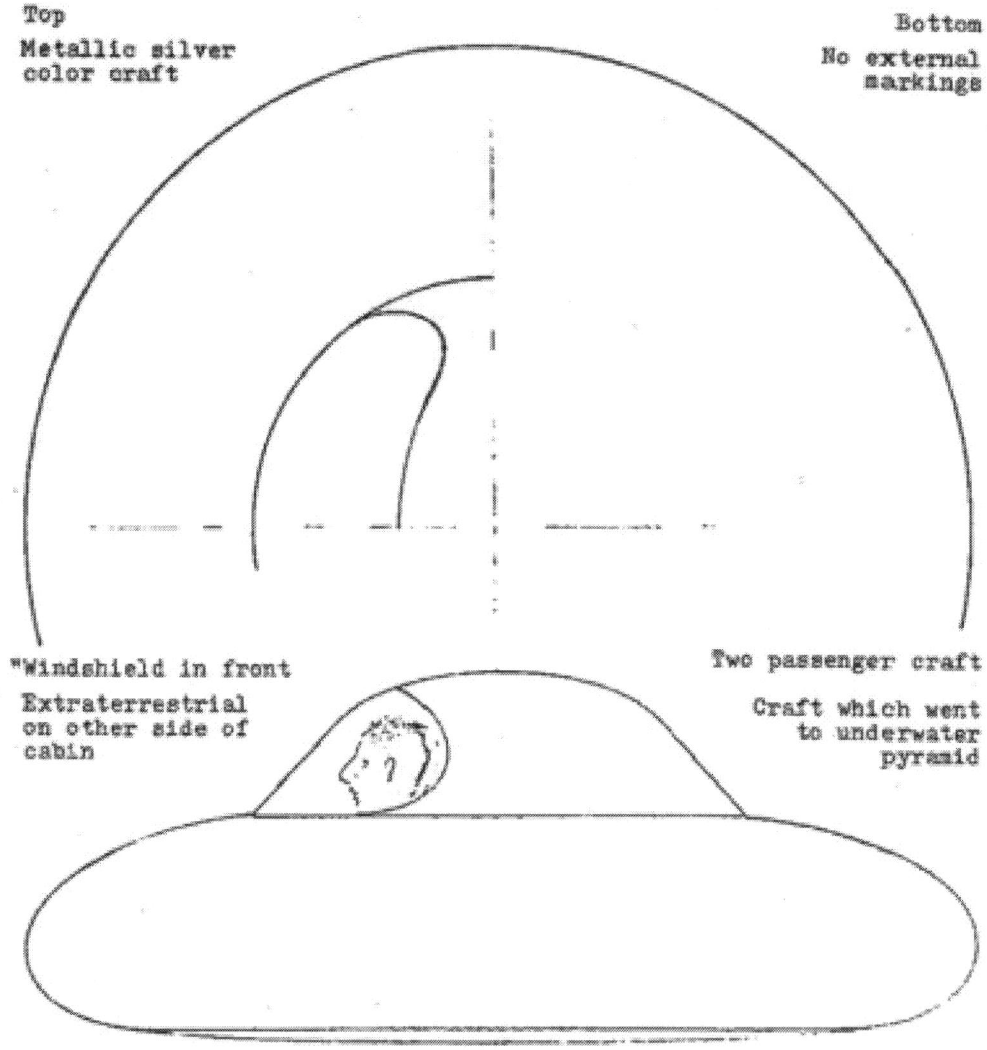

This ship traveled at very high speed underwater.

This craft debarked from a larger carrier vehicle of some kind

The witness was immobilized in place by an invisible force of some kind that held him firmly motionless

The pilot got out of this ship with a torchlike device that he used to open a "port" in a rock facing from which two more identical UFOs emerged and accompanied them to the underwater base. The abductee was returned from the underwater base in still another vehicle.

An erected line drawing of the underwater vehicle that carried Mr. Cardenas and one extraterrestiral pilot to the underwater base.

HYPNOTIST - Tell me?
FILIBERTO - Well, now I have come down out of that thing.
HYPNOTIST - Have they put you out? Take advantage and look at the time. What time is it?
FILIBERTO - It is seven and almost 40 minutes.
HYPNOTIST - Continue. What are they doing?
FILIBERTO - . . . (silence)
HYPNOTIST - Relate it. Come on. Tell me. What are they doing? What about the thing?
FILIBERTO - . . . (sigh)
HYPNOTIST - What was it? Louder, I can't hear you . . . Louder . . .
FILIBERTO - . . . (sigh)
HYPNOTIST - What is happening?
FILIBERTO - They are giving me something to eat. It is most strange.
HYPNOTIST - Is it a pill?
FILIBERTO - I don't know what it is . . .
HYPNOTIST - Is it liquid?
FILIBERTO - It is like a liquid, as if it were . . . a . . .
HYPNOTIST - What color is it?
FILIBERTO - I did not see a color. They put it there. It tastes something like honey . . . but no . . . sweet and bitter.
HYPNOTIST - They didn't tell you what it was?
FILIBERTO - No, they said it was to feed me. Now someone is coming out of the other part . . . They are opening a whole wall.
HYPNOTIST - You are out of the apparatus?
FILIBERTO - Yes. They have taken me out of the apparatus.
HYPNOTIST - Can you breathe good?
FILIBERTO - Yes. However I lack the ability sort of, to talk. I have the sensation as if I had much pressure on my chest. Like as if I were compressed. But I can breathe. I have some difficulty breathing, but not too much.
VIRGILIO - Breathe deeply to see if it gets better. Is it better?
FILIBERTO - It is that there are strange sensations, strange odors, and I am not accustomed. These things are very strange . . .
HYPNOTIST - Where did they take you?
FILIBERTO - Well, I am sitting on something like a stone. A thing here.
HYPNOTIST - Are you loose?
FILIBERTO - Yes, they left me free here.
HYPNOTIST - And the people?
FILIBERTO - Well, they pass by there . . . it is like I know the whole world. I don't know. It is like I am not a stranger . . .

HYPNOTIST - Are they the same as those who came in the apparatus?
FILIBERTO - Some. Some are like them, but there are others, other people who are distinct . . .
HYPNOTIST - How are they? Tall or short? How are they?
FILIBERTO - Well . . . Look . . .
HYPNOTIST - What is happening?
FILIBERTO - No, no, it is not . . . No, I saw one that looked like the other that I saw there, some months ago, but then this other looks like him . . .
HYPNOTIST - Where is "there"?
FILIBERTO - There, where I was before.
HYPNOTIST - Ha. Yes, yes.
FILIBERTO - And then . . . He says "welcome" . . .
HYPNOTIST - Did he say it in Spanish?
FILIBERTO - Fuck...shit...that sissified shit of fear ...mother fucker...son of a bitch... (inaudible)
HYPNOTIST - Speak up. I can not hear you. Who said "Welcome"?
FILIBERTO - What welcome shit, not a welcome. That is the Chilean or Argentino . . . a strange thing . . .
VIRGILIO - Can you speak to him? Does he understand you?
FILIBERTO - Yes, I am talking to him. He is telling me that I am welcome and he doesn't mean trouble. He talks like he is Chilean, a strange thing, like he is Argentine also.
VIRGILIO - Ask him where you are . . . in that place where you have met him.
FILIBERTO - . . . (silence)
HYPNOTIST - Has he answered you?
FILIBERTO - . . . (silence)
HYPNOTIST - Tell me?
FILIBERTO - It is that he is showing me a thing here that he has in his hand . . .
VIRGILIO - What is he showing you?
FILIBERTO - It looks like it is a pistol, or a revolver . . . of theirs something like the pirates of ancient times used. But it has a wide mouth or end. Now they have put up a televisor and he tells me that he can not make a test here, but that we are going to see in the televisor what it is capable of doing.
HYPNOTIST - Let us see . . . What is he doing? Tell me.
FILIBERTO - It is like a launcher, like those that I have seen in the movies, but it is short (and small). You can use with the hand . . . (silence)
HYPNOTIST - Good, let us do a marvelous thing now. When I

count to three, you are going to be able to ask all the questions you want and he will respond. One . . . two . . . three . . . Ask him his name.
FILIBERTO - . . . (silence)
HYPNOTIST - Are you asking him? Does he answer? Did he tell you his name?
FILIBERTO - . . . (silence)
HYPNOTIST - Speak loudly, one . . . two . . . three. Louder.
FILIBERTO - . . . (silence, and he began to move and became restless)
HYPNOTIST - Be calm, serene, relaxed, sleep soundly . . . (during this time we changed the recorder tape again) Now, when I count to three you will continue in the same situation in the same place, and you will describe all that is happening. One...two ...three. Now! Where are you now? What are they doing?
FILIBERTO - I have to question this guy. Because, this is the one that is going to translate to me, all this shit that they are doing to me . . .
VIRGILIO - Ask him. What are they doing?
FILIBERTO - . . . (silence)
HYPNOTIST - Did he answer you? What did you ask him?
FILIBERTO - . . . (silence)
HYPNOTIST - Answer me!
FILIBERTO - . . . (silence)
HYPNOTIST - When I count three you are going to answer me loud and clear. One . . . two . . . three. Now! What are they doing to you?
FILIBERTO - (He gave a great sigh and commenced to move restlessly.)
HYPNOTIST - Be calm, serene, relaxed. Answer loudly. What are they doing to you?
FILIBERTO - He says, this one, that he was afraid like me the first time, but he is working now for humanity, which I could do for the whole Earth. He has a technical device here, well, a technical power with these apparatus and things that he knows how to operate . . . He alone is equivalent to more than ten divisions of an army.
VIRGILIO - He is from Earth?
FILIBERTO - Him, the Chilean or Argentine, I don't know what.
VIRGILIO - What is his name?
FILIBERTO - When I asked him, he told me his name was not important (did not matter).
HYPNOTIST - Did he show you how to make anything? (Do anything)

FILIBERTO - Well, he was showing me things. I don't know what happened to this sucker.
VIRGILIO - Did he show you anything that you could do here on Earth?
FILIBERTO - What he was showing me was how if he wanted, he could frighten me . . .
HYPNOTIST - Look at your watch and tell me, what time is it? What time do you have on your watch?
FILIBERTO - . . . (silence)
HYPNOTIST - Quickly . . .
FILIBERTO - It is seven and 42 minutes. (It is only two minutes of watch time since he debarked from the apparatus.)
HYPNOTIST - Tell me, what does the guy say?
FILIBERTO - Now, here is another who is doing some things to me.
VIRGILIO - What is he doing?
FILIBERTO - I don't know . . . with an apparatus that he is passing over me and along the sides . . .
HYPNOTIST - Where are you? Are you still sitting on the stone or in some other place?
FILIBERTO - No, now we are in another place, where they have taken me.
VIRGILIO - What is that place like?
FILIBERTO - It is like as if it were a table. One of them is at like the side of the table and it is like one is sucked down to it. Then the table rotates until I am mouth up.
HYPNOTIST - Do you see any televisors?
FILIBERTO - No, now I am here seeing a small scene, like lights and they are looking in my eyes with lights. They also put lights into my ears . . . and they moved them along my shoulders and my arms. They used a thing like . . . One time I had an electrocardiogram, but with much more apparatus all over my body . . .
VIRGILIO - Do you feel any pain?
FILIBERTO - Well, it is like a sensation, something like a woman who is sucking on you, something like that. (They extracted semen.)
VIRGILIO - Who is doing this?
FILIBERTO - This is another, and there are things that come out of the wall and perform operations by themselves. They are like arms (mechanical), with things on the ends . . .
VIRGILIO - And the one, does he speak to you in Spanish? Is he there with you?
FILIBERTO - I can not see him now.
VIRGILIO - Then, are you alone?

UFO Abduction From Undersea

FILIBERTO - In the position I am in I don't know if there is anyone here.
VIRGILIO - You don't see anybody?
FILIBERTO - No. I am thinking that all this shit, I don't know when it is going to stop. I don't know when all this filthy business is going to end.
VIRGILIO - Is the room large or small?
FILIBERTO - The room comes to an end . . . like . . . like . . . the size is two lengths of my body long.
VIRGILIO - Can you touch the table?
FILIBERTO - My hands are fastened to the table.
VIRGILIO - Is it of crystal or wood?
FILIBERTO - I don't know what it is like.
HYPNOTIST - What are they doing? What time is it?
FILIBERTO - It is 42 with a little . . . and 29.
HYPNOTIST - What time is it now?
FILIBERTO - 7 and 22 with 49. (Evidently the 42 above was meant to be 22, or 22 minutes and 29 seconds, now 49 seconds.)
HYPNOTIST - What else is happening?
FILIBERTO - . . . (silence)
HYPNOTIST - Tell me, what else?
FILIBERTO - . . . (silence)
HYPNOTIST - Now a strange thing is going to happen. When I count to three we are going to go forward in time 30 minutes ... one...two...three, Now. What time is it? What time is it?
FILIBERTO - No... no... I feel very bad... no...
HYPNOTIST - What are you doing? What are they doing to you?
FILIBERTO - Nobody is doing anything to me. Here I am walking there to see the lights like that come . . . because . . . (Filiberto has returned to the moment after being let out of the ship near the Tamiami Trail.)
HYPNOTIST - Tranquil, serene, well relaxed. Sleep soundly . . . Now, when I count three, we are going to go back 30 minutes in time and we are going to be once again at 7:42 (on your watch). One . . . two . . . three, Now!
FILIBERTO - . . . (The sobs changed to intense crying and tears ran from Filiberto's eyes.)
HYPNOTIST - Be calm, serene, well relaxed. Now it is 7:42. Be calm, serene, relaxed . . .
FILIBERTO - (Continues to cry heavily)
HYPNOTIST - Now it is 7:42 and you are above in the room. Where are you?
FILIBERTO - (Begins to sigh and ceases crying)
HYPNOTIST - You are on the table, no? Tell me what is happen-

ing. Is the table of crystal or wood?
FILIBERTO - I am not on any table. (No longer crying)
HYPNOTIST - Where are you?
FILIBERTO - Now they are carrying me someplace.
HYPNOTIST - What time is it?
FILIBERTO - It is 7:41, almost to 7:42.
HYPNOTIST - And where are they carrying you?
FILIBERTO - They are taking me to another place. Now this guy shows me an apparatus that shoots flames.
HYPNOTIST - Continue speaking.
FILIBERTO - We are entering a very strange place.
VIRGILIO - That is in the cave?
FILIBERTO - Yes, this doesn't now look like a cave, it looks like a city!
VIRGILIO - Do you see buildings?
FILIBERTO - It is like we are entering a city through a tunnel.
VIRGILIO - But, do you see buildings?
FILIBERTO - No, what I see are walls, nothing else. When we came by the road, all that I could see was walls, walls . . .
VIRGILIO - Are the walls of brick?
FILIBERTO - They give me the impression of being . . . that . . . like the constructions of crystal fiber, like fiberglass boats.
VIRGILIO - Do you see doors?
FILIBERTO - Yes, but those doors open in a strange way . . . different from what we are accustomed to.
VIRGILIO - How did they open?
FILIBERTO - They opened half up and half down, others to the sides.
VIRGILIO - Do you see balconies or windows?
FILIBERTO - No. No, I don't see anything like that.
HYPNOTIST - Now, when I count to three we will go back in time only ten minutes (Filiberto interrupts).
FILIBERTO - Now they are putting me on the table.
HYPNOTIST - Correct. Who is putting you on the table?
FILIBERTO - Well, the table rotates and it is like I am sucked onto there. Now it is rotating.
HYPNOTIST - Does the table have feet?
FILIBERTO - No. The table is like as if it was a wall. I am fixed to the wall and it rotates me mouth up. I am mouth up with my arms fastened to the table.
HYPNOTIST - Are you in the air?
FILIBERTO - Yes, as it turned . . . I don't know what they do to the table to make it turn.
HYPNOTIST - Good. When I count to three you will go forward

five minutes in time. One . . . two . . . three, Now! Five minutes have passed. What time is it?
FILIBERTO - Now we are coming up on 47, for there . . .
HYPNOTIST - Where are you?
FILIBERTO - I am here, in a place of . . .
HYPNOTIST - Where?
FILIBERTO - This is very strange.
HYPNOTIST - Is it light or dark?
FILIBERTO - It is like they are doing something over my shoulder, but so I can not see.
HYPNOTIST - Why?
FILIBERTO - . . . (sigh) . . . I don't know.
HYPNOTIST - Can you speak to anyone?
FILIBERTO - I am talking now with the one who has the beard, a very strange beard.
VIRGILIO - What color is his beard?
FILIBERTO - It is like . . . like . . . a reddish color. But I don't know because these people are very strange.
VIRGILIO - And their hair?
FILIBERTO - This one has something like that on his head. It looks like a small lock of hair. But it looks to that of dolls, nylon strands.
VIRGILIO - And the eyes. How are the eyes?
FILIBERTO - They do not have eyes the same as ours. It seems to me that this person is disguised . . . this person is disguised!
HYPNOTIST - Now let us do a strange thing. Let us regress in this remembrance, when I count to three, to the most interesting conversation that you have had during this time, with the person who talked to you most and with the person who told you the most. One...two...three, Now. What time is it?
FILIBERTO - ... (silence)
HYPNOTIST - What time is it? Louder . . . What time is it?
FILIBERTO - . . . (silence)
HYPNOTIST - Answer me loud and clear.
FILIBERTO - . . . . (He began to become restless and a little agitated.)
HYPNOTIST - Be calm, serene, relaxed. Be calm . . . calm . . . Now when I count three, you are going to tell me, in that same situation, the things most important that he told you. One . . . two . . . three, Now! What time is it?
FILIBERTO - . . . (silence)
HYPNOTIST - What time is it? Loud and clear so that I can hear. What time is it? What time is it?
FILIBERTO - 7:36.

HYPNOTIST - Where are you? With whom are you talking?
FILIBERTO - . . . (silence)
HYPNOTIST - Loud and clear.
FILIBERTO - . . . (silence)
HYPNOTIST - Quickly, quickly . . . Where are you?
FILIBERTO - . . . (He began to sob and cry intensely.)
HYPNOTIST - Be calm, serene, relaxed, sleep . . . sleep . . . sleep . . . Now when I count to three you are going to return in time to today, the present date. When I count to three it will be 8:29 of January the third. One . . . two . . . three, Now. Now it is 8:29 of January the third. We will continue returning in time and now when I count to three it will be 5:00 in the afternoon of the day, 10 January. One . . . two . . . three. What day is it?
FILIBERTO - . . . (continues crying)
HYPNOTIST - Loud and clear . . . loud and clear . . . Now it is the 10th of January. Answer me loud and clear. When I count to three you will continue sleeping and you will answer my questions. What day is it?
FILIBERTO - . . . (More relaxed, Filiberto guards his silence.)
HYPNOTIST - Loud and clear.
FILIBERTO - . . . (silence)
HYPNOTIST - Let us continue regressing in time and hour. When I count to three, we will be in Saturday 3 January 1979 at 7:20. One...two...three, Now. What day is it?
FILIBERTO - ... (silence)
HYPNOTIST - Now when I count to three, we will return to today's date, Saturday 10 February. One . . . two . . . three, Now.
FILIBERTO - . . . (Filiberto shows some agitation.)
HYPNOTIST - Be calm, relaxed, serene, sleep soundly . . . soundly . . . Now it is the day 10 February, Saturday. Now when I count to three, you will answer all my questions, loud and clear. One...two...three, Now. What is your name...your name?
FILIBERTO - Filiberto Cardenas.
HYPNOTIST - Very good. What day is today?
FILIBERTO - . . . (sighs)
HYPNOTIST - What day is today, Filiberto? . . . loud and clear . . .
FILIBERTO - 3 January.
HYPNOTIST - Now we are going to return rapidly to 10 February. When I count to three, one...two...three, Now. What day is today, Filiberto?
FILIBERTO - 10 February.
HYPNOTIST - Very good, be tranquil, serene, relaxed, sleep soundly and continue answering my questions. Now when I

count three, you are going to tell me, only, one thing that was most important that they told you on the trip you have taken.
FILIBERTO - . . . (silence)
HYPNOTIST - Loudly and quickly.
FILIBERTO - The most important of all the things was when they told me that the conference of the three was a failure and that was to bring a great war on all the world.
VIRGILIO - To what three are you referring?
FILIBERTO - It seems they are referring to the American President, that of Egypt and that of Israel.
VIRGILIO - When is this going to come about?
FILIBERTO - They said that was a failure, that it will not endure much time, and that each time it will get worse and then if we don't take measures rapidly that is going to bring on the great war.
VIRGILIO - Did they tell you how you could communicate with them?
FILIBERTO - Yes.
VIRGILIO - How?
FILIBERTO - I have a place where I can communicate with them.
VIRGILIO - Where is the place?
FILIBERTO - . . . (silence)
HYPNOTIST - Tell him, loud and clear.
FILIBERTO - . . . (silence)
HYPNOTIST - Well, tell me it, loud and clear.
FILIBERTO - They don't want anybody to know the place.
HYPNOTIST - Where is it?
FILIBERTO - I cannot tell you for they made me a compromise. They have told me that whichever of those groups I am aiding and they want to have an experience, to come out with me some day and then perhaps, if he wants to have tests, we may give them to him.
VIRGILIO - But, if we go out with you and nothing happens, why won't you tell me the place?
FILIBERTO - (silence)
HYPNOTIST - Now, when I count to three, you will tell me, one . . . two . . . three, Now.
FILIBERTO - . . . (silence)
HYPNOTIST - Now, loud and clear.
FILIBERTO - . . . (silence)
HYPNOTIST - Louder, I can't hear you.
FILIBERTO - It is that I have promised. I cannot tell you.
VIRGILIO - Can you write it? So. You are no longer under your

promise.
FILIBERTO - Yes, but I cannot write it either, because if I do that, they are watching me though it is not of my own desire to do so. I would like to comply with what you tell me, but I do not want them to ... I don't know if they would take some kind of reprisal against my family or me. All these things you are asking me I have been forbidden to tell, and possibly my whole family ... (Here Filiberto began to sob and cry again.)
HYPNOTIST - Be calm, serene, relaxed. Nobody nor anything can wake you except me. Sleep calmly, relaxed, serene . . . What is your name? Loud and clear. Your name?
FILIBERTO - (Now a little more calmed) Filiberto Cardenas.
HYPNOTIST - What day is today?
FILIBERTO - 3 January.
HYPNOTIST - When I count to three, you will return to today's present date. One . . . two . . . three, Now. What date is today?
FILIBERTO - 10 February.
HYPNOTIST - Very good. Now, tell me . . . What is your name?
FILIBERTO - Filiberto Cardenas.
HYPNOTIST - Very good. Now, when I count three you will awaken happy and content, pleased and very tranquil . . . very relaxed . . . you will remember this whole trip you have made and all the things you have told us in full consciousness. One . . . two . . . three, Now.

At this moment Filiberto opened his eyes, smiled and asked, what happened . . .

CHAPTER 5

The Captive

After having been paralyzed by a combination of mysterious light and sound Filiberto woke up in a seat that seemed to hold him in place by some kind of suction which restrained all his movements. He was in a small room. At his side were three strange figures. One of them, though of human form, seemed more like a robot. The other two also had a human appearance, and seemed to have life. They were of small stature, a little smaller than Filiberto (who was a smaller man himself), and they were dressed in very tight fitting suits, contoured to the body. One of the strange beings approached carrying a special kind of helmet in his hands. He raised it and placed it on Filiberto's head.

This helmet seemed to be full of small needles and came down to the shoulders. The beings tried to communicate with Filiberto, speaking in a language that sounded like German. Coming to realize that Filiberto did not understand, one of the beings rotated a button on the right side of his chest and then began to speak in English. Filiberto indicated that he did not understand that either. Again the strange being rotated the button and began this time to speak in Spanish, with a Portuguese or Italian accent. Meanwhile they continued making tests on Filiberto's body that left 108 marks.

In this place where they had him detained, though he could not see outside, Filiberto experienced the distinct sensation of flying in the air. Later he felt like the velocity was diminishing, then he felt some jerks, and a port was opened. The extraterrestrials made him pass through to another bigger room. There, on a high seat, like a throne, was seated an individual wearing a cape. His body was similar to a human body. He wore a chain on his collar that fell to his abdomen, from which hung a triangular-shaped stone that rotated in many directions. A bright light came from the wall, which impeded Filiberto's ability to observe closely the facial features of this alien entity. The walls of this place were in resplendent colors and seemed to be made of some kind of lucite material, or perhaps like a transparent resin acrylic. This person, who seemed to be in charge, perhaps their chief, addressed Filiberto in perfect Spanish while at the same time transmitting ideas telepathically. The conversation revolved in turn from the subjects of human beings to humanity. On the walls they projected images, something like television pictures, that showed scenes from the past, the present, and also the future. All of this equipment apparatus was controlled by some buttons that the extraterrestrial had under his control in the arms of the seat or throne, and also on the floor there in front of the seat.

After this they opened another port and the captive Filiberto was carried to a small room, where he was placed in a seat similar to the first which sucked him down and impeded his movements as before. He was now in a small ship that was discharged from the mothership. Nearing the end of this flight, Filiberto could see what looked like a stretch of narrow beach approaching. There the extraterrestrial who seemed to be the pilot of this ship disembarked from the craft and, with something he carried in his hand, made a signal toward the base of a high mountain. In this place the captive could see large rocks, some vegetation, and a "small horse." The animal was later identified as a llama. One of the rocks opened up and became like "a tunnel toward the sea." From there came other flying objects. The pilot reentered the ship carrying Filiberto and it whirled toward the sea with the others. In front of Filiberto there appeared a kind of windshield, very close to his face. The space ships began to move and dived into the sea and submerged travelling at a fantastic speed. The captive at this time could not see what was in front of him. All was obscured by the incredible velocity.

The ship veered to the right and began to lose speed. In front of them Filiberto could now see a tunnel with illuminated walls, as if they were phosphorescent. The ship went into this tunnel and later came to a stop in a place completely dry. It looked like a large cavern but he noticed that it did not have any stalactites or stalagmites. It was a very big place. Here was a place made out of rock where he noticed two symbols. One of them had the form of a serpent. It was of great size, as big as an "electric light pole." The other was similar to the first but smaller. In that place the extraterrestrials disembarked from the ship with their captive and took him to a rock, where they let him sit down. They make him drink "a liquid that tasted like honey," which they told him was for nourishment.

UFO Abduction From Undersea

They opened an enormous door, that was like a whole wall, and a number of "people" came out. Filiberto felt pressure in his chest as if he could not breathe. The sensations and odors were very strange in this place. At this point someone came up to Filiberto and said "WELCOME."

This individual who received him spoke in perfect Spanish with a South American accent. He looked like an Earth person. He informed Filiberto that he was "from Earth and had been for some time working with the extraterrestrials." He also said that "he should be happy, because he was going to receive some instructions from a human being like us."

After they had taken Filiberto through another door toward a street of what seemed to be a city, they crossed it and entered a small building. In that place Filiberto felt like he was sucked up against a wall. This panel revolved a turn and converted itself into a sort of table. Paralyzed, the captive observed the ceiling, while at the same time he could see figures moving around him doing things. At one side of the wall he could see his clothes "floating" in the air, and he now knew he was nude. They put a light in his eyes, something in his ears (which they later told him was a transceiver so they could communicate with him), and examined him with other instruments. From the walls came mechanical arms full of instruments with which they looked at and tested almost his whole body. One of these arms connected something to his penis and sucked and ejaculation of semen from him. He felt no pain but he could not move because of some kind of invisible restraint.

Upon terminating the examination they let him get up and get dressed again. They went down a corridor until they arrived at another room. This place was the same, or very similar to the control room of the mothership. It had the same kind of high seat that rotated, an individual wearing a cape, television displays in the wall, etc. He demonstrated, by means of the televisions, to Filiberto, new and different things that were going to occur. Later he signaled to a reflection in the floor of "three triangles or pyramids united by a halo of fine light." He explained that "Those are the controls that we have here in the Earth. One in the Pacific Ocean (where we are now), another in the Atlantic Ocean, and the other deep in the earth.

Another extraterrestrial came up to the captive, and conducted him to still another distinct place. Along the way at times, he stopped, putting a hand on the captive's shoulder, and made him sleep. Later he would awaken him and ask, "Are you rested," and they would continue the march. When they arrived he showed

Filiberto a book, with many photographs of distinct places. He made Filiberto think that this had taken them 18 months. For food he gave Filiberto "some things like pills." For a time, Filiberto felt like he was going crazy. They passed another habitation where there were two individuals "who looked like Earth people" that were all gray "like the ones they use in laboratories." He was taken to another habitation where there was a party going on like some kind of a reunion.

After that he was taken to a great room where there was a great ship in a vertical position "like our big rockets." They went inside of this, and encountered in this spaceship three more extraterrestrials, who placed him in one of those suction seats as before, and then they set up the controls and manipulated the ship for departure.

The captive could see nothing of what was happening outside. After a short trip the door of the flying machine opened and Filiberto was put out of the ship, in a pasture. The space people opened his mouth and made him drink something. At this time the captive began to feel bad. The ship took off vertically at high speed and was disappearing from view high in the sky, and Filiberto made a supreme effort to orient himself. He didn't know where he was. He began to move his feet on the Earth again.

UFO Abduction From Undersea

CHAPTER 6

The Experience of Maria Elena
19 February 1979

On Monday 19 February 1979, about 6:30 in the morning, Filiberto called us on the telephone. At that time of day I was driving on the road to work with my wife. When Maria Elena returned home and got the note she returned the call only to be informed that Filiberto was sleeping, and not to call back until after 10:30 that morning because Filiberto had spent the whole night out and needed to sleep some. Maria Elena relates the events as follows:

"At 10:30 in the morning I called Filiberto back. He immediately informed me that they (the extraterrestrials) had said that he could bring me and other persons to the place where his abduction had taken place. He told me that in life a most important thing is LOVE and that I had been selected for something because of something. He also informed me that one of my daughters would also be selected, that we should have faith. Filiberto continued the conversation talking about the sentiment of LOVE, its importance, and that I should go and meet the extraterrestrials."

"We ended the telephone conversation and I hung up the phone. Almost immediately it rang again with Mario Rodriguez on the line and I talked to him. At this hour I could not communicate with Virgilio, and so I related the conversation with Filiberto. He wanted us to get together that evening to discuss the things that were happening and coming to pass, and so we arranged it. There were the three of us, Mario, Virgilio and I seated in the salon speculating on what Filiberto had told me when, at 11:30 the telephone rang and it was Filiberto saying that it was now the time to go to the place."

"Mario and Virgilio began to give me instructions about what could happen or could not happen in case there was a contact and they took me. They didn't want to frighten me and tried to analyze everything from a logical point of view, though none of us allowed any assurance of a contact."

"After certain instructions we all went to the Cardenas' home. I asked Mario and Virgilio not to get out of the automobile because I didn't want to risk breaking the connection or interfere with the presence. Upon entering Filiberto's house I came to realize my suspicions about who the other person would be. It appeared to be the parapsychologist Patricia Hayes. Patricia had been since the first days near Filiberto experimenting and studying the case. Some time later Filiberto told me that her experiments were not exactly scientific, but on the contrary speculatively bringing her students, as part of the program, to the Cardenas' house to receive, according to her, extraterrestrial energy, but instead receiving more delusion than anything else. From that time Patricia went away until she separated herself completely from the case. Nobody had anything to say about that."

"When we entered the house, the only thing Filiberto talked about was LOVE (in an altruistic sense) and that we should go to the encounter. At 12:00 midnight we went out to meet them. Before arriving we could see the sky through the window of the car. It was clear and full of stars. I studied them and thought, which of them could be a UFO. Upon arriving at the entrance to the side road, Filiberto put out the lights of the auto and parked at the side of the road. There in the darkness we held hands and kissed on the cheek in a sign of LOVE. With the lights out, Filiberto proceeded along the road until we arrived at the place where the first abduction occurred. Filiberto got out alone and began to walk a little behind the car. We couldn't see him in the darkness of the night but in a minute he returned to the car. Then he told us he felt that the place of the first contact was a little more ahead. He got back in the car and we continued some two blocks. We stopped again as he informed us that we had arrived at the place and we could get out. The place was well known to me, having been there in the company of Virgilio and Mario many times. Sometimes we had waited until sunrise. For this reason we were not in the least afraid. What most preoccupied was the sentiment of LOVE we should have, when in reality I didn't feel any and I was more curious about what might happen. Also I didn't want to unduly influence anything. Patricia asked me if I didn't feel a certain heat at one side of the road more than the other. I answered yes but very slowly. Filiberto began to walk and got away from the rest of us, until he disappeared in the darkness. Patricia, a little nervous, asked me if I knew where Filiberto had gone, and I answered no, and we continued waiting. Some time passed and it became apparent that fear was growing in Patricia. I was amazed that I didn't feel the same thing."

"Finally Filiberto appeared in the darkness and came up to the car, and we asked him, 'Did you see anything?' He answered no, that he only had felt a little heat on one side of the road, but nothing else. Then Filiberto discovered a mark in the form of a cross that had been painted on the asphalt of the road. This mark had been made by surveyors tracing a curve at the end of the road. Filiberto asked me to stand in the middle of the cross and so I did. I don't know why but I stood erect, closed my eyes and my ears, and commenced to ask that they come and appear at that time. I was in the act of doing that when there immediately commenced to blow a strong wind that beat the trees on the other side of the road. Every moment the force of the wind increased. Soon I became afraid and opened my eyes, turned to the others and said, 'What is happening? Why is the wind so strong?' In the confusion one could see Patricia, who up to this moment had been at my side, give one jump and was standing at the side of Filiberto who was some 15 feet from me. In our faces one could see surprise and a little fear on the part of Patricia. In those seconds I didn't know whether I wanted to go toward them or remain where I was standing. Then I decided to go toward them, and I noted as I walked that I felt a little seasick. I could see that my feet were not standing on the road! At first I attributed this to having smoked a cigarette, something that I do not do frequently. The calm returned again and the trees returned to stationary shadows of the night."

"Filiberto, without saying any words, returned to walking and disappeared in the darkness. In about five minutes he returned and said we should go, that nothing was going to happen. He said this in an agitated tone. I began to dispute going with Filiberto, saying that now is the time we should wait, that now was when the extraterrestrials would be likely to come. But he insisted no and we all got into the automobile. I still had the feeling that something was going to happen. We had not gone but a few meters when, looking through the window toward the shrubs, I saw some eyes that looked at me. I continued looking until I lost them in the obscurity of the distance. I didn't say anything to the others about what I had seen."

"When we were, after returning, in the house of Filiberto, he called me aside and asked insistently if I had seen anything. I was afraid to tell him anything and so I denied it. Filiberto, with tears in his eyes asked me if I was telling him the truth. He judged that he had seen me, when I was standing on the cross and the wind was strong, ELEVATE SOME TEN INCHES from the road. I thought this explained the seasickness and hope I felt when I walked toward the others. But 'THE EYES' . . . 'Really, didn't you see them?' I took a little time before I affirmed those things. Today I am sure that what happened was a very strange experience."

Days later we put Maria Elena under hypnotic regression and reviewed the whole thing that happened, confirming the above. Since she is my wife, these experiences put me in a delicate position. I don't want any of the investigation group to think that I am involved in a farce, and that my wife is also involved. For my part, I can not think that my wife would fool me, and the same for Mario Rodriguez, who for many years has investigated the UFO phenomenon as Uruguayan representative for MUFON, an important and serious organization here in the United States. The only one who could have prepared a farce was Filiberto whom we have known for only a few days. But it all seems to indicate with witnesses, doctors' statements and police reports that he has in truth suffered an experience. I lived those moments at a time when I was pressured by friends who insisted that I should not follow this case with the objective of assuring myself that it was all a lie, that it could not be true. They obliged me continually to proceed seeking the help of international research groups to work together with us in examining the accounts. In this manner I felt supported. Also, if the circumstances began to involve me also (as I hoped), there would still be other investigators to take over the investigation immediately, and I would pass over to be a new witness in this case. I always felt that the investigator should not in any way become involved in the circumstances of the case. He should remain outside the case in order to be able to make rational deductions based on the evidence without being unduly influenced. The fact that my wife Maria Elena was now involved in this case could endanger my position as an impartial investigator. But at the same time I felt that her inclusion would give me an opportunity to live, together with her, the experience itself, taking the investigation to a level of understanding that justified our inquiry on this basis.

The "eyes" seen glowing in the tall scrub that grew along side of the road at that point. Filiberto was desperate to know if Maria Elena had seen them during the wind and levitation demonstration. She had but hadn't told anyone yet.

UFO Abduction From Undersea

CHAPTER 7

Second Abduction

On the night of 21 February 1979, Filiberto and his wife Iris could not stay asleep and decided to go to the place where Filiberto was abducted. It was around 5:00 A.M. when the second encounter with an extraterrestrial ship and its occupants took place.

After returning to his house, Filiberto called me by telephone and told my wife what had happened. He said that they were very tired and that he would call back again after 10:00 in the morning. They would lay down and get some sleep. That afternoon I received a call from Manuel Rodriguez, Investigator of the Centro Investigador De Vida Extraterrestre, our local group, who has maintained a little distance from the Cardenas case, calling to inform me that he had received notice that people at Miami International Airport had observed a UFO that morning.

Rodriguez had recorded a conversation by telephone with one of the older employees at the airport, in which the employee said that at about 10:00 in the morning he had observed a large mothership and various smaller objects flying around it. In the conversation the woman, Sra. Julie Gonzales, said, "I and four companions saw a large round thing like a plate very well illuminated. At first my companions saw the one. Then soon we saw two more objects come out of the larger one. They were very high. I saw like a reddish ship which moved around among the other three. The aft part had the form of a fish, elongated, without wings or a tail. The upper metallic part shown with a brilliance. We were in the 'satellite' of the airport and we were observing from a part near the runways. The four ships were of the same size. Then we do not know how they disappeared. We continued to observe the sky to see if they would come back into view. The sky was cloudless and very clear. We did not see anything else. The other witnesses are Ricardo Sanchez, Francisco Valdez, and the other two I don't remember their names. We all work on the morning shift."

Days later we were able to obtain the address of Sr. Ricardo Sanchez and he accepted a visit to his house. This is how the conversation went:

"I was on the rest break when my companions told me they were observing a light in the sky. But because there are many airplanes, I thought it was one of them. Then I saw that they insisted on looking toward the sky, so then I decided to look also. I could see one disc. Then I went to the other work companions, Francisco Valdez and Julie Gonzales and said that I was looking also to know what they were looking at. Our supervisor, Harold, was also with us and he too was there looking. There were five or six of us there. The object seemed fixed in the sky. It was round and had like three lights, one very white, one yellow, and the other one also white but more opaque than the first one, or you could say that it had one white light that shone brighter than the other, and also a yellow one. At the sides of the ship one could see two other ships a little smaller, of the same form but smaller. They had only one light each. It looked like one object with two more alongside it. The bright white light in the center was fixed but the yellow and the more opaque one pulsated. We watched them for twenty to thirty minutes. We got tired of looking at them."

VIRGILIO - Toward where were they? Were they in front of you? Toward the north . . . south . . . east . . . west?

RICARDO - I was standing facing the west.

VIRGILIO - If you divide the sky like a clock with 12 directly overhead and 9 on the horizon, in what angle did you see the UFOs?

RICARDO - The objects would be at about 10:00.

With these two answers we were able to localize the mothership with the other UFOs DIRECTLY ABOVE THE PLACE WHERE FILIBERTO WAS PICKED UP, which is the same place where only hours before this observation, the second abduction of Filiberto had taken place. Coincidence? This can all easily be seen by reference to the map of the city of Miami. The main runway of the airport runs parallel to Highway 27, better known as Okechobee Road. Without imagination one can see that Ricardo Sanchez and the other witnesses were standing facing the contact place. If they observed the UFOs at an angle of 60 degrees they would have been situated directly over the contact point. But let us pass on to the experience of Iris and Filiberto Cardenas that morning.

UFO Abduction From Undersea

Iris and Filiberto Cardenas as they waited for the spacecraft for the second trip aboard. It arrived in only a few minutes and picked them up.

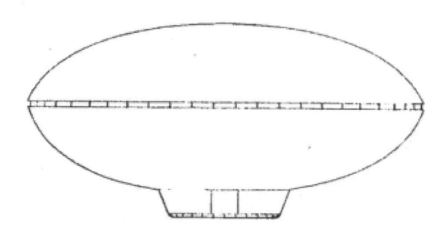

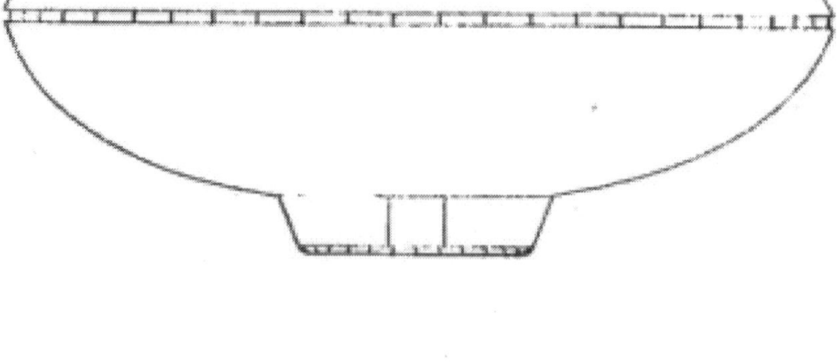

UFO Abduction From Undersea

"The ship appeared from behind us as we stood there. It made a turn at about 60 to 80 feet altitude above our heads, descended and hovered just above the ground, without touching it. It maintained like a foot of altitude above the ground without any type of landing gear, tripod, wheels or anything. We could hear a sound that didn't seem like it should be coming from a ship so large. We could see that the ship had like two levels or stories, one level a little smaller below and another larger one above. I (Iris) stayed in the lower level and did not see above."

"Iris saw the ship arrive. She took out a cigarette and lighted it, very naturally. I told her I didn't think she should do that because they might not like it. Then she did not know what to do with the cigarette. In comparison I would say that the ship was a little larger than a truck or autobus, though of a very distinct form. We entered (the ship) up a ramp about eight feet long. We could see inside but nevertheless, it gave me the impression, or better, the sensation that my body passed through the body (transparent material, like glass) that was there. It was like I was going to collide with something but passed through, It was like a window of crystal, which upon passing through, we felt a distinct atmosphere, almost like we were out of this world! I felt myself floating. I felt like my body did not weigh anything. My thoughts and ideas were of great intensity. When I looked back outside through the 'door,' it seemed as if it were a division between two worlds, very distinct and separate."

Referring back to the extraterrestrials, they gave me the impression that there was not much physical difference between them and us, despite the fact that I had not seen them without those suits. They all looked to be of strong constitution. I got the bright idea that they covered their whole body, head and face with something as a protection for the walking ones that surrounded us, and it was that that made it difficult for me to see well their configuration."

They were dressed in a suit of very special brilliance. It was the color of silver and reflected the lights around them. (Iris) They were not very tall. They were shorter than Filiberto and seemed to be light in weight. I saw four of them among whom there was a woman. I was only aware of this because of the form of her tightly fitted suit. The suit covered her whole body, and hands and feet, leaving only an aperture for the face, and it came down and covered half of the forehead. On the right side of the head for where the ear should be, they had a bulge in the suit like an audiophone, but inside the suit. From the nape of the neck to the bottom of the back near the waist, they had five cables or flexible

UFO Abduction From Undersea

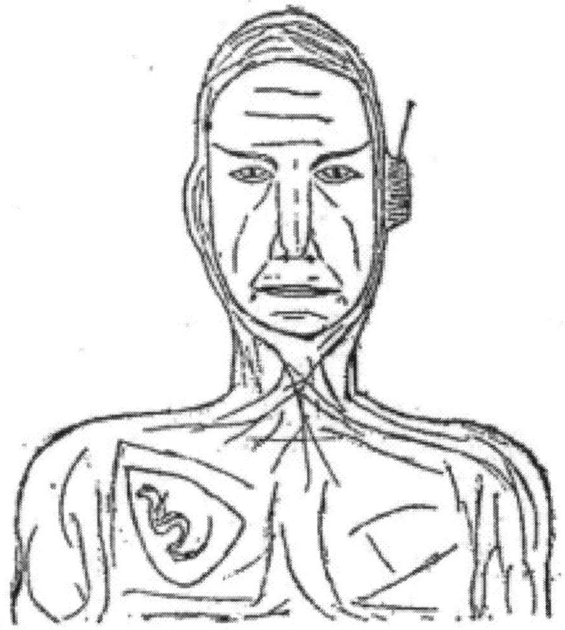

Herbert Schirmer's drawing of the crew leader.

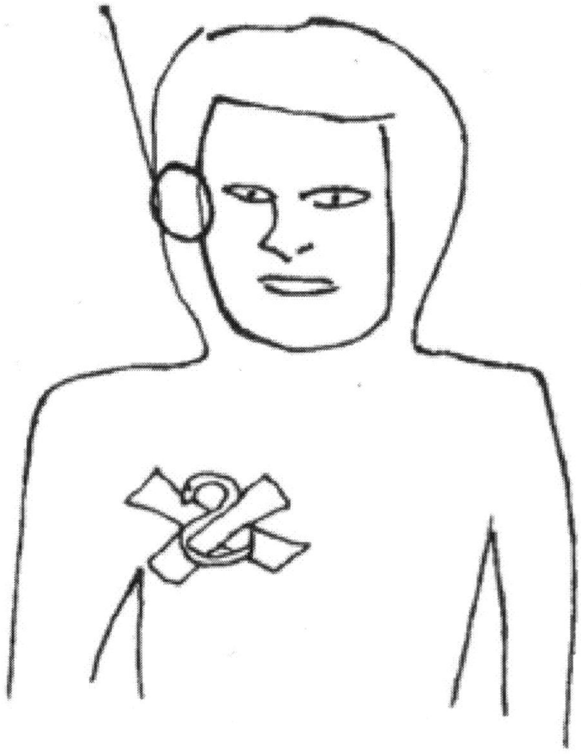

Iris Cardenas sketch of the alien being seen aboard the spacecraft.

transparent tubes, which did not impede their movement. Besides this they had other buttons and controls on the breast of the suit that could be operated by the alien being."

"The face was normal, much like ours, but the eyes were elongated and had eyelashes like ours. I could not see the eyebrows. Either they were covered by the suit or they did not have any. The nose was smaller and a little flattened. The mouth was large and long without having much lip, or rather the lip was quite fine. They opened their mouth to talk but I could not hear their voice. The face ended in a small light beard."

"On the suit, on the right breast, they had an emblem made up of a serpent in the form of an 'S' or maybe more like a 'Z' with rounded corners, with a wide 'X'-shaped cross lying down underneath. I could not see their hands because they were covered by the suit extending down over the fingers like a glove. They sneezed constantly. (They later explained that the sneezing was caused by the near presence of human beings.)"

Iris Cardenas is still talking.

"Inside the ship there was a sound something like that of parrots, a great number of parrots. I could hear them perfectly but I could not see them. They must have had several cages for them installed in this ship. (Iris did not connect the parrot sounds to the beings at that time. As an afterthought one wonders if that might not have been the language of the beings themselves.)

"The extraterrestrials paid a great deal of attention to my painted nails, both fingers and toes. I was wearing sandals at the time. They looked at them constantly, my painted nails, that is. There was only one that spoke to me. He communicated mentally because I could not hear his voice. He spoke very fine and delicately to me. I felt very well with them, they did not frighten me. It seemed like I was floating and I felt very tranquil. Instead of feeling afraid and wanting to run, I, on the contrary felt peace and tranquility."

"At a point I asked the one who talked to me if he would permit me to touch him. I was like St. Thomas in wanting to see for myself before believing and I wanted to touch him. He (the extraterrestrial) said to me, yes, that I could. He raised his right arm and I could see that he had a body under the suit. The suit material seemed to have a soft scaly texture."

"In the lower level of the ship where I remained the whole time, there was a small cabin full of televisions in rows, one alongside another, many in double banks. There was a narrow seat with a high back, as if it were for the captain of the ship. It was very

UFO Abduction From Undersea

Sketch done by Mrs.Cardenas during second encounter. 2/24/79
-"They had 5 thin cables that came from down the seat up to the neck"-

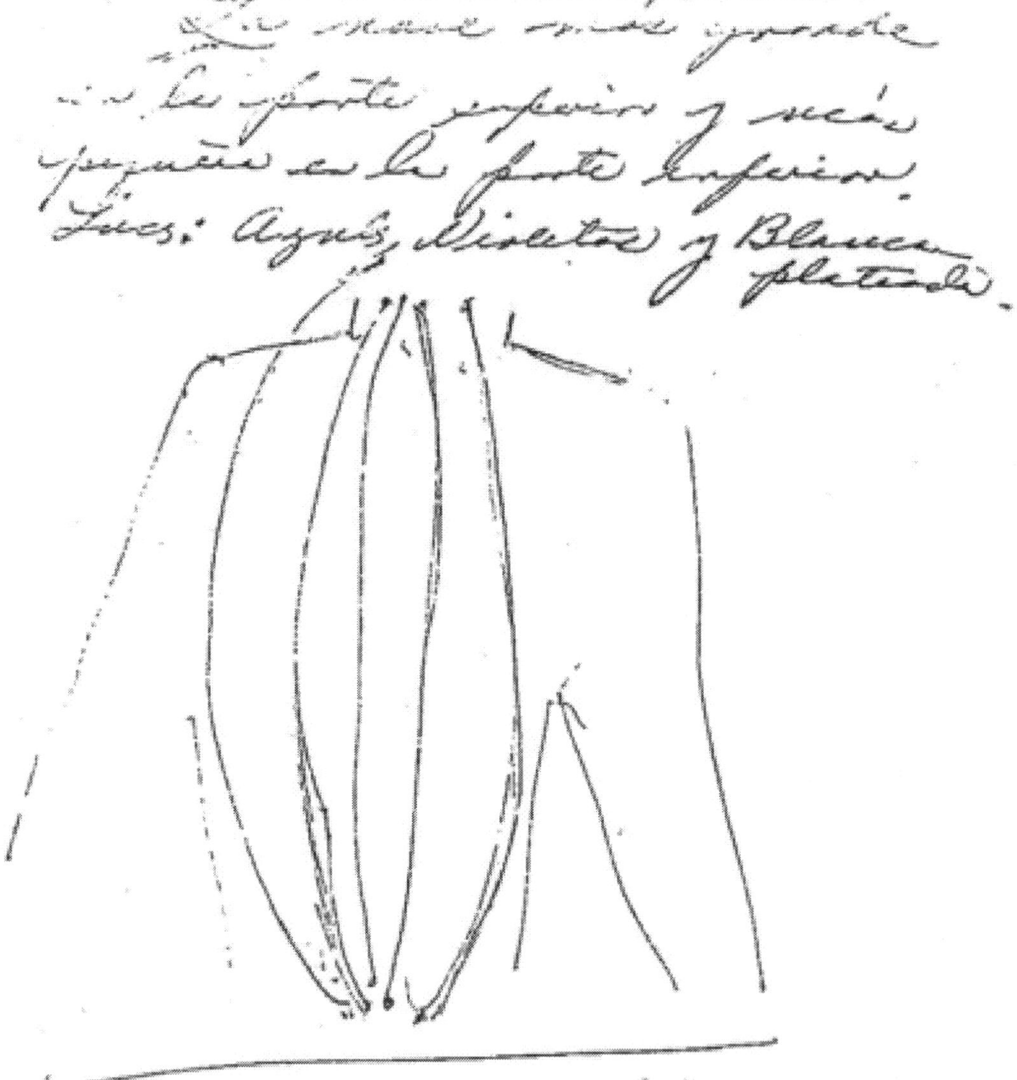

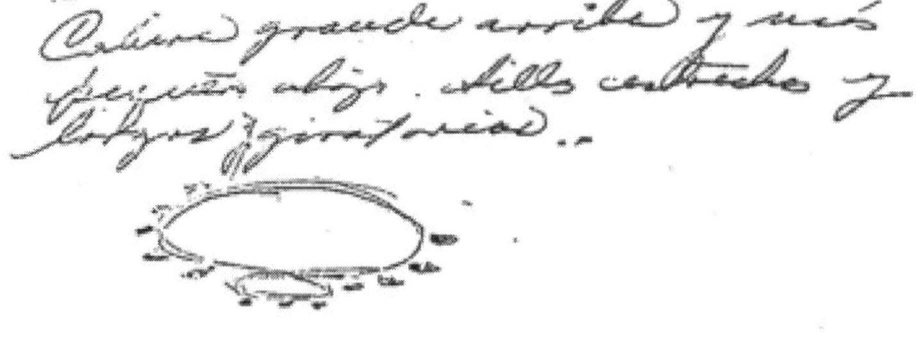

Sketch of the UFO. -" The craft was smaller in the bottom and bigger on the top"-
-"The light: Blue,Violet and bright white"-

UFO Abduction From Undersea

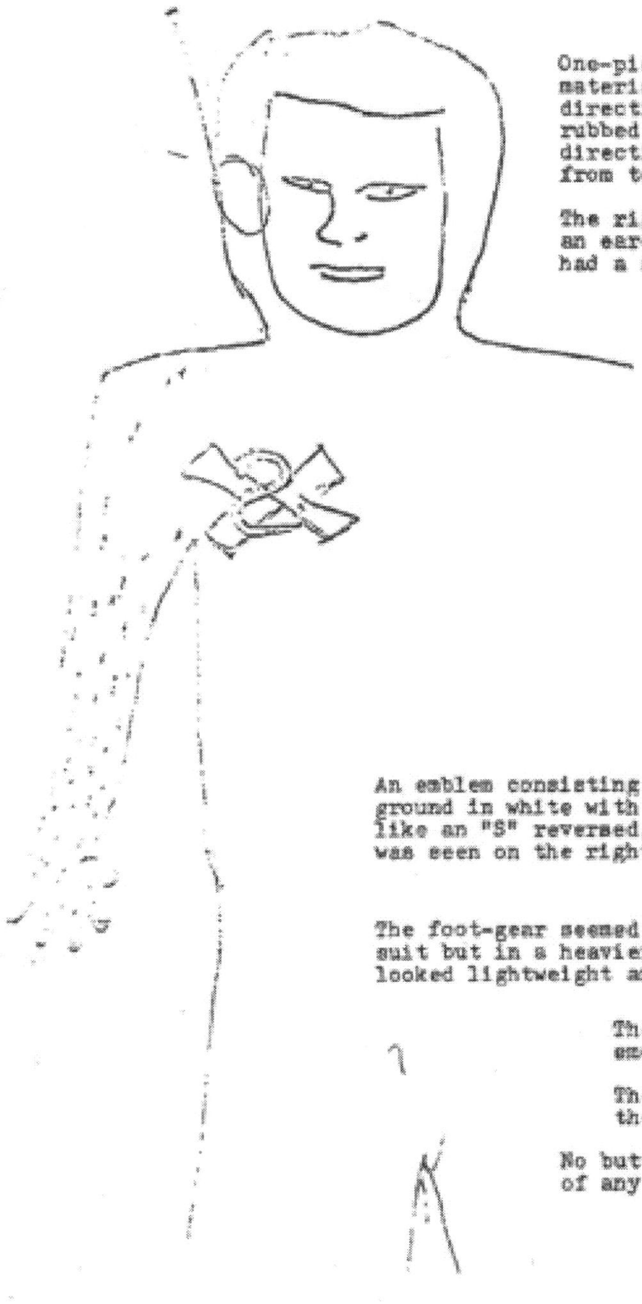

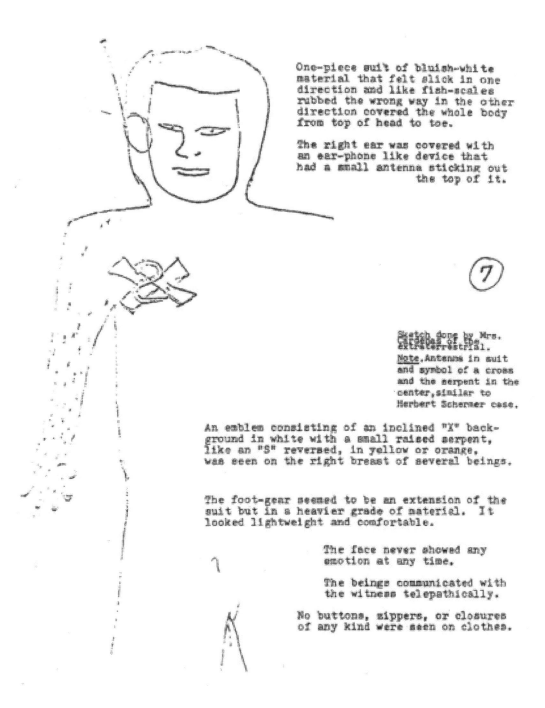

One-piece suit of bluish-white material that felt slick in one direction and like fish-scales rubbed the wrong way in the other direction covered the whole body from top of head to toe.

The right ear was covered with an ear-phone like device that had a small antenna sticking out the top of it.

(7)

Sketch done by Mrs. of the extraterrestrial.
Note. Antenna in suit and symbol of a cross and the serpent in the center, similar to Herbert Schermer case.

An emblem consisting of an inclined "X" background in white with a small raised serpent, like an "S" reversed, in yellow or orange, was seen on the right breast of several beings.

The foot-gear seemed to be an extension of the suit but in a heavier grade of material. It looked lightweight and comfortable.

The face never showed any emotion at any time.

The beings communicated with the witness telepathically.

No buttons, zippers, or closures of any kind were seen on clothes.

prominently placed. This seat rotated. There was another seat in which nobody was sitting and they seated me there. On that floor around me there were many small lights. When I sat down I observed the lights around my seat, which began to brighten in different colors. The white light to which we had become accustomed went out and I couldn't see it any more. The lights were clear and brightly transparent, such as nothing that we have here. The floor was made of a very strange material. It was not plastic, but it was a smooth flat material. It was of some kind of material completely unknown to us. Also it had various levels of elevation. I didn't see any walls as such. Everything was covered with apparatus or was 'windows.' Inside the ship one had the sensation of not standing on the floor, but more like he was floating. For the whole time I was there, some twenty minutes, I was conversing with them, but in a form very strange, not like I am talking to you now. The one who talked to me was sitting in the high seat in front of me, and as he spoke he looked at me intently. Filiberto was standing at one side on foot, though in a moment they took him to the upper level in the ship."

"They, the extraterrestrials, walked very rapidly there inside the ship. You would see them there and then almost immediately they were here. The one in front of me smiled. They had a language of their own which they used to communicate between themselves. It sounded to me like they were talking in some kind of Arabic dialect. I did not understand them. They were very small. They smiled at me as they were saying, 'Be calm, nothing is going to happen to you.' In the conversation that I carried on with the one seated in front of me, in the high seat, he talked of LOVE, UNIVERSAL LOVE. He told me much about universal love. He said that they came on a mission to Earth and that they selected any person for contact simply by accident of time and place. These persons were subjected to a series of tests. If that person felt LOVE toward them, then they often continued the contact. But if, on the contrary, they did not feel any LOVE they did not contact them again."

"They allowed the contactee to say that he had seen them (the extraterrestrials) without interfering with his memory. He said that they did not come to harm us and that they are messengers. They told me that this is the only way they can come here to Earth, without causing fear or panic. Many for this reason have been contacted only once. If the person contacted does not feel LOVE, or if he does not report his experience, or does not respond to the needs of others contacted, then they leave him. For that reason, they told me, there are here on the Earth, many who have been contacted only one time and no more. But if, on the other hand, a person contacted comes to know them and does not fear, they often continue contacting him. At the same time they are studying the people. They bring many messages. For example: Cancer can be cured. They told me that the time has come. They are going to tell us with what we can cure cancer. It will come from a plant, the sap of a plant. Also they told me that we must make our lives more healthy. They say that we are very contaminated, that we do not have here a very healthy life. They do not want from us any goods of the Earth. They live more naturally than we do, and the suits and the tubes installed in them is to protect them from the contaminating Earth elements. They control everything with the power of the mind which, they told me, was of extreme importance. At a moment in the conversation I asked them, 'Why did you select my husband for this problem?' And they responded that any person here in the universe could be selected. Right now is a period of experimentation, but later, there will be millions who will see them. They do not want to endanger humanity. They come here to help us. We are super backward in everything, they say."

"There exist other planets much advanced over us. In 1993, we Earth people will make contact with other planets ourselves. There we will be able to see the life and the advancements of the other planets."

Then Filiberto Cardenas spoke to the investigators. "I can not repeat all that they told me aboard the ship, but they reaffirmed that they came to planet Earth to aid us in all they could, and very especially in all that related to health. They ratified their universal love concept. They do not come to endanger nor to conquer us, nor do they want to be recognized as saints or saviors. This has happened before. They say that they are beings of other dimensions, of other worlds, but that they are not gods, and they do not want to be considered such. They do not want to be attacked. They are wanting me to be one who talks to the public about these messages, messages designed to prepare for the coming of them on Earth. These messages have been given to six other people of Earth who have been contactees of this kind or will be contacted soon. I do not know for sure whether these other six are abductees or whether they are being contacted mentally to receive the messages. I have the impression that some are abductees, having the opportunity to see and feel directly the same as I."

"Among the things that I was told was an assurance that women will rise to important positions in our society. It is to be that many women throughout this Earth will rise to high positions in politics as well as in business. There will be a tendency to defer to and to vote for women in those positions with the hope of a change, and to see if the world can grow up. This tendency, the extraterrestrials see in the very near future."

"When they come to make definite official contact with us, the illnesses will be something of the past. The sick will be cured easily. The state of anxiety, our peroccupation of mind, is precisely for the moment of evolution in which we are living. In actuality this is one of the worst illnesses. The excessive preoccupation with material existence, without feeding the spiritual, produces the immense majority of the illnesses. Preoccupations such as fear of illness in us, produces illness. Fear that something will occur produces illnesses, and fear in general, of many things, produces premature aging. They told me that we, in a period very near, and after their coming, will undergo radical changes. Some people who already have been contacted, and who possess certain powers, could live easily more than a hundred years. Perhaps even to a hundred and ninety years. At first certain people with psychic faculties and strong spirits capable of assimilating knowledge and controlling their emotions could live even up to three hundred years."

"They possess great destructive power through their scientific advancement, but they told me that they have no desire to destroy us. They live looking for and giving LOVE. The Pope who is now in the Vatican (Pope John Paul) is one of those contacted by them. The function of this Pope is to evangelize throughout all corners of the Earth, or at least that is what he is trying to do. What the Pope is going to do, what he has done, and what he is doing is of great importance."

"After my abduction I received the help of distinct religious groups, and all of them asked me, what is the message for humanity. And they all were pleased when I told them, but more so that the extraterrestrials spoke of universal love. The pope is one of those most greatly worried about the lack of love at these times in this world."

"I believe at this time that those who believe in God do not have to look in others or elsewhere for Him but within themselves. If they have faith, God is within them. Christ is within every person. Here is where you have to look for it. The Pope is a beacon of light for humanity. Not only for Catholics, but for all, including the atheists. Those who desire to have a change in the world should heed the gestures of the Pope."

"Before this I worked excessively, working with the logical

aspiration that any person could achieve a good social position. I must confess that I did not dedicate enough time to the questions of spirituality and aid to less fortunate people. Or rather that I gave a little love to all those people who did not need it. I believe that the whole world must begin to give more LOVE. Not only to the man in the street, but to begin with your parents, your children, your families and friends. LOVE must begin in the family, which is the base of our heritage, and radiate out from there. I ask of all who hear me that they give more time to LOVE that inspires love in humanity. This is how we will achieve our majority sufficiently great in this system in which we are living at this time."

UFO Abduction From Undersea

Wendelle C. Stevens and Filiberto Cardenas outside the Miami International Airport.

CHAPTER 8

Coincidental Cases

The experience of Filiberto Cardenas did not end with his return to our familiar world there along the Tamiami Trail. On the contrary, it only began for the rest of us and for those have been following these developments with interest.

The subject Ufology comprises a great scientific base for the study of this phenomena. Evidence exists in many of the abduction cases. The witness is identified and followed for a time, then isolated and taken aboard a craft, often examined physically and sometimes by other methods, and then returned. Sometimes there are landing marks on the ground, artifacts of different kinds and sometimes a residue of some kind. There is often evidence of the physical examination on the body of the abductee. Occasionally there are other witnesses to the abduction or to follow-on events.

Other cases of abduction can be compared to that of Filiberto. For example the disappearance of Travis Walton on 5 November 1975, when he also was taken aboard an extraterrestrial spacecraft in full view of other witnesses. There various beings of different appearance put a mask of some kind over his face. In Brazil in the Bebedouro case, witness Jose Antonio Da Silva was introduced through a door into a cubical compartment. He felt pushed and obliged to sit on a seat and they placed over his head a helmet like the one they wore. In Argentina, in the Urruti case of 1976 he says, "After the luminous flash it seemed like I was swallowed by a species of (huge)oyster that went into a tunnel of intense violet and yellow color. I felt them (the beings aboard) put a helmet on my head that had various cables coming out of it. I felt it pressing on my parietals and the maxillaries." As in the Cardenas case, the extraterrestrials transported Urruti to a submarine base where also there were human beings.

During the UFO wave of 1973, in October, Charles Hixon and Calvin Parker were abducted by strange beings from a UFO.

Here also there are coincidences. During my interview with Hixon he said, "They were only five feet tall . . . my feet never touched the floor . . . I was moved about floating . . . Calvin and I have talked about this and we have come to the conclusion that they could have been robots or machines. We felt that they were programming us. They came here to do something specific and they did it. They were not distracted by anything. I will believe until the day I die that they were robots communicating with a mind someplace else."

Herbert Schirmer, patrolling the roads of Ashland, Nebraska, was abducted and carried someplace aboard an extraterrestrial craft on 3 December 1967. In his narration of his abduction and what took place we find, "There were pictures like television . . . On the left side of the breast they wore an emblem of a serpent . . . (And the sketch of that emblem was almost the same as the sketch Iris had made of the emblem they had seen in this case.) Their uniform ended on their heads in the form of a helmet with an antenna from an earphone on the left side. They told me that they have bases under the ocean near the coast of Florida, also at the North Pole, South Pole and off the coast of Argentina, all below the sea. They used the word 'invasion' in a friendly manner. They said that in one day they would show themselves completely. The public has nothing to fear from them. We should give serious consideration to the fact that they are not hostile. We have nothing to fear."

The abduction of Betty Andreason occurred on 25 January 1967, one of the biggest years for UFO activity, and was investigated ten years later by Raymond Fowler, a Regional Director of MUFON in Seguin, Texas. This story was not published until six months after the abduction of Mr. Cardenas. Mrs. Andreason was abducted by small creatures who took her to a base underground. Here also there are similarities with the Cardenas case. Mrs. Andreason said, "They (the extraterrestrials) love the human race. They have come to help us . . . Love is the great force . . . They want no harm to come to anybody . . . They said they had contacted others here . . . Others have their minds programmed . . . They put a secret in my mind . . . It will be revealed when the time arrives." (It seems that many of the abductees have been programmed for the future.) "I saw a pyramid . . . one of whose sides was white . . ." (Here also we have a pyramid described.)

In June of 1979, five months after the abduction of Filiberto Cardenas, in a construction near the town of Mirassol, in Brazil, Antonio Ferreira, the guard of the place, was abducted by extraterrestrial beings. Two hours later he was returned to the place displaying the same marks on his body as Filiberto and he gave the same descriptions of events under hypnotic regression. This case is being followed to see if Ferreira is in fact one of the other six mentioned to Filiberto.

Other details often encountered in abduction cases are the light or lights and sound seen at the moment of the abduction. These factors of light and sound are reported in the majority of abduction cases, and very frequently in sighting cases as well. The complete loss of power in automobiles and electrical systems is also frequently reported in UFO cases of all kinds. In other UFO cases there has been observed loss of line voltage in electromagnetic systems up to and even including complete line failure for systems up to total blackout of whole large cities.

The physical characteristics of the extraterrestrials are fairly common. There are differences in some aspects and in size but in general they are very similar to humans, having a head with 3-D vision, stereo hearing and other senses, a body, two arms and two legs, and they are invariably bi-ped and walk erect.

The suits or uniforms worn by the extraterrestrials are surprisingly similar in general terms. They are usually one-piece close-fitting garments of simple design with no evidence of closures such as buttons, zippers, etc., and occasionally have provisions for environmental systems for the occupant.

The physical effect of floating instead of walking is another factor that comes up often, as does the loss of a sense of motion and time. Also it seems that inside the ship the witness loses his sense of weight and seldom sits to rest. Another common aspect is that the extraterrestrials themselves float a little bit above the floor instead of walking.

The configuration of the ship is often rounded, in the form of a plate, curcular, etc., looks metallic, often has lights and sometimes sound which is frequently described as an electrical hum.

A physical examination of the abducted human also seems to be a frequent occurrence in this kind of case. Often this treatment leaves marks on the body. Sometimes the extraterrestrials take special interest in the reproductive organs of the human being such as in the Cardenas case. Others have been submitted to tests of various kinds. In the case of women there are recurring reports of the insertion of a needle in the abdomen resulting in some pain. There are cases, as in that of Antonio Villas Boas of Brazil (abducted 15 October 1957), where the captive human is obliged to have carnal contact with an extraterrestrial woman, evidently in connection with some genetic experiment of theirs. Filiberto's abductors told him that they had conducted similar experiments ultimately resulting in 81 hybrid half extraterrestrial, half human beings alive and well on our Earth today.

The list of such cases and data is interminable and it is not our intent to explore it all. We offer this data to be numbered as a simple reference for the student and lecturer. We do not seek to impose our ideas and deductions on anyone and leave the proper judgment of the Filiberto Cardenas case to the future.

CHAPTER 9

Personal Points of View

I can not terminate this report without exploring several points of general interest in the Cardenas case as well as in the entire UFO phenomenon.

I have tried to be as objective as possible, maintaining a scientific attitude and basing our actions exclusively on the information obtained during the investigation, which often was cold and monotonous. But this was our task, to present the evidence as we studied it. But we could not let pass our reactions and emotions. Without doubt it was a great adventure for us and the emotions were most varied, sometimes confused and other times doubtful. I believe that from the first inkling that I was confronted with a serious contact, I decided to try to involve myself in it. I tried to experience together with Mr. Cardenas, the consequences of his encounter and I must confess that this was not difficult. The psychological impact of the phenomena could be transferred to those concerned. The physical aspect of such contact could be studied extensively such as flight patterns, velocity, marks left on the ground and also on a witness's body, photographs, radar returns, etc., but the psychic or paranormal aspect has always been a difficult situation to understand, not only because we lack instruments to study it but also because it still is not acceptable to orthodox science. Not only do we not give it scientific validity, we call it scientific irresponsibility.

Nevertheless, the number of events continues to grow and they become more and more spectacular. New aspects develop which cannot be divorced from the rest of the phenomena as such. Among these are, new and different information coming from the abductees, materializations and dematerializations, not only of the extraterrestrial vehicles but of the apparent humanoids operating them as well. There have been changes of form, instant accelerations and sudden changes of position that could only be explained by aberrations in time. Many of these reports and worried a great deal about the insecurity of return. True, they returned Filiberto Cardenas, but in the hypnotic regressions we learned that there are others that had not been returned.

Many times I thought that if I involved myself much in this case, I would have to seek help from other investigators, from another with some experience in this subject, who could continue the investigation from outside the phenomena that were going on. I did not welcome this sensation and believed that it would take a will of iron to become involved to any extent without beginning to fantasize. Still by becoming involved in the case itself, one could also "taste" the phenomenon. In my case I believe I lived the phenomenon without any aftereffect. Because of this it is my opinion that an investigator should become a part of the case going on, especially since there are seemingly no two cases the same. To the paranormal aspect of this phenomena different people react in different ways. They understand what they perceive from different points of view and relate it positively or negatively according to their inclination. The cultural and religious status of contactees and abductees enormously influences their interpretations and descriptions of their perceptions experienced.

We are extending the physical phenomena of the UFO question into the metaphysical. We must use our imagination therefore to carefully guide the course of the investigation, neither disillusioning ourselves nor ignoring the evidence. As well as the physical aspect, the psychical demonstrates the plurality of the phenomenon at hand and its impact on the life of man. We must be careful, however, of the importance we place on the predictions of future events even though they come true as outlined. There is a danger of this evolving into a religious fervor and false hope that the extraterrestrials are some kind of super beings who are here to save humanity. We must take into account the popular interest in this whole phenomenon. More than 65% of our population now believes that there is something to the UFO question and many of these think that we are in fact being visited by beings from another world. More than fifteen million North Americans have reported seeing UFOs or knowing someone else who has seen one. We have even observed the creation of sects admiring the UFOs and their occupants, and some are preparing actively for the arrival of these extraterrestrial beings. In some cases the occupants of the UFOs have told their Earth contacts that all of the problems that vex our society are our own creations and that nobody is coming from anywhere to save us from ourselves.

UFO Abduction From Undersea

This has been going on for more than 30 years now in its modern interpretation and it continues today in ever increasing intensity. The messages delivered and the predictions made are very similar but they are soon forgotten in the excitement of the next major case to come along. They leave their mark in time, marks that may be leading up to something of which we are at present completely ignorant. Perhaps one day we will get to the bottom of this phenomenon. Until then we must continue our investigations and documentation of data for study and file. Time will provide us the key to this mystery.

Dr. Virgilio Sanchez-Ocejo
P.O. Box 313
Opa Locka, Florida 33054

END

APPENDIX 1

A Similar Case in Puerto Rico

Reverend David Delmundo (a pseudonym I have used to protect his real identity), an ordained minister in the Southern Baptist Conference, has been having direct contacts with UFOs and their occupants for over 15 years. He is at the same time an executive in a successful company in San Juan, Puerto Rico and minister of his church which also operates a mission and clinic in the mountains above Bayamon.

His UFO contacts all began back in 1964 when his mind suddenly went blank and he couldn't think. Then he heard beeps in the air above his head. It got louder and an object passed in the sky and then the beeps stopped and his head cleared. Later, in 1952, when he lived in New York he woke up with a start feeling like someone was in the room. He got up and looked around and then looked out the window and saw a bright disc-shaped metallic object with a yellow-orange halo around it flying very low above the Hudson River near the tri-borough bridge. It was so low that he thought it would hit the bridge but it raised up and passed over safely. He heard the beep . . . beep . . . beep sound again as the object operated in the vicinity.

Then the beep contacts began in strength in late 1968 or early 1969 and for a three month period he heard the beeps four or five times daily. Then they progressively increased in intensity and came more often until every 15 minutes he heard in his ears a very fine strong high pitched noise which lasted for only a small fraction of a second. This happened frequently and it was very high pitched and loud. Then he noticed a new development. Every time he got near an electric motor the device made strange noises and sounds—even if it was turned off. He felt a strong electrical charge about his person at these times, which grew and increased in intensity steadily. Then he seemed to notice that every time he heard the beeps in his head, he could look up and see the object in the sky somewhere in the vicinity.

In 1971 many UFO sightings were reported on the north side of Puerto Rico Island, so many, in fact, that UFO watch parties were organized by various groups to observe the phenomenon. The activity became common knowledge in the area and everyone seemed to at least know somebody who had seen the strange aerial objects. Scores of sightings of from one to more than a dozen flying, luminous, disc-shaped objects were reported almost nightly. The Baptist mission group, like many others, went to the main UFO activity area near Bayamon and Aguas Buenas to observe. They said that they saw many, even scores, of the low flying luminous objects coming and going. At a point near the intersection of County Roads 879 and 812, from Aguas Buenas to San Juan, they all got out of the cars and watched for many minutes. They saw Puerto Rican Air National Guard jet fighters unsuccessfully trying to chase some of the UFOs. They flew everywhere, hundreds by day and night, during this flap. There were thousands of witnesses to these activities. So many people were on the mountain tops watching that there was no space for more cars or people.

An airline pilot and his crew, flying for a Puerto Rican air passenger line, about that time, observed one of the greenish-blue lens-shaped luminous objects close to the airliner in flight. He called the passenger's attention to the UFO and many others saw it also. Upon landing he reported the experience to his company and to Air Traffic officials. Later he consented to a newspaper interview and the story was published by the paper and subsequently was also picked up by others and re-printed. The airline at this point issued a denial and a short time later dismissed the pilot from service with their company. He has been unable to find airline pilot employment since.

The frequency and intensity of the sharp high-pitched tone increased daily and bothered the witness considerably by this time.

Then came a day late in 1972 when Delmundo heard the beeping sound again, and the loud high pitched tone came every few seconds, and he observed the strange flying machine in the vicinity. Suddenly it seemed to fly off and disappear. Then he became aware of a very strange human-like creature standing beside him. He did not see him arrive. The being was estimated to be about 5′3″ tall and he was dressed in a thin one-piece uniform-like coverall garment which covered him from feet to head. He had thin lips and a small nose and looked very stern. Delmundo could see no teeth when he opened his mouth which was seldom. The stranger had wide wrap-around eyes of an elongated oval shape that slanted up on the outer sides. He wore a sort of wrap around turban-like headdress that had a 10 or 12 pointed star set into the front of it. The turban was thin and light weight and of a dark color. The eyes were the most striking thing about the figure. They were a pale bright green, almost the color of new grass or a new leaf shoot and the whole eye was the same color throughout, having no "white" as we are accustomed to. The eyes also had no pupil like ours. At times he thought he detected a ladder of slits in the green color of the eye but he couldn't see them all the time. The green elongated orb of the eye had an uncountable number of flecks of what looked like sliver points of light that appeared and disappeared in the green of the eye that seemed to make them scintillate and gave them radiant light. At times the eyes seemed to flash and the gaze was very intense. The skin was pale gray.

The uniform-like garment was of some very lightweight material and was a pale gray to smokey gray in color. The hands were covered with a long gauntlet and the feet were covered with an extension of the uniform that became a little heavier and formed a kind of boot. The neck of the outfit ended in a narrow band of material sort of like a minister's collar. There was a silvery colored metallic rib-like device fastened to the uniform that came over the mid-shoulder from back to front, and below the ending of that in front there was an angled "U" shaped device of the same metallic material that was mounted on the breast with the open part of the "U" pointed toward the center of the waist. They seemed to be emblems of some kind.

The alien being's nose was a small fleshy nub with no bridge structure. It had two nostrils like ours but they turned into the head in a different way. The ears were also small and not much more than a firm ridge but they didn't have any openings. The ear structure seemed to consist externally of a pair of membrane covered pits in the head. There was no jaw development and very little brow or cheekbone giving the head an almost melon-like appearance. The face muscles were also underdeveloped and the face had little mobility, giving the head a stern expressionless appearance. When asked about this later the being said that they had essentially overcome their emotional natures and there was little of that nature to be expressed in the face. The eyes were the center of attention in the face and they seemed to be very alive. They seem to flash and the image is very intense.

"He took me by the hand and I became totally controlled. He was shorter than I am. That's why I say about 5'3", very thin

UFO Abduction From Undersea

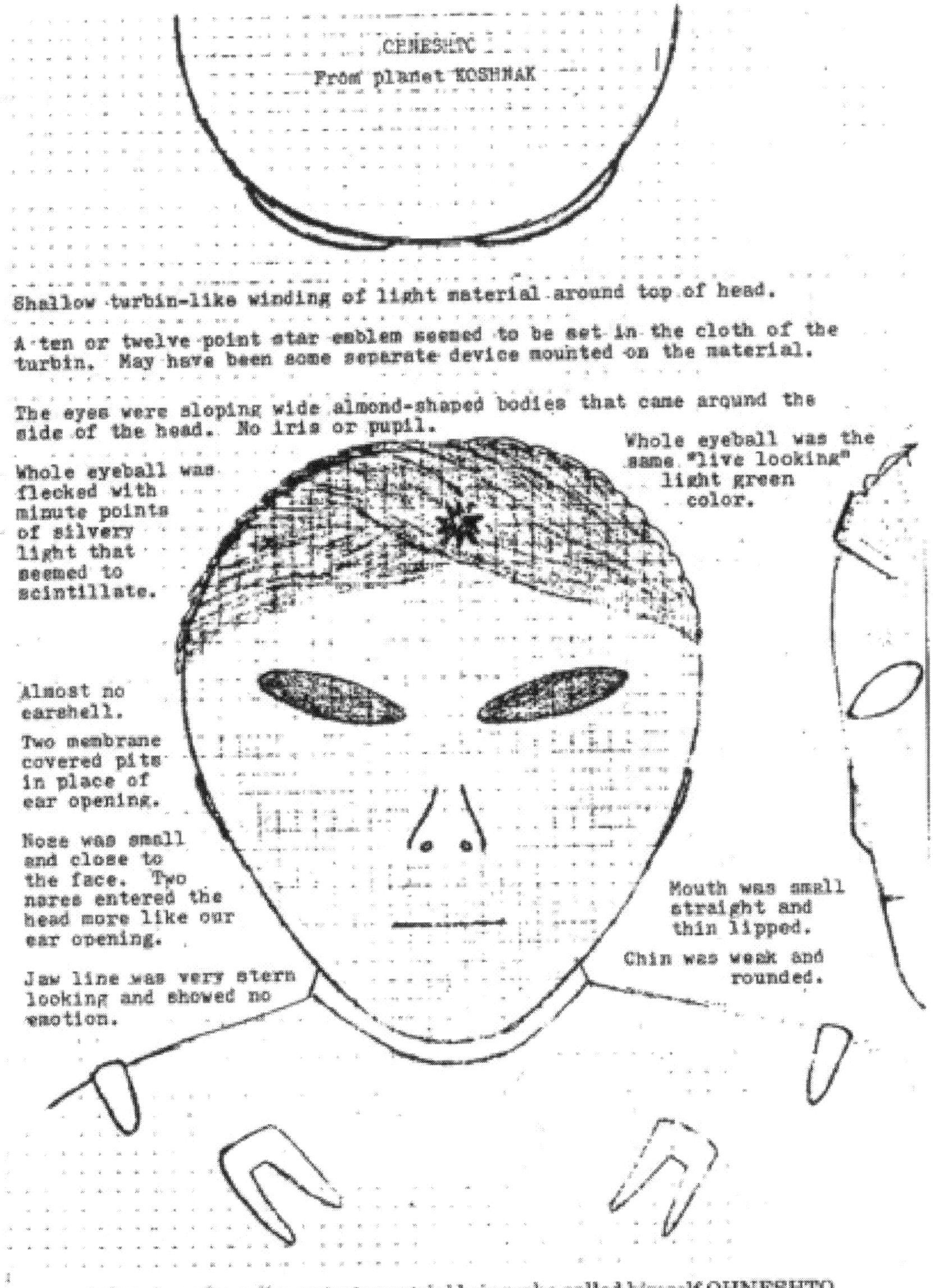
CHNESHTC
From planet KOSHNAK
Shallow turbin-like winding of light material around top of head.
A ten or twelve point star emblem seemed to be set in the cloth of the turbin. May have been some seperate device mounted on the material.
The eyes were sloping wide almond-shaped bodies that came around the side of the head. No iris or pupil.
Whole eyeball was the same "live looking" light green color.
Whole eyeball was flecked with minute points of silvery light that seemed to scintillate.
Almost no earshell.
Two membrane covered pits in place of ear opening.
Nose was small and close to the face. Two nares entered the head more like our ear opening.
Jaw line was very stern looking and showed no emotion.
Mouth was small straight and thin lipped.
Chin was weak and rounded.

A drawing of an alien extraterrestrial being who called himself OHNESHTO and said that he came from a planet he called KOSHNAK in a star cloud in the star group we call Orion.

with a garment similar to a coverall but tighter fitted . . . I would say something like a nylon type of fitted overall, grayish white in color. It was completely closed but I couldn't see how it was fastened. The material looked thin because it was right against his body."

"We walked, say like a distance of a couple thousand feet over a hilly type of terrain. All of a sudden there was the craft, waiting. The ship must have been 30 feet or better in diameter—from this point to this point. As soon as we . . . yes, it was sitting on three legs . . . and as we got close he used his hand again. That little box he had in his hand showed a thin beam that went straight into the . . . this was completely dark . . . the ship was dark . . . it wasn't shiny or anything . . . but as soon as he flashed the beam it became bright . . . this lower part . . . just this part (indicating the lower half of the ship below the rim) . . . luminous . . . radiantly luminous . . . bright . . . just this part. And then a part of this came down . . . like a ramp . . . and there was a greenish light inside . . . luminous pale green light throughout. And we walk in . . . and as we walk in there are four cushioned seats . . . just four . . . all cushioned . . . two at the controls . . . just four seats . . . two in front and two in back. And then I could see that if we were to look behind . . . it was like in front. It was all transparent . . . all around . . . and we could look out all around. The whole cabin was enclosed in the same metal. And we could see through it . . . even sideways and so on . . . The seats were of a leathery type of material . . . soft . . . very wide . . . very comfortable . . . and very low . . . similar to an airplane, but completely different. It (the material) was a sort of pale . . . like tan color . . . pale brown, and as you sat the hind part sort of sank, and something came up and held you this way . . . holding. It was an automatic thing. There wasn't any seat belt of any sort."

"No word . . . nothing was communicated to me at that time . . . I knew as I sat over here . . . in the seat . . . I saw the whole panel arrangement . . . no gages . . . completely different . . . all kinds of colors going on and off . . . yes, colors, colors, colors . . . every little section had more colors, and there was at one point a lever . . . right here (indicating), that's all. And this lever moved that way, that way, that way and that way . . . and here everything was . . . At one point I did notice that there was something that was . . . like when you draw a graph . . . You know, when you draw a graph you go this way and this and like this . . . and that was right on the panel . . . on the panel. The line changed at first and then it got to a point when it stabilized, and all of a sudden I see myself looking outside and we are above the west northwest side

UFO Abduction From Undersea

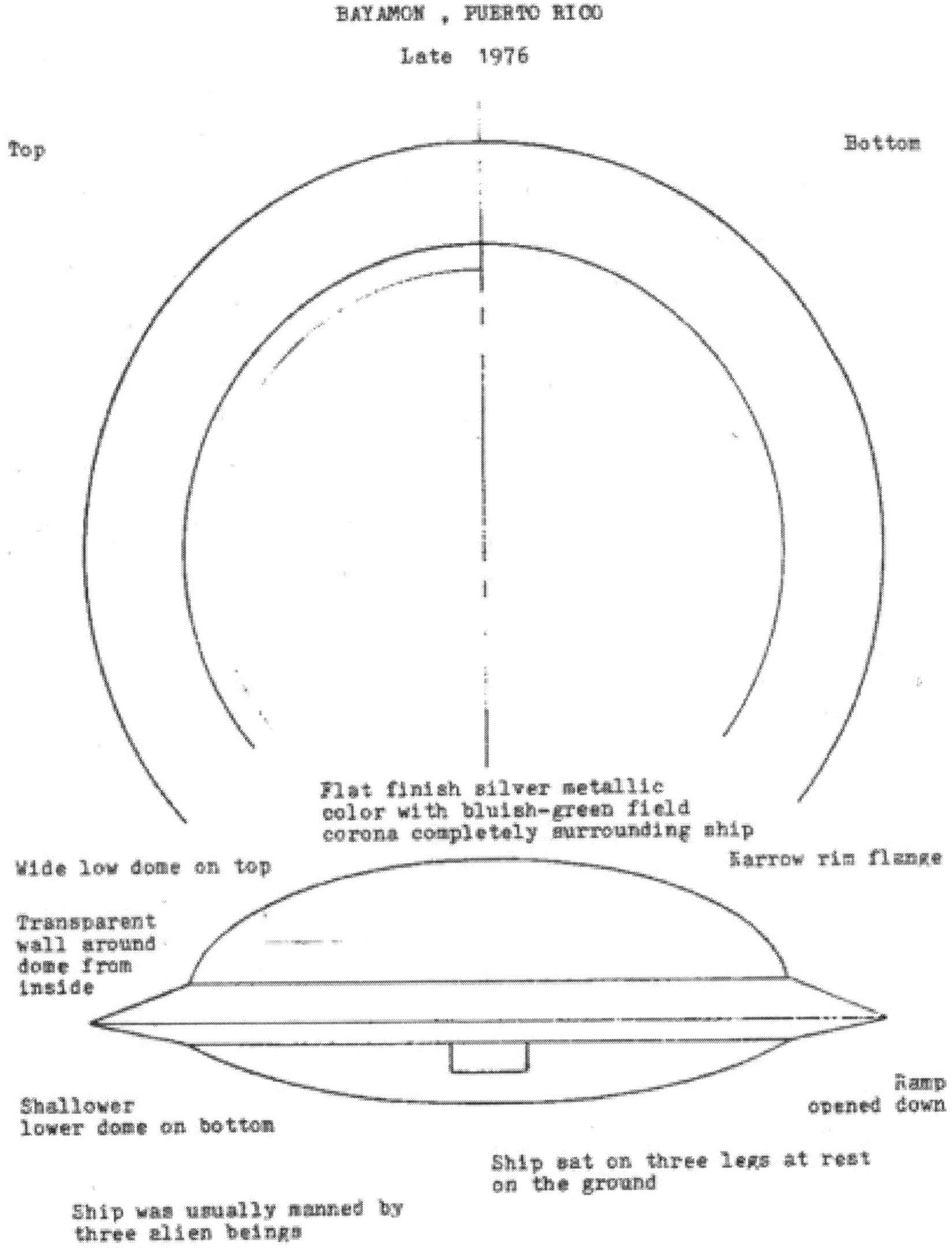

A line drawing of the ship from KOSHNAK that picked up Delmundo and took him to a large undersea base operated by the aliens.

of the island (Puerto Rico) shifting toward the southwest. I remember very distinctly that we came over one of our cities . . . and that village is called Agua Dia. I remember very distinctly going over Agua Dia. And I looked down and I recognized the village. Ramy Air Force Base was to the right side . . ."

The being said that Delmundo could call him Ohneshto, that his origin was a planet called Koshnak located in our heavens in the direction of Orion. It would be considered about 1,200 light years from Earth. He said that there were many many other beings in our universe, some from Orion, some from the Pleiades and many from other places.

Ohneshto discussed energy briefly and explained that we are limited in time and space, and therefore he could only speak of simple things. He discussed the Law of Parallels. He discussed matter and anti-matter of the universe and why man dies, and why he exists at all. Delmundo suddenly realized that he was now aware of knowledge he never had before, he now had the answers to many things that had vexed him all his life and he was alerted to many many mysteries of our vast universe—unknown to contemporary man. He felt enlightened in many ways.

"All of a sudden we shift at that point south by southwest . . . and he said, 'We are moving at a very slow, slow speed, and we're not utilizing the normal travel energy that we use for high speed travel through the universe.' There was an alternative propulsion system, like a little motor, for coasting this way. He says, 'Now we are going,' and then is when I saw this graph-like instrument very clearly. And he said . . . 'Thirty-five miles southwest of your island . . . ,' and they gave me latitude and longitude . . . And now we're going down, down into the water, and there wasn't any splash . . . They had enough energy to displace any type of matter . . . because they create their own field around the ship to displace, not only air, but also more solid things like water and even other matter . . . They came down this way 9,000 feet . . . and there was a drop . . . the water was displaced and we went down . . . and it wasn't dark. There was enough energy around the ship to see where we were headed."

"And then . . . this is the way they went . . . and they came this far . . . in . . . to a rock formation under water . . . got this close . . . and when it was close to the wall here he used exactly the same beam and the water was displaced between the rock and the wall . . . and an opening appeared and we went in and it closed back again . . . and we found ourselves in a very deep cavern . . . and

UFO Abduction From Undersea

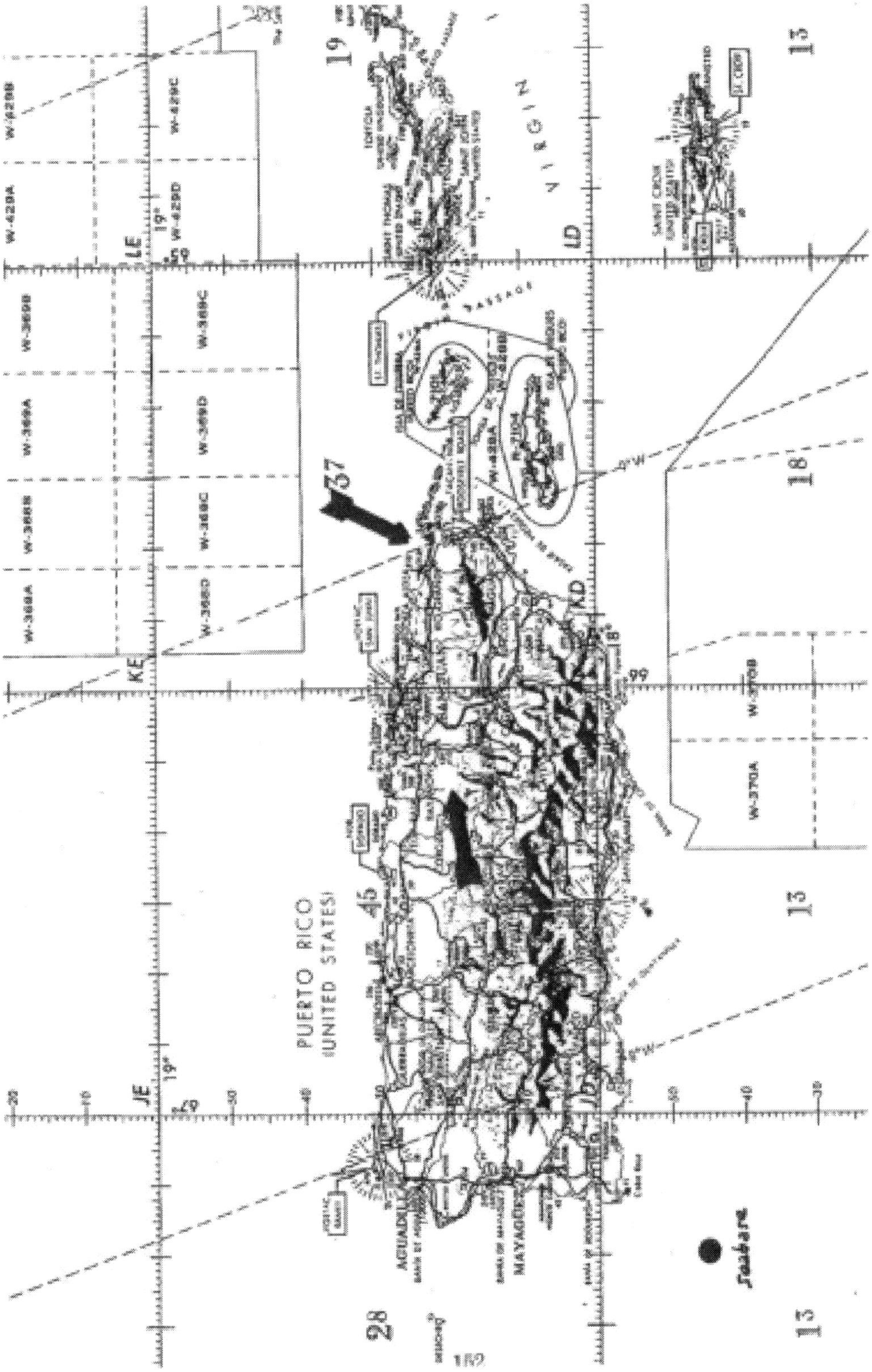

this was very . . . there was no water there . . . just a cavern . . . and they propelled the ship onto an area . . . and I could see no less than 25 or more of the same (ships) . . . Other similar ships . . . smaller ones and a real big one . . . but many, many small ones and many similar ones. And we stepped and walked on solid ground . . . and when that took place it was just like being home . . . and we then started talking. There were no lips . . . just an opening . . . slant . . . just like that . . . an opening. When you said teeth it didn't occur to me, you see, because only I spoke . . . He never opened his mouth. I was so over whelmed by the whole thing . . . and then he said there are close to 700 (individuals) here in this camp. I saw many of them . . . He, Ohneshto, walked into an area that looked similar to an eating place. And there were these small round tables . . . like transparent . . . like plastic, and there were sitting stools, like this . . . like an inverted 'U,' more or less . . . and someone handed me a platter with a funny looking bowl . . . and they had a creamy stuff in it. It was a white creamy . . . similar to cornmeal . . . and it was semi-solid . . . It was given to me . . . and they each took one and we had chow . . . we all ate . . . the three and myself . . . four . . . we who had arrived in our spacecraft. The food was like a . . . something cooked . . . like a . . . I've always tried to memorize that taste . . . because it wasn't sweet . . . it wasn't salty . . . it wasn't like anything . . . it was like something, and it was very nourishing. It was very good. It had everything you needed and it was very good. It was not a matter of flavor . . . it was just nourishing . . . that is all you need. That was the way I was feeling in my mind. I was very satisfied."

"Then they took me to another area, which stood from here, and we went into another location where they had a complete panel . . . similar to the one they had here . . . and there we could sit like if we were watching the sky . . . right from there, and we could see the stars and all . . . People were standing in front of panels . . . and it was just like a big, big, laboratory."

"At this point we are talking about pretty deep down underground. It is something that just breaks my mind because I just don't know how to think of this. They said we were down 9,000 feet. There were in the vicinity of 700 of them at that time, and that is also when they advised that they were working on six other camps, to make it seven camps throughout the world . . . and this was just one of them . . . and that there were 83 contactees eventually through them for definite reasons that they were being needed . . . and they were requested by higher forces unknown to us to aid and help at convenient times . . . and at that time they said 1976, and that was 1972 . . . and it (the contacts) will continue for the next years. They said, 'You will be hearing from us oftener and in different ways . . . different people . . . we cannot be here too long because we cannot be exposed to your environment too long. We are allowed to be only six months here at a time. . . . The north of Puerto Rico is favorable for our operations because it is highly magnetic and helps trap energy that we need to leave your atmosphere. And that is why we have chosen this point. Also we cannot give you any more than six months (of our own time before we are rotated) . . . and the most favorable times are usually around the middle of March and the middle of September for leaving and coming. That is when others come and replace those about to leave.' The alien being said, 'We are allowed to operate in our specialized field (space travel) only seven years out of our lifetime. Otherwise it can hurt our civilization . . . by being exposed for more than that period of time.' "

"They showed me a type of sleeping cot right in the same rocks . . . on different levels . . . and they were fat but yet small . . . no luxury . . . nothing out of this world . . . The thing that impressed me most was that I could see all of this and also the laboratory . . . The rest of the installation was like normal but austere . . . like eating and sleeping."

"The aliens were not super beings . . . they were humanoid and very similar to us . . . just of a different shade of color and unique in many ways . . . and they looked very much alike . . . all of them. I couldn't tell them apart. Without expressive features they seemed so alike . . . so strange . . . but yet I could sense LOVE . . . but they don't show it. They have 83 other human beings on this good earth that they are in contact with. I am not the only one. They told me that I am not their only property (contact). If I wanted, they could get someone else. I don't know how long I am going to be contacted . . . I don't know. I am not irreplaceable. Once I stop serving them they will get another . . . someone else. I only serve a purpose. As long as it works it will continue."

Ever since going aboard the UFO, whenever in presence of someone deceitful he sees a warning beacon of light on their head. He has developed other remarkable faculties that he cannot explain. He remembered that the alien being spoke of the law of the speed of thought . . . which he did not quite understand. Ohneshto had also said at one point that one hour of our time compares to 200,000 hours of their time in their own dimension. He had also mentioned that molecular structures can be made to travel in a linear direction at up to seven times the speed of light. . . . He said it took about four hours of our time to come to Earth from Koshnak in Orion. He said they travel in the seventh and eighth dimensions, unknown to Earth humans, and that they are aware of 13 dimensions of being. Ohneshto pointed out references in our bible pertaining to UFOs. He said that their normal span of life is about 800 to 1,000 of our years. Their normal intelligence would be over 200 by our scales. He explained that they could continue life forever with only one cell of the body. Ohneshto said that the axis of the Earth has changed four times as far as they have checked this out, that it tilts about every 20 to 25 centuries. He said that man is as old as his Earth, that more ancient races were the ancestors of nearly all the inhabitants of this planet.

The Orion said that other beings in our universe become very active other Earth, studying and recording just before each tilt. They are standing by to assist and help prevent the total loss of life on Earth in these catastrophes, to aid in the re-growth of humanity on a new scale. They are much concerned about avoiding the mistake of 1943 where the development of atomic sciences ooccurred before they were due.

On subsequent contacts where the aliens had occasion to communicate between each other he heard the language used, which was articulated, and it sounded slow and slurred to his ear. They used a lot of gla, o, a, l, ll, and m in their intercommunication.

They didn't seem to communicate much between each other. Everyone seemed to be occupied at his particular task and they all seemed to be quite busy. They appeared to be well organized and they operated with great efficiency.

From this time on the electrical charge around the person of David Delmundo increased until 1973. Whenever he got near an electrical device it would make those strange noises. He seemed to be carrying some kind of electromagnetic charge on his body because if he touched grounded metal or electrical circuits, or even water if it was grounded, he would draw sparks and he could see a flow of bluish energy from his fingertips to the object. Even if the electrical current to the object was turned off he would feel a strong electrical charge.

The beeps continued on a more or less frequent basis, and every time he heard them he could look up and see the bright and often luminous object in the sky above, even in bright daylight.

In 1973, during another UFO flap over Puerto Rico, seven people from the mission, including David Delmundo and his elder daughter Moira and son David Junior, were driving the highway below Mayaguez near Cabo Rojo on the southwest corner of the island. When they were about ten miles from the lighthouse they began seeing the now familiar bright greenish-blue disc-shaped self-luminous objects flying all around them. As they made a turn and came in sight of the water south of the cape they saw several objects go into the sea and disappear beneath the surface. They could see the glow in the water for a few seconds after the objects submerged. It was just dusk and they could see the objects and the skyline quite clearly. The most notable part of the observation was that the objects had a glowing greenish-blue field around them and they entered the water at considerable speed without any splash. The water just parted ahead of the visible field and the objects flew into the hole and it closed up behind them with only a flurry of ripples. Other disc-shaped objects came out of the water the same way and flew northeast over the island. After the UFOs entered the water there was a greenish glow for a few seconds that faded as the objects presumably went deeper. Conversely, when they came out of the water they were preceded by the greenish glow and then the water would part and the ship would emerge—again with no splash and no water dripping from the object.

As the mission group drove away some minutes later, two very bright greenish-bluish-white discs of light rose out of the water south of the lighthouse and flew away to the south.

In the early part of 1978, Mr. W. Mendez of San Juan, a 34 year old airline transport pilot and his girlfriend (now his wife) were driving from State Road 174 and were nearing the intersection of state roads 812 and 879, when they saw a brilliant bluish-white ball of light in the sky to the north. It was close to 20:30 in the evening and he called his girlfriend's attention to the light and then slowed the car to watch. He saw that the brilliant ball of light was descending in a smooth glide when all at once the ball seemed to flatten out, like a plate standing on edge being turned down on its rim upside down, and now he could clearly see its true outline despite its brilliance. He could easily distinguish its disc shape with a low dome raised in the middle on top. As soon as the disc was level horizontally it dropped like a stone to the ground and the light went out. He drove up to where he thought it had landed but couldn't see anything more. He waited a few minutes, looking, and then tried his CB radio to see if anybody else had seen the light. He couldn't raise anybody at all and then tried a base station nearby for a radio check. He couldn't contact the base station either. Later he learned that all CB radios in the area had been unable to receive or transmit for over two hours at about the time of his observation. They all reported hearing strange noise interference in the background which they hadn't heard before and which they have not heard since.

UFO Abduction From Undersea

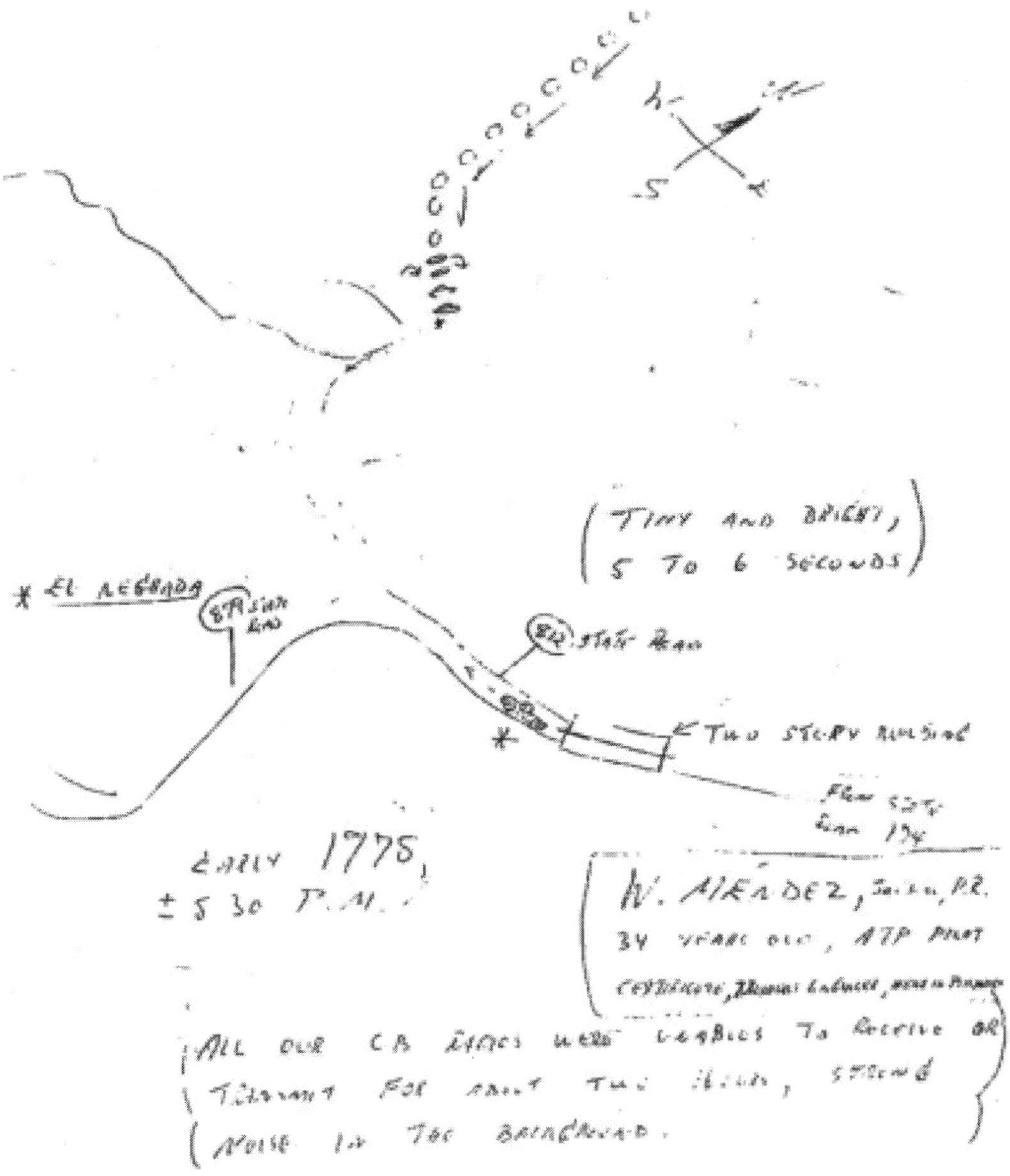

This approach and descent was witnessed in early 1978 by Mr. W. Mendez, an Airline Transport Pilot and his girl friend during the great sighting wave of that year.

UFO Abduction From Undersea

On the twelfth of April 1980, young David Junior saw one of the alien beings from through the window in his father's home. It was between 01:00 and 02:00 A.M. and all were sleeping with closed doors and closed windows, something unusual because they do not usually close both. David Junior got up to go to the bathroom and turning, closed that window, too. As he closed the bathroom window he saw the alien standing just outside—less than six feet away. He froze in astonishment . . . closed the window . . . thought, "Can it be?" . . . opened the window again and the alien was still there and they stared each other in the eye for several seconds. He was very impressed by the intelligence and power he felt in those eyes. This alien was dressed in the same kind of garment as described earlier by his father, and the descriptions given by his father fit this one very closely also. On a later contact his father learned that this being was from the same ship as Ohneshto and that he was called Orenox.

In August of 1980 Mr. Hector Vasquez of the mission was awakened at 2:00 A.M. with a very severe pain in his side that seemed to move to his lower back. He sent one of his children to see if David Delmundo would drive him to the hospital for treatment. He had had the pain before and it had been diagnosed as a kidney stone. He knew what he faced. David came for his and put him in the car and they started out for the hospital—a 20 minute drive.

Hector was lying down, doubled up with pain, in the back seat when David, who was driving, noticed an orange glowing luminous disc of light in the sky a few hundred feet above the car. It was quite large and close, and illuminated the foliage and ditch on both sides of the road. He called Hector's attention to it, but Hector, who was still lying down in the back seat, thought David was only trying to get his mind off the pain and made some remark like, "Yes, and the New York Yankees are out there waving flags at us, too." But David insisted and Vasquez turned to look. Then he saw the light, too, but from his lower viewpoint he could see it more clearly, and watched it carefully. It moved to one side of the car and paralleled its travel only a few hundred feet away to the right and a few hundred feet above the ground. Then it moved ahead of them and when they came up to the turn it was waiting. It moved ahead again and waited, and did this several times. Then Vasquez noted that the pain was gone. They arrived at the hospital about that time and Hector went in to be treated. He couldn't bear the pain coming back again. When he was examined, however, the kidney stone was completely gone—and it hasn't returned since. When they started home an hour later they saw the orange colored luminous object in the sky again, but this time it was much higher in the sky and it flew away. Hector is convinced that the object had something to do with the disappearance of the kidney stone.

A few days before this event there was a small greenish UFO hovering over the clinic. It could be seen clearly with binoculars. Part of the telepathic communication received at that time by David Delmundo stated that there was a sketch in a book on its way to him (UFO . . . Contact From The Pleiades) that was similar in shape to the one under observation, and would show that such craft do in fact exist. (The sketch referred to is the one of the 15 foot diameter remote controlled disc-shaped craft.)

In 1977 the mission group was advised in detail about this visit taking place now in 1980, and were given a message to be relayed to this author at that time. On 12 April 1980 another message was delivered to be mailed to me prior to this trip, but Delmundo hesitated to mail it. He handed it to me at the end of our first day of examaination of his UFO experience. The message read:

"Please be advised once and for all of our presence here on this, your Earth. We must emphasize (that) you must come out in the open and go forth as you have been previously used . . . You Earthlings have . . . for it is time for action. The second year of this decade (1981) will leave us no other choice but to come out in the open and (we) certainly hope that encounters will be throughout (the world). Nonetheless, should you fail, your own personal life is in great danger and leaves us no choice but to connect sufficient and more serious structures to go forth."

"Now we are . . . just one point . . . from 700 are only 84 dispersed throughout your world. Should there be any need we could go to 600 thousand. We are agreed that the consciousness re-awakening of your society should have given to the decade 50 what we are now striving to do in decade 80. Thus within three decades of foolishness and waste we should perceive not to wait as long as three years for a book to be published, but rather go on nationwide networks, otherwise WE shall intervene personally, and WILL do so. The start of awakening of those we call gods (authorities) has been done individually already, and the broadcasts are just a call, as a key word, to those who have already been advised as such."

"The tragic moments expected are due soon, and although this society is cherished much, because of circumstances beyond your understanding, we have no choice but to proceed in accordance to writings, scriptures, and foreplans. We certainly hope to come forth in closer communication to the Navajos in your mainland and in the state of New Mexico. You will understand your Indian nations, hopefully."

Orenox

That message, though stilted in style and poorly worded in English is a sincere communication from another intelligence visiting us on our planet and should not be taken lightly. They are very serious. It at least gives us some clues as to why they are here.

Then Delmundo said, "There is more to this—I have four implants, three in my heart and one in my head. I was seven months in the hospital and the doctor said I would not survive. The aliens installed miniature devices (micro circuits) in my body—that is why I do not wear any metal—it interrupts . . ." Delmundo has had several heart attacks and been hospitalized for it.

"During the seven months, when I was in intensive care, I spoke in many languages unknown to me. My heart stopped many times and I was near death. The doctors told me that part of my brain was damaged by a lack of circulation. I have my medical records here. . . . I am not supposed to be able to see, or hear, of move my limbs, and I am walking and driving, and I listen better than ever. I have a bit of short vision, but who does not at my age, anyhow?"

When the witness was five years old he was stricken with spinal meningitis—an almost always fatal disease—and he was given up by the doctors as incurable. His parents were told to take him home and isolate him because "he contaminates everyone and everything" and he will die. And he died. Then something happened and he started to revive and to recuperate. He lived and began to recover. He had to go through all of his learning processes again—learning to crawl, to eat, and toilet training all over again. It took almost a year but he slowly came back. He thinks now that the aliens had something to do with his miraculous survival, and he dedicates his life to their cause if need be . . . but working silently and out of the UFO limelight. He seeks no attention or recognition and doesn't want any. In fact, he thinks it would hinder his work and that is why we have carefully disguised his real identity.

His work goes on to this day and his contacts still continue with the successors to Ohneshto and Orenox, and he serves in the best way he can.

If only the rest of us were inclined to follow his example we wouldn't be trying so desperately to destroy our beautiful planet.

Wendelle C. Stevens

Upper Photo—A view of the Baptist Mission from the pinnacle overlooking the mission property. The spacecraft ovten hovered here near the peak.
Lower Photo—A view of one of the landing sites from the Mission grounds near Del Mundo's cottage.

UFO Abduction From Undersea

Upper Photo—Del Mundo leads Jun-Ichi Yaoi of NTV in Tokyo to one of the landing sites.
Lower Photo—Del Mundo and Yaoi confer at the landing spot. Sparse stalky grass grows there now.

UFO Abduction From Undersea

Upper Photo—View of the most recent landing site in the dense jungle vegetation. The foliage was badly seared but began to grow back almost immediately. Small trees were broken off.
Lower Photo—Close-up of one seared area.

APPENDIX 2

UFOs From Undersea Eastern Argentina

One could safely assume that any vehicle capable of deep space travel might also be capable of operating under water. Both conditions require completely self-contained systems aboard the vessel.

Since our planet has a great deal more water surface than land, and since human beings inhabit more land than water, one might also assume that any space travelers desiring to observe us clandestinely and unmolested would likely resort to use of that medium for certain operations.

We have just examined a case containing evidence of a submarine base off the west coast of South America manned by extraterrestrial beings; and then we looked at another case off the north shores of South America, where extraterrestrials operated disc-shaped flying vehicles from an underwater base in the Puerto Rican Basin.

We may have, as well, a similar operation going on off the southeast coast of South America in the vicinity of the Argentine Basin; and we are here considering only the local waters around one continent of our great planet.

We are aware of but have not reported an extensive underwater operation discovered on the Pacific Ocean by United States Naval Officers which shows that sub-marine bases may in fact be worldwide.

We have encountered evidence of this situation before in our investigations. For example, in July of 1967 a Dutch multinational businessman was contacted in the Oostscheld, below Amsterdam, by extraterrestrial beings who said they came from a place they called Iarga, some 11 light years from our sun as we calculate distance. They were observing us from underwater and they took the witness underwater to deal with him. This is a very extensive case filling more than 400 pages of a book called "UFO Contact From Planet Iarga."

UFO Abduction From Undersea

Then we got into investigation of another case of extraterrestrial contact with a witness in Switzerland. Here we discovered that the alien beings had some kind of operation going on under the North Sea.

Two years later, in 1978, we began investigating still another case where extraterrestrial visitors described to their abductee an underwater operation going on in the Rio Salado in Northern Argentina. Another extensive 400 page report of this case was published in 1981 as "UFO Contact From Reticulum." There are hundreds of other lesser cases in our files.

Is there, in fact, a submarine UFO base in the South Atlantic off the Patagonia Coast of Argentina? More and more incidents seem to point that way.

Ever since ten years before February 1960 when the Argentine and United States Navys' combined forces tried for two weeks, with uncounted tons of explosives, to bring two unidentified objects maneuvering under the waters of Golfo Nuevo, an area of only 20 by 40 miles, to the surface, reports of UFOs in that area have continued.

Near the end of June 1950, Sr. Romero Ernesto Suarez, walking the coastal road between Rio Grande and San Sebastian in the Territory of Tierra del Fuego, late, about 23:00 hours, suddenly heard the sound of turbulent water, which increased and became more violent. He was puzzled and became a little frightened. There was no wind, storm, or water currents that could explain this noise. He peered into the darkness in that direction, and suddenly a huge, luminous, oval-shaped object emerged from the sea about 500 meters from shore. It ascended vertically to a certain altitude, made a quick 90 degree turn and disappeared rapidly to the northwest, toward Rio Gallegos.

Escena del fenómeno luminoso que surgió del mar, según observación del señor Romeo Ernesto Suárez practicada en junio de 1950.

UFO Abduction From Undersea

Fifteen days later, again at night, when he was between Rio Gallegos and Santa Cruz, ascending a hill near Puerto Coyle in the province of Santa Cruz, he witnesses a similar occurrence. This time four small luminous domed discs surged up out of the water vertically, in perfect formation, leveled off and flew up the coastline a ways and then turned left in the direction of the Cordillera de Los Andes.

Twelve years after that, and even 2½ years after the February 1960 case so well reported in Flying Saucer Review Vol. 6, Number 3 and Vol. 10, Number 4, UFOs were seen to enter and also to leave the water again. In August 1962, Sr. Vicente A. Bordoli, a truck driver from Mar del Plata, while in the South, driving along National Highway Route #3 bordering the Atlantic Coast, with his son Hugo, observed strange formations of lights in the sky that entered the water in the Golfo San Matias, Province of Rio Negro. A few minutes later they emerged and ascended into the sky and disappeared. San Matias is a deep gulf with 500 foot depths in some places.

Según el testigo Vicente A. Bordoli, periódicamente se sumergen y emergen del Golfo San Matías extrañas formaciones luminosas que cobran altura rápidamente.

Two hundred miles south is another deep gulf, the Golfo San Jorge. On 28 July 1964, at 21:24, the subprefectura at Puerto Madryn, Chubut Province, received a message from the Argentine tanker "Cazador," saying that at 21:10 the captain and crew had sighted a strange light that fell into the water. They had plotted its bearings as latitude 45 degrees, 56 minutes and 06 seconds South and 64 degrees, 00 minutes and 00 seconds West longitude. They and another tanker, the "San Antonio" searched a five mile circle looking for survivors and debris. In the afternoon of the next day, the Norwegian ship "Sumber" arrived in port and the captain reported to the authorities, "Yesterday at about 21:10, as we were approaching the Argentine coast, we observed the fall of an aerial object or small comet (into the waters of the Gulf). It came from the northeast, horizontally, towards shore. It radiated a brilliant light."

Two months later, in the same Golfo San Jorge, a public personality known for his honesty, who prefers to remain anonymous, declared that on 20 September 1964, while driving at night to the city of Comodoro Rivadavia, as he was leaving the town of Caleta Olivia, northbound up the coastal highway, he saw four small luminous lens-shaped objects describing a parabola in the sky as they flew in perfect formation. Suddenly they dipped, and still in formation plunged into the waters of the gulf and disappeared. He stopped his car and got out but could see nothing more.

A little later, while driving north of that position, he saw four similar luminous objects, possibly the same ones, emerge from beneath the sea, veer in his direction as they accelerated, and climb out at a steep angle at prodigious speed and disappear into space above.

El 20 de setiembre de 1964 se vieron objetos luminosos que —describiendo parábolas— se introducían y salían del Golfo San Jorge.

Also in the Golfo San Jorge, on 18 March 1966, Sr. Carlos Corosan, a well known resident of the area, walking the beach 15 kilometers north of Puerto Deseado, at 16:00 heard a strange rumbling sound. Looking up, he saw a strange cigar-shaped craft 18 to 20 meters long, moving about 30 meters above the waves off shore. A grayish vapor was coming from the rear of the object. It was dark gray colored and its surface shined with a

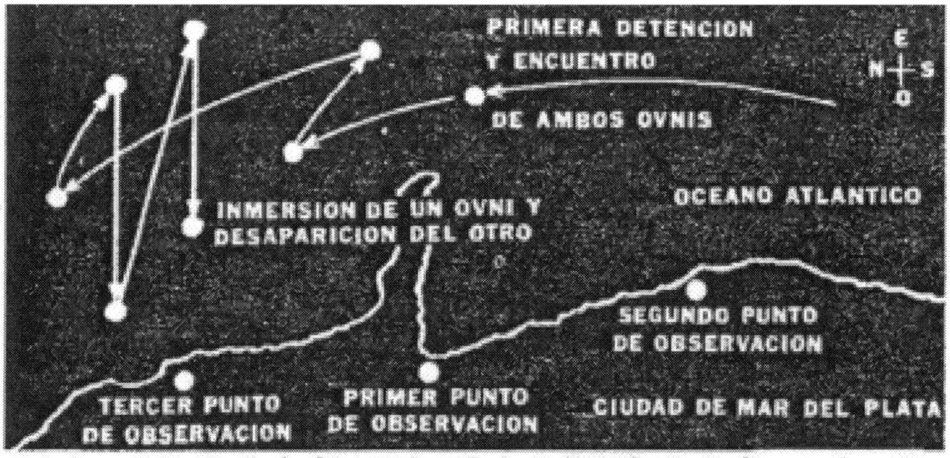

Evoluciones de los dos Ovnis vistos por los señores Raúl y Ricardo Benítez, según gráfico del diario "La Capital" (M. del Plata). Uno de ellos se sumergió en el Atlántico.

metallic finish. The finish was completely smooth with no wings, windows, ports, or breaks of any kind and no markings. Suddenly it stopped ten meters above the water, commenced to vibrate with the rumbling sound increasing in intensity, and then he heard a muffled explosion. The smoke from the rear became denser and very black. The nose came up and it began a slow ascent to the north northeast, though visibly erratic. He heard another explosion followed by a reduction in the rumbling, and it descended rapidly and entered the water with a splash and disappeared beneath the waves.

Farther north, off Buenos Aires, in front of the Pinamar District, at night on 31 May 1971, psychologist Zulema Bruno, driving her car along the shoreline road, saw a strange luminous lens-shaped object surge from the sea as it rotated on its vertical axis and radiated orange rays of light. It followed her automo-

Surgimiento del océano de un elemento volador con forma de trompo, según descripción de la sicóloga Zulema Bruno.

bile for some 300 meters and then, putting on a burst of prodigious speed ascended and disappeared into the sky above.

So far we have no photographic evidence, but wait. On 2 December 1971, at Punta Norte, on the Valdez Peninsula, in the Golfo San Matias, Province of Chubut, at 15:00, mid-afternoon, Sr. Ricardo Jorge Espindola and several companions were hunting seals in the cold clear deep waters off the north cape of Punta Norte. They had taken a number of seals and he was shooting a picture of two of his friends with some of the seal carcasses. He

2 December 1971, Punta Norte, Peninsula de Valdez, Province of Chubut, Argentina. 15:00

On 2 December 1971, Sr. Ricardo Jorge Espindola and several companions were hunting seals in the cold clear waters of the Golfo de Matias off the north cape of Punta Norte. At about 15:00 in the afternoon they had taken a number of seals and he was shooting a picture of two of his friends with some of the seal carcasses. He had color slide film in his camera.

Suddenly the water about a quarter of a mile off shore began to roil violently and a large circular craft emerged from the turbulence coming directly towards them and then curved away and flew out to sea. He snapped the picture and lowered the camera in stunned surprise. The object was far away before he recovered his composure and remembered to try for another. He decided it was too distant and did not take the second picture.

He object was circular and of a dark color, and was closely surrounded by a reddish haze or halo effect that gave the whole craft a reddish cast.

We have been unable to substantially verify this case because the photographer is a transient sailor aboard ship and we have not been able to catch up with him. He gave the pictures to a friend who later revealed their existence with the story described above.

From a personal letter from Sr. Guillermo Carlos Roncoroni.

had color slide film in his camera. Suddenly the water about a quarter of a mile off shore began to roil violently and a large circular craft emerged from the turbulence coming directly towards them, and then curved away and flew out to sea and disappeared. He snapped the picture and lowered the camera in stunned surprise. The object was far away before he recovered his composure and remembered to try for another. He decided it was too distant and did not take the second picture. The object was circular and of a dark color, and was closely surrounded by a reddish haze or halo effect that gave the whole craft a reddish cast. The object was soundless and left no trail.

Two hundred and sixty miles south of the Valdez Peninsula, along the coastline of Golfo San Jorge, which has figured prominently above, another new case developed. At 19:40 on 23 March 1974, near coastal highway Route #3 just before reaching the town of Caleta Olivia, Sr. Cesar Elorda saw a silvery metallic domed disc approaching from the east, from the Golfo San Jorge. It was moving west on a steady course at low altitude and he could see it very clearly. He had time to get his camera ready and take one beautiful color picture on Ektachrome film. It was completely symmetrical and smoothly finished in a low conical form almost like a "coolie hat." It had no projections, ports or windows of any kind and no markings. The dome rose in a smooth unbroken curve from the flange of the disc to the top, and was smoothly rounded. It flew almost directly overhead and to the west into the sunset sky. By the time he got his camera ready it had already passed over and he shot the picture at an angle into the sunset. He could still see the silvery finish when he snapped the picture but when the slides came back he was surprised to see that it had photographed completely black.

Ten months later to the north, near San Antonio Oeste on the north shore of the Golfo San Matias, an almost identical domed disc-shaped craft was photographed. This event happened at Las Grutas Balneario (Resort) at 09:15 on 3 January 1975. The day was cold and cloudy with occasional rain and a low overcast sky. Sr. Francisco Moreno was on the second floor of a beach cottage reading a novel when his attention was called to a strange hissing sound, something like a television set tuned off station. At first he paid little attention to it, but it began to intensify and it intrigued him. He thought it might be the vacuum cleaner, but then it noticed that it was outside the house. It was not very loud but loud enough to irritate him. He went to the only window in the room and looked out to see if he could identify the source of the noise. It was then that he saw a dark object suspended in the air outside. It was a dark gray "coolie hat" shaped object and was just hanging in the sky. Then he noticed that it was slowly coming towards him. He had a distinct impression that the sound was coming from the strange object.

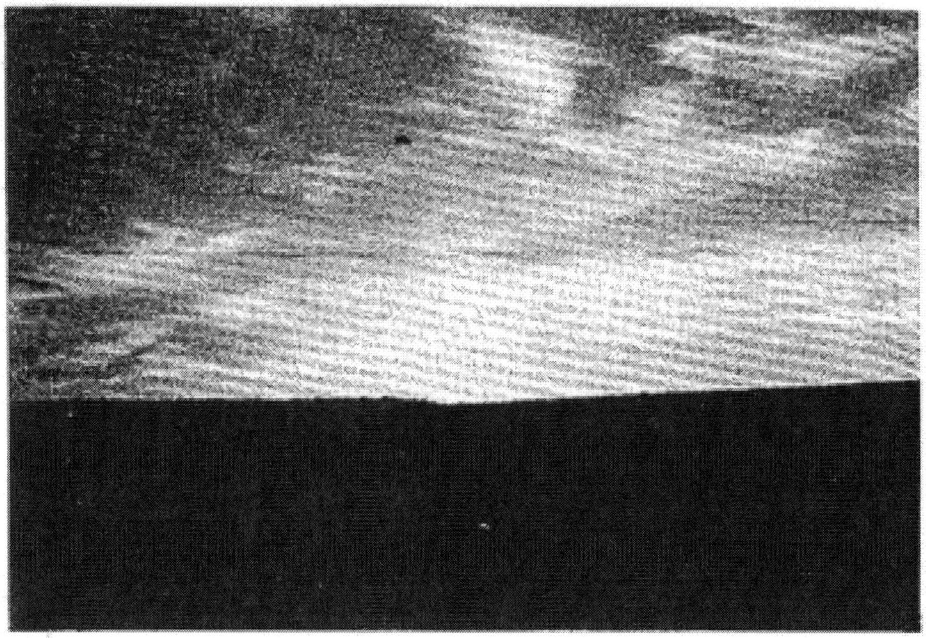

23 March 1974, Caleta Olivia, Pcia. Santa Cruz, Argentina. 19:30

At 19:30 on 23 March 1974, as Sr. Cesar Elorda, senior employee of Y.P.F. in Comodoro Rivadavia, was 16 kilometers out of Caleta Loivia driving from Comodoro Rivadavia along a coastal highway paralleling the shoreline of Golfo San Jorge, he noticed a strange circular aircraft approaching from the ocean to the east. It was traveling in a westerly direction, across the highway at not a very great speed. When he first saw it, it was coming from the gulf, from over water, and was about 200 meters from land. It continued its course and passed over the highway as he came abreast of it, passing over his car also. He could clearly see now that it was no airplane like he had ever seen before.

He stopped the car and got out with his camera, a Voightlander Bessamatic, and was able to get one good color photograph before the object was too far away as it flew to the west and into the sunset.

The object was a circular lens-shaped craft with an indictinct flat bottom and a dome on top. It was a dark dull grey and looked metallic. It flew lazily along, making no sound and leaving no trail. He did not see any lights of any kind. The sun was already below the horizon when he snapped the picture but the sky was still quite bright.

People in that area see UFOs quite regularly, especially around Golfo San Jorge where many think that they go into and come out of the clear waters of the gulf. Some UFO researchers think there may be a submarine UFO base near there.

Courtesy Sr. Guillermo Carlos Roncoroni.

At first he seemed paralyzed with surprise, and then he remembered the camera left in the room downstairs. He shouted for his wife and daughter to come up and bring the camera. He wanted them to see it, too. They both heard him and grabbed the camera and raced upstairs. "By the time they arrived on the upper floor and brought me the camera I had calmed down but was afraid that the object might disappear before I could get a picture of it. I took the camera and pointed it and saw that the photo meter needle showed underexposure. I adjusted the diaphragm aperture. The object continued its slow movement in the sky, but I was trembling so much that I had great difficulty in focusing correctly." Sr. Moreno pressed the release and took the first picture. He rolled the film to the next frame as he looked at the object. It was still almost stationary and sort of balancing on the air. Then it began to move, a little faster at first and then began to accelerate. He quickly raised the camera and took the second picture. As it began to accelerate the hissing sound began again and increased as it accelerated. He tried to get a third picture, but from where they were standing he could not get the picture before it disappeared beyond the window's view. It flew towards the south. They could still hear the sound rising and falling after it passed from view. They ran downstairs and out into the street but did not see it again.

The witnesses were unable to estimate accurately the size or dimensions of the object, or its altitude or distance from them. Sr. Moreno guessed that the object might have been from 150 to 200 meters above the ground and about 300 meters distant when he snapped the first picture. Neither of the three witnesses saw lights, reflections or any other significant details, except that the upper part was lighter in color than the lower. They all noticed the balancing on air motions. The object was in view for about 2 minutes in all. Sr. Moreno estimated that he heard the sound for about one minute before he went to the window to look, and about a minute and a half after he saw it until he took the first picture. He thought that no more than 15 to 20 seconds had elapsed between the first and second photos. The object was smoothly contoured from flange to dome with no breaks in the surface. The object shows strangely dark and featureless in the developed photos.

The camera used was an Asahi Pentax 35mm with standard 50mm lens set for shutter speed of 1/250th second and a diaphragm aperture of f5.6. The film was Kodak reversible, ASA 64, processed normally. Examination of the diapositives with a 300 power Zuhio microscope shows normal emulsion grain distri-

UFO Abduction From Undersea

3 January 1975, Las Grutas Balneario, San Antonio Oeste, Pcia. Rio Negro, Argentina, NW Golfo San Matias. 09:15

On a cold and cloudy day with occasional rain, Sr. Francisco Moreno (on vacation) was on the second floor of a borrowed cottage reading a novel when his attention was called to a strange humming sound, something like a television set tuned off station. At first he paid little attention to it, but it began to intensify and it intrigued him. He thought it might be the vacuum cleaner, but then he noticed that it was outside the house. It was not very loud but loud enough to irritate him. He went to the only window in the room and looked out to see if he could identify the source of the noise. It was then that he saw a dark object suspended in the air outside. It was a dark gray sombrero-shaped object and was just hanging in the sky. He had a distinct impression that the sound was coming from the strange object.

At first he seemed paralyzed with surprise, and then he remembered the camera left in his room downstairs. He shouted for his wife and daughter to come up and bring the camera. He wanted them to see it, too. They both heard him and grabbed the camera and raced upstairs. "By the time they arrived on the upper floor and brought me the camera I had calmed down but was afraid that the object might disappear before I could get a picture of it. I took the camera and pointed it and saw that the photo meter needle showed underexposure. I adjusted the diaphragm aperture. The object continued to stand still in the sky , but I was trembling so much that I had great difficulty in focusing correctly." Sr. Moreno pressed the release and took the first picture. He rolled the film to the next frame as he looked at the object. It was still stationary and sort of balancing on the air. Then it began to move, at first slowly and then began to accelerate. He quickly raised the camera and took the second picture. As it began to accelerate the humming sound began again and increased as it accelerated. He tried to get a third picture, but from where they were standing, he could not get the picture before it disappeared beyond the window's view. It flew away to the south. They could still hear the sound rising and falling after it passed from view. They ran downstairs and out into the street but did not see it again.

The witnesses were unable to estimate accurately the size or dimensions of the object, or its altitude or distance from them. Sr. Moreno guessed that the object might have been from 150 to 200 meters above the ground and about 300 meters distant when he snapped the first picture. Neither of the three witnesses saw lights, reflections or any other significant details, except that the upper part was lighter than the lower. They all noticed the balancing on air motion. The object was in view for about two minutes in all. Sr. Moreno estimated that he heard the sound for about one minute before he went to the window to look, and about a minute and a half after he saw it when he took the first picture. He thought that no more than 15 to 20 seconds had elapsed between the first and the second photo.

The camera used was an Asahi Pentax 35mm with standard 50mm lens set for a shutter speed of 1/125th second and a diaphragm aperture of f5.6. The film was Kodak reversible ASA 64 processed normally. Examination of the diapositives with a 300 power Zuhio microscope shows normal emulsion grain distribution throughout the whole picture frame of both slides.

Letter from Sr. Guillermo Carlos Roncoroni

UFO Abduction From Undersea

UFO Abduction From Undersea

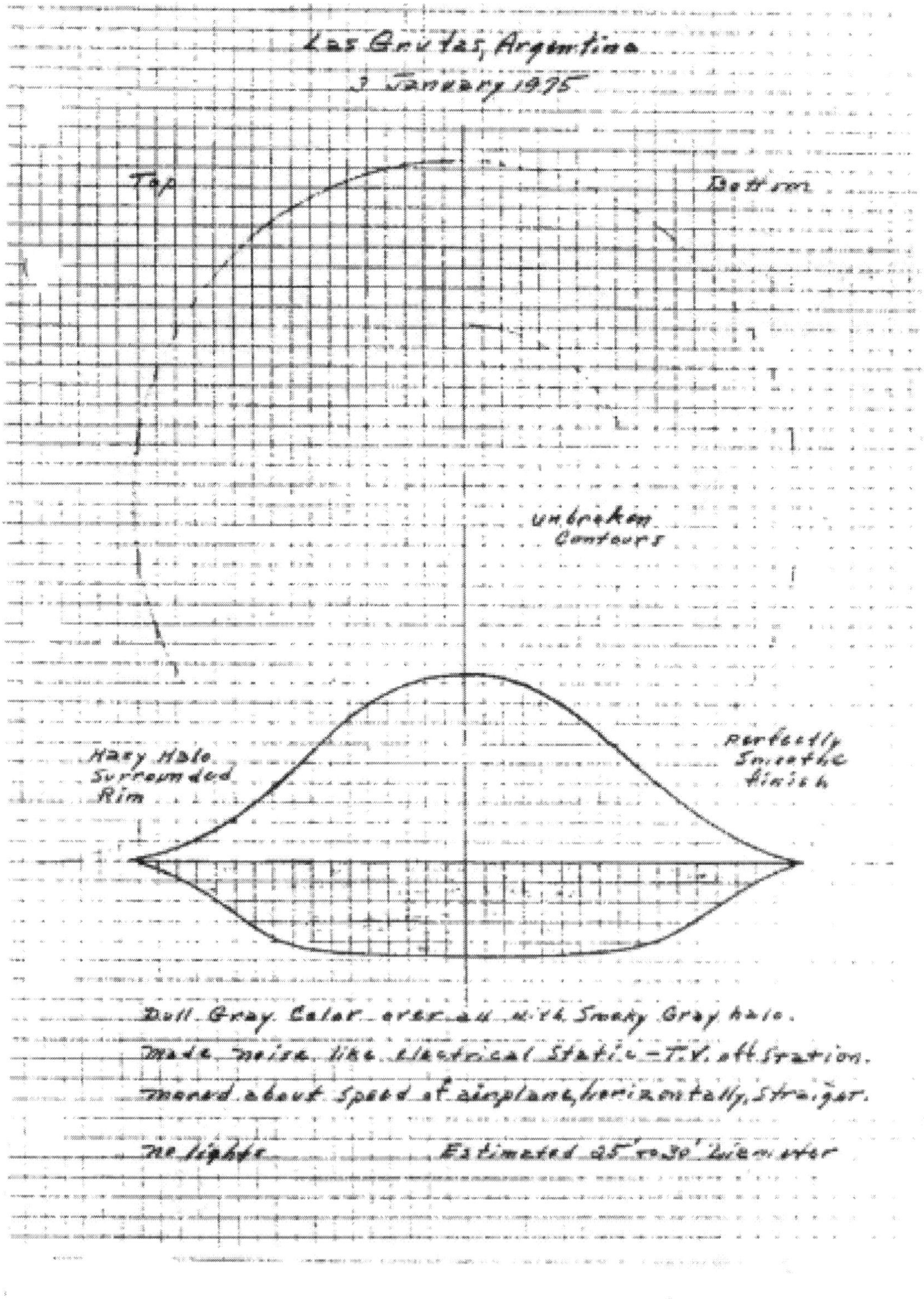

bution throughout the whole picture frame of both slides.

Early last November a letter arrived at the central offices of ONIFE, a UFO study group in Buenos Aires. The letter described a UFO sighting and included a photograph which the writer said he had taken. The letter reads as follows:

"City of Trelew, Privincia de Chubut, 24/10/75. Dear Sr. Zerpa: I am an avid reader of your magazine, Cuarta Dimension, although it is quite difficult to obtain copies of it here in Trelew. Excuse me for not identifying myself but I prefer that my name not become known, and the best way to be sure of this is to remain unknown to you also. With this letter I am sending a photograph which I took on 18 February of this year in the outskirts of Puerto Madryn. As a reader of your magazine and a real UFO fan I am sending you this information on the experience believing that you would be interested concerning my experience. Day: 18 February 1975. Hour: 15:20. Place: outskirts of Puerto Madryn, more precisely at the place called Punta Cuevas. Duration of observation: Approximately one minute. To clarify, I took five photos in all, and the one I send you is the second of the series and the best. Also the UFO appeared silver and shiny metallic, but as you can see, in the photo it appears black, which is very strange, as it was silver and reflected the sun's rays. The UFO came from the west and veered along the coastline to the east. I heard no sound of any kind."

"I believe this is all I can tell you in this respect and I know you will understand my caution. Saludos and my best regards. R. E. S."

"PD: Believing that you are interested, I advise that I used a Pracktika Pentacon camera and a roll of Kodak slide film. The enclosed photograph shows a black object, very small but well defined, moving against a bright blue clear sky. Below that is the

18 February 1975, Punta Cuevas, Pcia. Chubut, Argentina. 15:20

This photo was sent to O.N.I.F.E. by mail, by a correspondent who refused to identify himself, claiming that it would be injurious to his business. The witness says that the object was coolie-hat shaped, and that it was a silvery metallic color. He was quite puzzled by the fact that the developed print showed a black object and asked O.N.I.F.E. if they had any explanation for this phenomenon, and had this happened before.

His letter, in part, says, "City of Trelew, Provincia de Chubut, 24 October 1975. Please excuse me for not identifying myself, but I do not want my name revealed, and the surest way to be sure of this is for you not to know me. With this letter I enclose a photograph that I took on 18 February of this year in the outskirts of Puerto Madryn. As an interested reader of your journal and an ardent student of the UFO phenomenon I include the details that I think you will want to know, and this will be my only communication regarding my

UFO Abduction From Undersea

experience. It was about 15:20 hours, and I was in the outskirts of Puerto Madryn, more precisely at the place called Punta Cuevas. The observation lasted about one minute. I took five photos altogether, and the one which I enclose is the second one of the series. Also the UFO was silver in color, but as you can see, in the photo it appears black, which is quite strange because it was shiny silver and reflected the rays of the sun brilliantly. The object came from the west and flew toward the sea, or to the east. I heard no sound from the objedt and saw no trail. I think that is all I can tell you in this case and I hope it answers your questions . . ." He used a Practika Pentacon camera and Kodak color film. The photograph showed a small dark object clearly defined against a deep blue sky. The foreground showed a typical arid desert hill of that part of Patagonia along the coastal highway.

Sr. Guillermo Carlos Roncoroni of O.N.I.F.E. carefully studied the picture and offered the following observations: 1. According to the witness the UFO was a shiny silver color and reflected the sun's rays. The witness does not explain why the object appears black in the transparency, flat black, without reflection of any kind. He could not account for the discrepancy either. The object is not backlighted, and is not over anything white or bright that could cause the effect. He speculated on the possibility of rays in the light spectrum beyong the visible range, but thought that there should still be some reflection. 2. The witness stated that he had taken five pictures but only sent in one. Do the others actually exist? 3. Enlargements showed a dark object, well defined, in the form of a "coolie hat." The shape and proportions are exactly the same as the object photographed on 3 January 1975 at Las Grutas, Argentina. An almost identical object was also photographed on 23 May 1974 at Caleta Loivia, Pcia. de Santa Cruz, Argentina.

The photographer is being sought in an attempt to view the other four photographs taken at this time.

Cuarta Dimension, Number 34, p. 26. Courtesy Sr. Guillermo Carlos Roncoroni.

arid Patagonian landscape along the road at this point."

Sr. Guillermo Carlos Roncoroni of ONIFE studied the photo very carefully and observed that although the witness reported that the UFO was silver and reflected the sun, he is unable to explain why it appears in the picture as a flat black, without reflection of any kind. The ONIFE laboratory is likewise unable to account for this effect as there is no strong back lighting, or anything in the foreground, or anywhere else in the picture for that matter, bright enough to produce that condition. It might be an unknown light radiation that would affect the human sight one way and the film another, but he feels that there would be some reflection of some kind anyway. This is pure speculation, however.

The picture shows a small dark "coolie" hat shaped, circular craft, almost identical to the one photographed at Las Grutas, moving in a bright blue sky over a light colored sand dune with sparse scrub growing on it. The object is quite low in the sky as in the Las Grutas case, and is headed out over the beach towards the Golfo San Matias. This object is also seen at about the same elevation in the sky as in the Las Grutas case.

Another interesting and possibly related event happened 12 days later, on 2 March 1975. That night a group of fishermen observed a very bright light moving horizontally at low altitude in the sky, and coming from the Patagonian mesa. The men were aboard a fishing boat a few kilometers north of the Valdez Peninsula. The light, which had a definite form and emitted a loud buzzing hum, stopped suddenly over the waters of the gulf and dived beneath the waves and disappeared under the sea. The witnesses insist that this was not a meteorite nor an airplane of any known kind.

Many UFO investigators and students of the phenomenon feel that much evidence points to the possibility of a submarine base for UFO operations somewhere beneath the waters of one of these deep gulfs. The water here is over 500 feet deep in places. The area is sparsely populated and inhospitable to humans, and is well protected naturally from disturbances of civilization.

END

UFO Abduction From Undersea

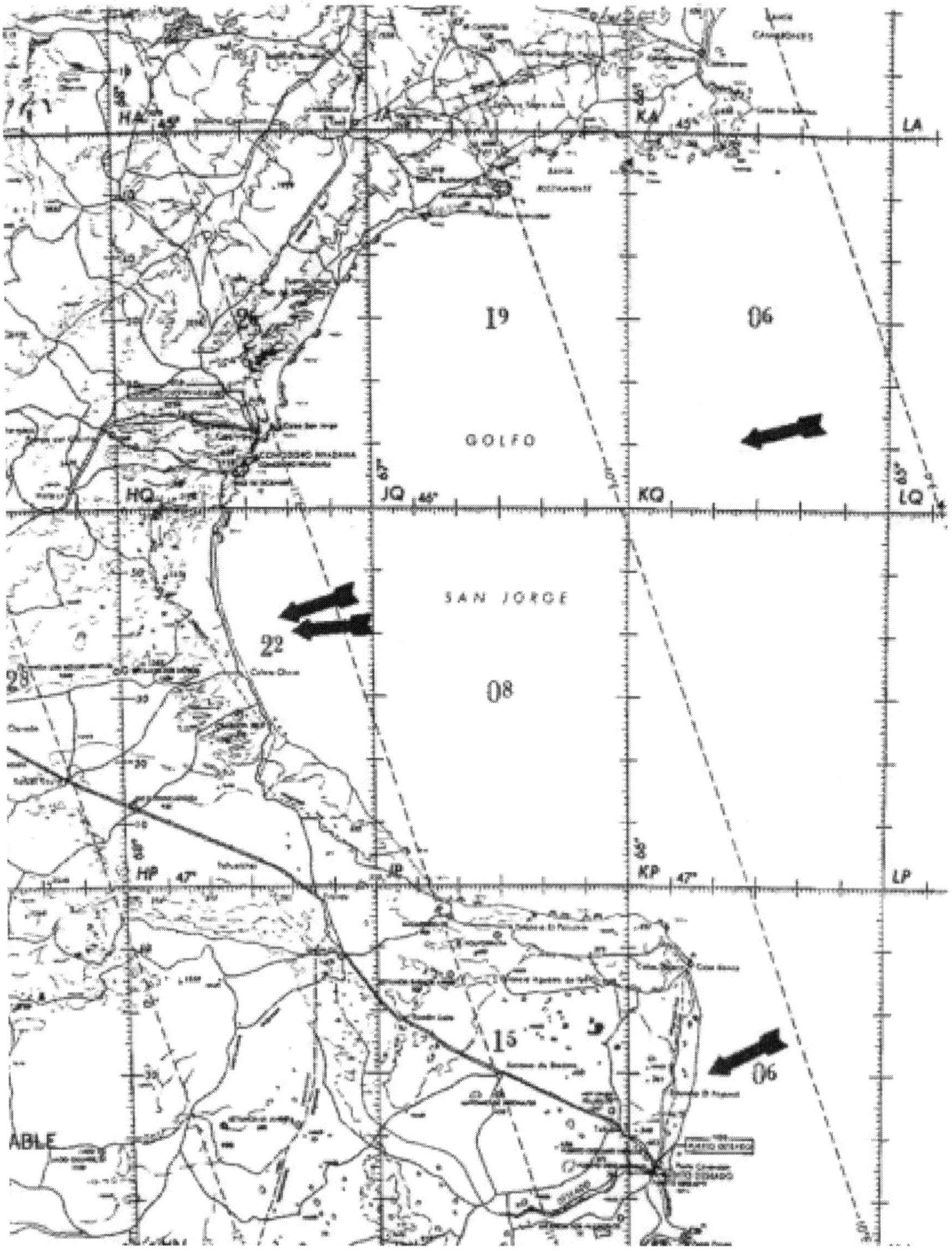

UFO Abduction From Undersea

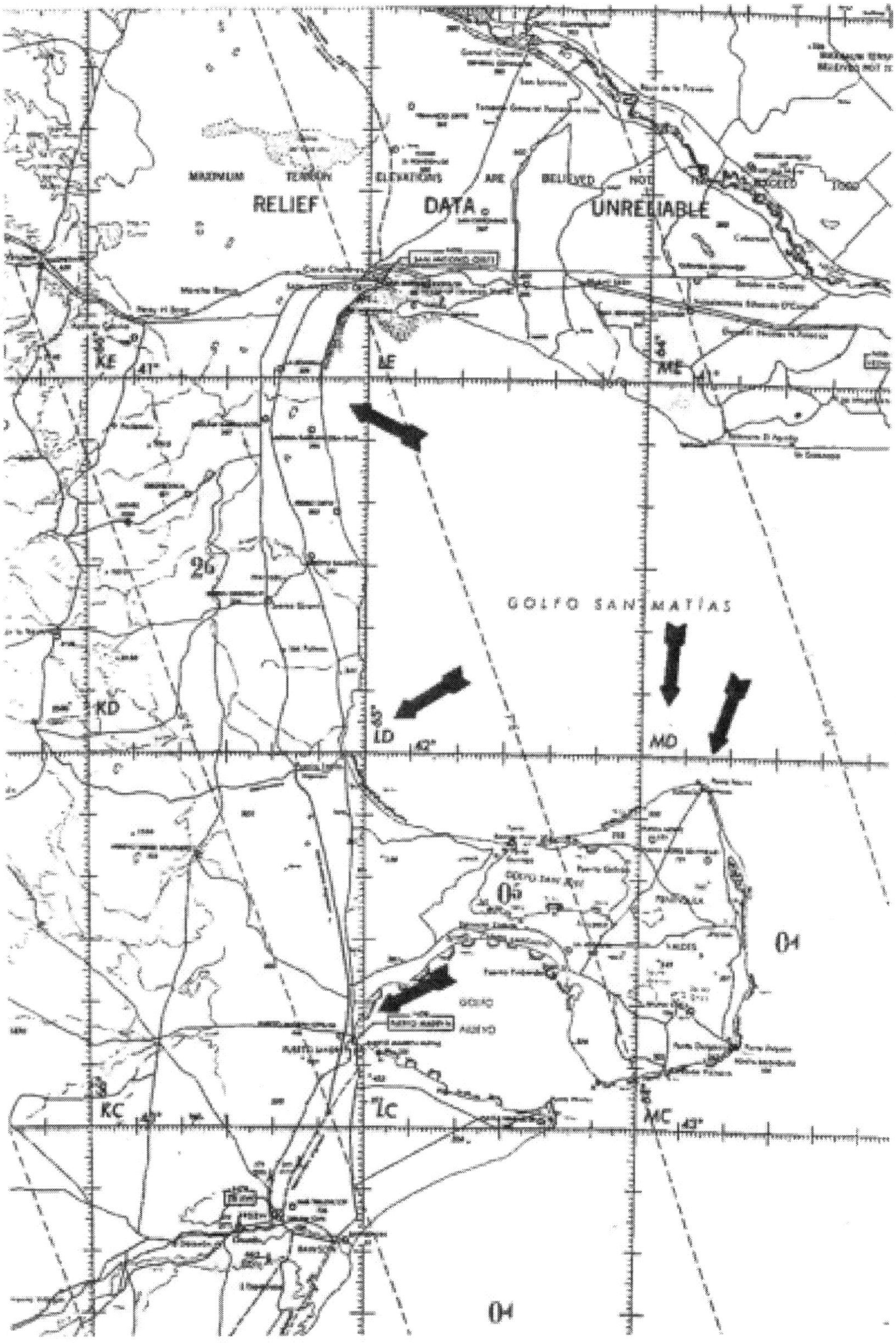

UFO Abduction From Undersea

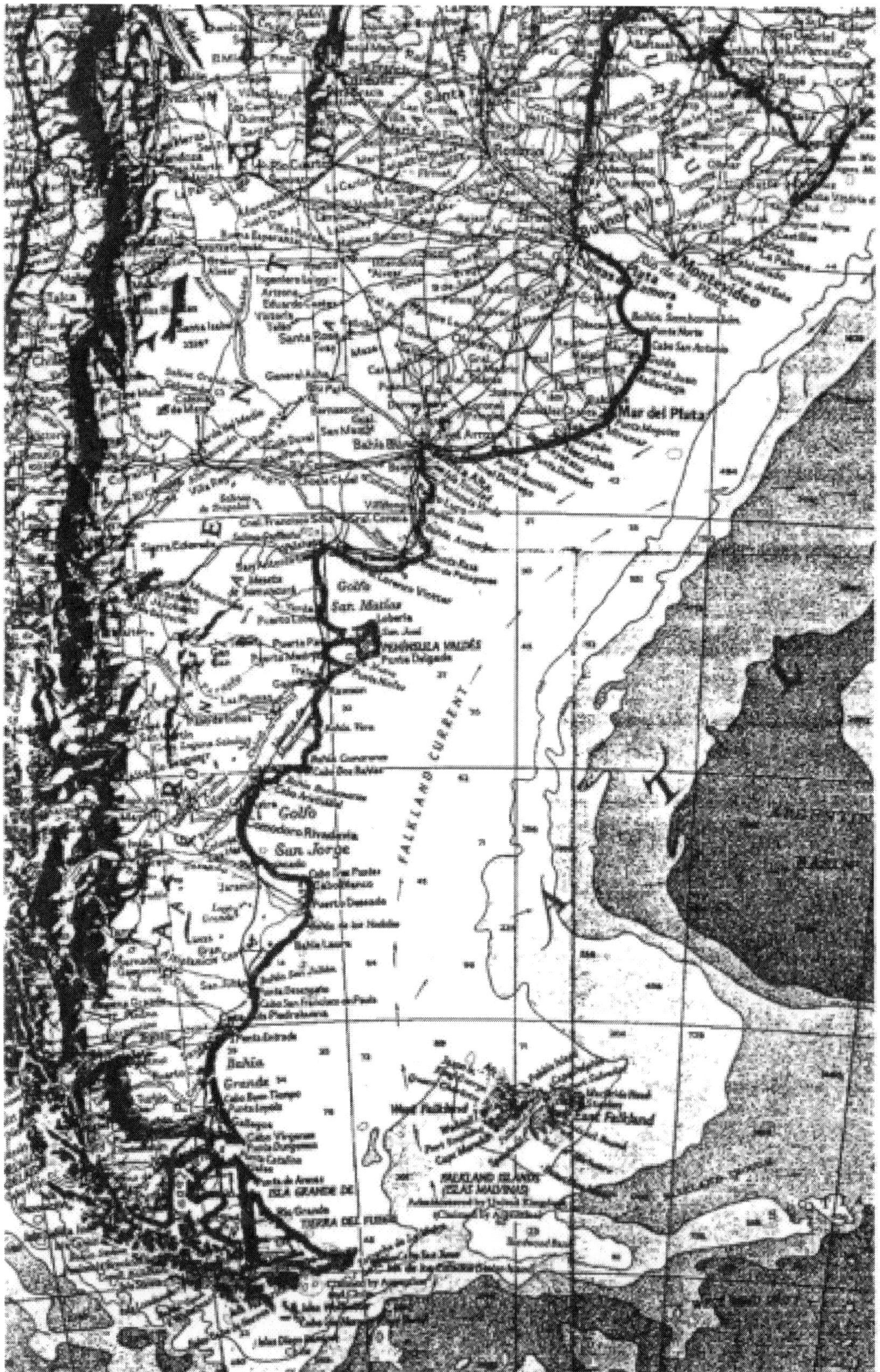

APPENDIX 3

Submarine Bases?

The following information is translated from Chapter 11 of "El Gran Enigma de Los Platillos Volantes" by Sr. Antonio, published in Spanish in Barcelona by Editorial Pomaire in 1966, and is reproduced here with permission of the author.

"For some time I had had under consideration a possibility that seemed truly fantastic, but is not really so fantastic when we consider the evidence accumulating. Do the crews of the mysterious UFOs have bases under the sea?"

"Remember that the oceans and seas cover about three quarters of the surface of our globe, 71% to be more exact, and that their depths go down to 4,000 meters. This translates to about 1,300 million cubic kilometers of water constituting as such an ideal hiding place which we are only beginning to timidly explore with the bathyscaphs and the 'Submarine Disc' of Commander Cousteau. An interplanetary visitor arriving from space would be more likely to encounter water than land upon arrival, especially if he came to our surface in the Pacific Ocean area."

"From antiquity we have reported strange phenomena in the seas that could be related to UFOs. In various times unidentified objects have been seen falling into the sea or, which is even more strange, EMERGING from it.

"I reviewed my files and uncovered various notes relative to strange marine observations. I published some of this in my article titled 'UFOs And The Sea' which was printed in the Flying Saucer Review for November-December 1964. Consider the following items:

"On 18 June 1845, according to the Malta Times, we find the bergantine Victoria some 900 miles east of Adalia (near east), when her crew saw three luminous bodies emerge from the sea into the air. They were visible for ten minutes flying a half mile from the ship. Other witnesses also saw this phenomenon from

Adalia, Syria and Malta. The luminous bodies displayed an apparent diameter five times the size of the full moon!"

"On 22 March 1870, in the equatorial waters of the Atlantic Ocean, the sailors of the English corvette Lady of the Lake, saw a curious object (like a cloud in the sky). It was a cloud in lenticular form with a long tail, and it ADVANCED AGAINST THE WIND. This form was visible for an hour, wrote Captain F. W. Banner in the ship's log. The drawing by Banner in the log looked extraordinarily like a flying saucer."

"Near midnight of the 24th of February 1885, at a point between Yokohama and Victoria, the Captain of the bergantine Innerwich, according to Charles Fort, was awakened by his second mate who was seeing something strange in the night sky. The captain went up on deck and saw the sky all lit up. 'The following instant a great luminous mass appeared over the ship, completely blinding the crew and spectators.' The burning mass fell into the sea. Its size must have been considerable, because the sea that it raised struck the ship in gigantic waves and produced a roar that was 'deafening.' The captain, an old wolf of the sea, said 'The spectacle can not be described in words.' It is possible that the object causing this impression on the brave sailors was a bolide, but this could by no means explain the object seen on 12 November 1887 from the steamer Siberian. That object, described as a great ball of fire, surged from the sea near Cape Race and ascended to an altitude of 15 meters, then advanced toward the ship and passed alongside, remaining visible for five minutes. (For more details see the Meteorological Journal No. 6-448.) Captain Moore, in command of the Siberian, said that this was not the first time he had seen this apparition in this same region. Is there a submarine UFO base in this vicinity?

"The sea is an ideal refuge for the extraterrestrials that visit us. We cannot disregard the possible existence of submarine bases of operation. The water should be an ideal medium from which to operate because of its abundance and distribution throughout our world. It is no more hostile a medium than deep space."

"Another underwater occurrence of this kind was reported during the great UFO wave in the summer of 1965. It happened on Tuesday the 6th of July. At about 21:52 GMT when a ship navigating from Puerto La Cruz (Venezuela) to Santa Cruz de Tenerife was at a position 24°40′ N by 41°15′ W, wind NW at force 5, barometer 1.023 and 20° C temperature, the crew observed a great tongue of intense blue flame as it surged from the sea and came in the direction of the ship. 'I ran for the telephone and called the captain,' said a crew member, 'and without waiting his response ran to the locker there on the bridge and grabbed the binoculars. Then I could see a great object (in the air) that passed in front of the ship. The object came very near the poop at between 200 and 400 meters altitude and well below the broken clouds at that time. The sky was clear between the clouds and I could see the stars and the light of the moon. I could see perfectly the fuselage of the object and its upper part. It was cigar-shaped and had a line of windows from which a bright yellow-orange light shown. There was no sign of wings or tail. It had a narrow trail of bluish fire following it. A little behind the object, in the trail of fire, one could see something like a conjunction of incandescent balls in trail formation, which each emitted strong rays of blue light parallel to the direction of travel of the object. I thought at first that those balls of light were aircraft pursuing the object, but later I could clearly see that they were not. The trail of fire must have been some hundreds of meters long. the object itself was bigger than any aircraft known today. It travelled at an enormous velocity, and remained visible for 30 to 40 seconds, passing from north to south on a heading of 100 degrees. Despite its great velocity and its near approach, we could not hear any sound."

"The watch, seaman Ambrosio Hernandez, said that at first it looked like the huge object came out of the sea heading north and then it changed its direction toward the ship. The helmsman, seaman Narciso Guillen, said that he watched the object from the poop. Repairman Juan Hernandez and carpenter Ignacio Suarez made similar declarations. All of this took place aboard the Norwegian tanker Jawesta in the North Atlantic on 6 July 1965 and was reported in the ship's log by First Officer Torgrim Lien."

An almost identical event was observed and photographed by Sr. Antonio Gonzalez Llopis from the south of Gran Canaria Island, less than 30 kilometers away and 14 years later. This sighting, which occurred in the evening of 5 March 1979, was independently photographed by at least three different witnesses unknown to each other, and was kept secret by the Spanish Government for more than a decade. We are indebted to Sr. J. J. Benitez, a very active Spanish UFO investigator and prolific author on the subject for the details of this report and the copy photographs. This case was first published by Benitez in his latest UFO book, "La Gran Oleada," published in Spanish by Editorial Planeta of Barcelona in 1982.

Antonio Gonzales Llopis, 26, had been photographing night

UFO Abduction From Undersea

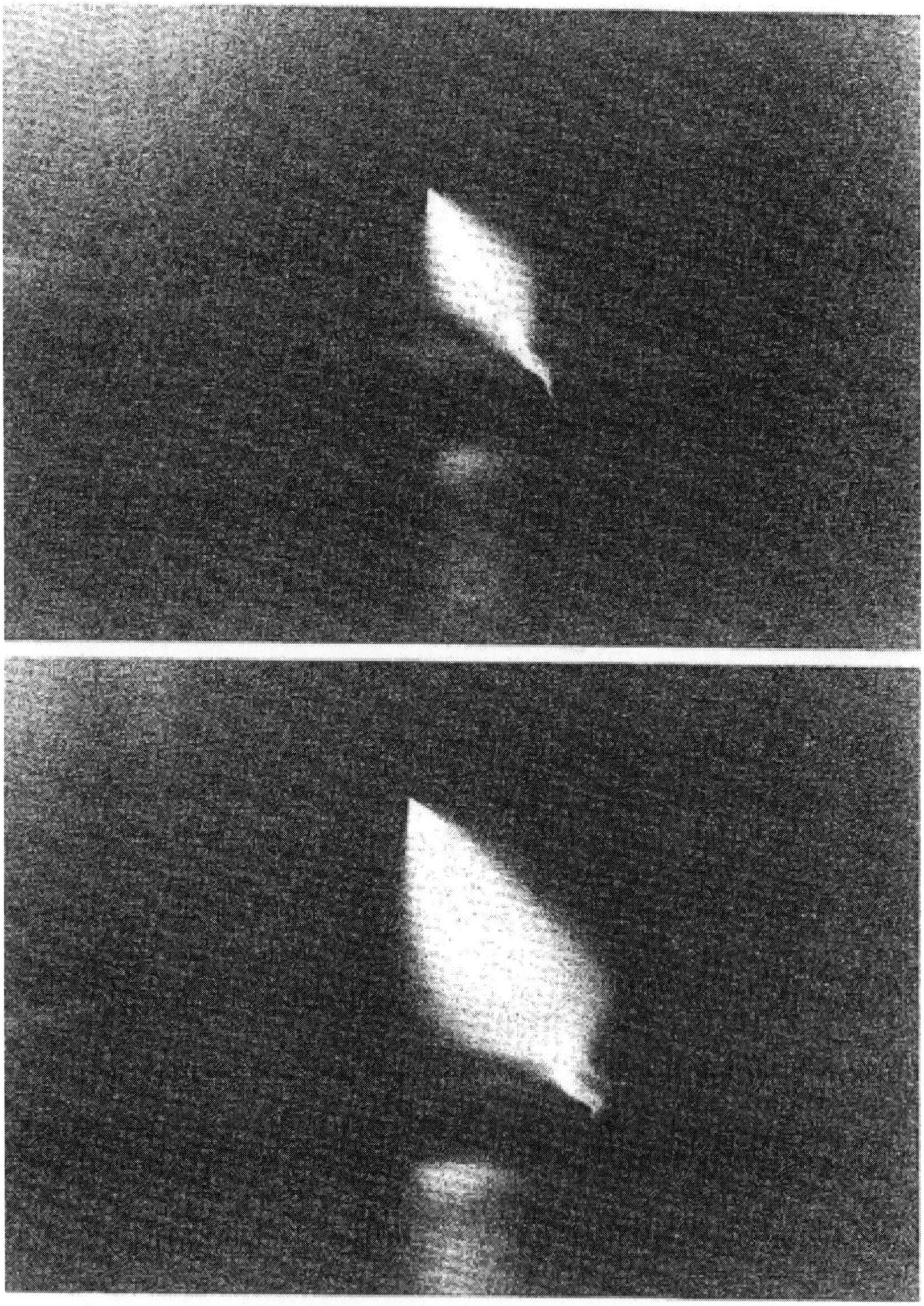

Above—5 March 1979, 20:08, Gran Canaria. This is the fourth photo by Sr. Gonzalez Llopis, showing the object emerging from the sea.
Below—This fifth photo made a few seconds later shows the object as it continues to ascend.

views of the south bay area of Gran Canaria at about 18:45, when he noticed a peculiar effect in the evening sky out over the sea. Suddenly a huge dark object surged from beneath the waves and climbed steeply into the sky on top of a bright ball of fire. Llopis snapped pictures quickly, changed position and checked camera settings, and continued shooting for the three minute duration of the sighting.

The bright light from the object's "tail" obliterated any details in the object itself. It accelerated rapidly leaving behind a glowing trail and a luminous cloud which took over a half hour to fade away. The event was witnessed by thousands of people, many of whom also photographed it, providing evidence for an objective scientific assessment of the phenomenon.

Sr. Gilberto Naranja, an engineer at the transmitting station on Mount Teide said, "Thank God I have been allowed to witness this spectable." He had his camera with him and also snapped photographs of this same event that same day.

An almost identical display was observed and photographed very near the same place five years earlier, giving credence to the statement by the captain of the Siberian that he had seen a similar display in this area before, and this spans 85 years of time!

On 12 June 1974, another photographer, Sr. Guillermo N. Lijtmaer, from Tenerife was taking pictures when he observed a change in the sky and saw a dark object leaving a great trail of flame suddenly surge from beneath the surface of the sea and ascend at a steep angle into the sky. He made photographs of this fantastic spectacle as quickly as he could. Two of Lijtmaer's color photographs correspond almost exactly with two of those shot by Gonzales Llopis. They differ only in minor detail but are clearly two different series of pictures. Experts say that this is not an underwater missile launch, or if it is, it is nothing like they have seen before. Remember, the earlier reports of this peculiar phenomenon, by the crews of the Siberian and the Jawesta was before we had successful underwater launches of missiles.

Ivan T. Sanderson, the great naturalist, wrote an entire book on intelligent life operating under the waters of this Earth, including extraterrestrial visitors or the possibility of such. The title was "Invisible Residents" and it was published by The World Publishing Company of Cleveland, Ohio, copyrighted 1970. The first chapter starts off with one of the classic undersea UFO reports of all time.

One evening in the Antarctic, during the U.S. Navy's Operation Deep Freeze, a Brazilian scientist by the name of Dr. Rubens

UFO Abduction From Undersea

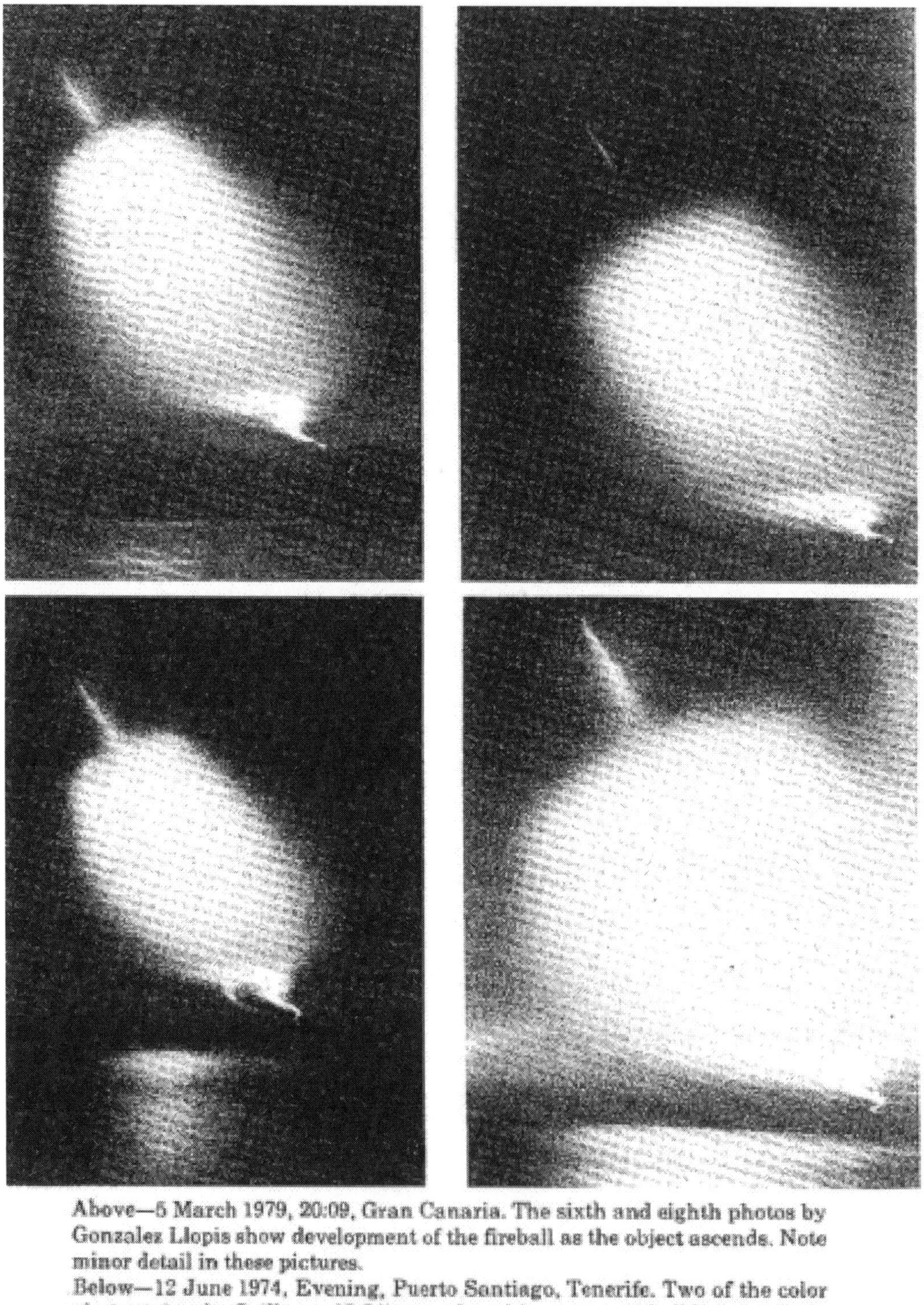

Above—5 March 1979, 20:09, Gran Canaria. The sixth and eighth photos by Gonzalez Llopis show development of the fireball as the object ascends. Note minor detail in these pictures.
Below—12 June 1974, Evening, Puerto Santiago, Tenerife. Two of the color photos taken by Guillermo N. Lijtmaer from his apartment building overlooking the south bay and Gomera Island, show the very near similarity of the pictures but differences in minor detail.

UFO Abduction From Undersea

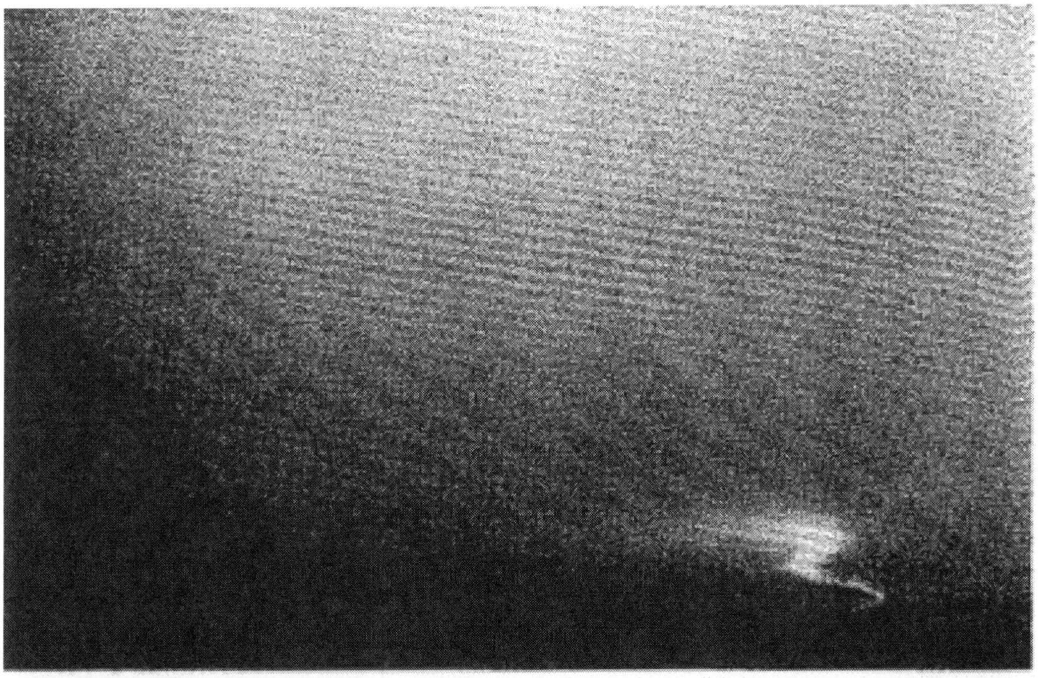

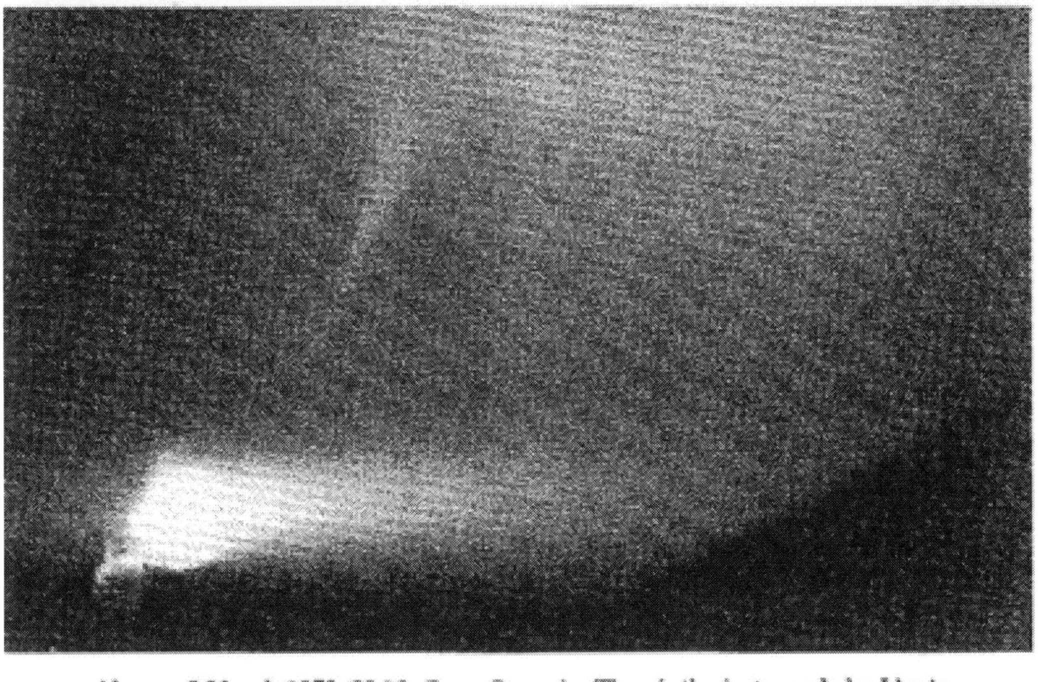

Above—5 March 1979, 20:10, Gran Canaria. The ninth photo made by Llopis shows full development of the fireball.
Below—5 March 1979, 20:11, Izana, Tenerife. Sr. Gilberto Naranjo, from the Observatory of Izana, photographed the same visual display as Llopis from Gran Canaria. This is one of his photographs showing the fading fireball after the object was gone.

UFO Abduction From Undersea

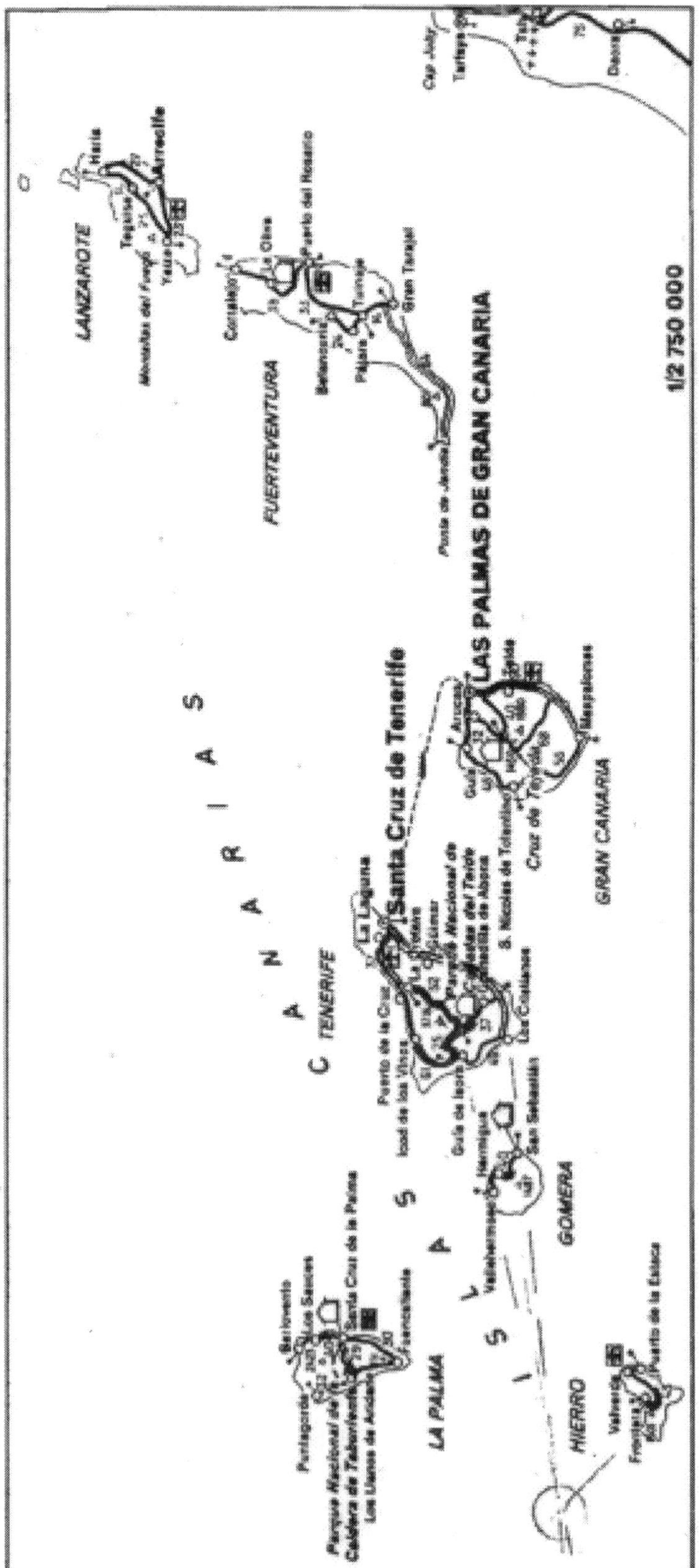

Map of the Canary Islands. A plot of all the sightings shows a focus just northwest of Hierro for the point of emergence from the sea. This also agrees with the locations reported by the ships much earlier. Is there a submarine UFO base here?

UFO Abduction From Undersea

J. Villela, assigned aboard a U.S. Navy icebreaker, was literally jolted almost out of both his body and his mind by a "something" that suddenly come roaring up out of the sea through no less than 37 feet of ice, and went on up into the sky like a vast silvery bullet. The ship was in Admiralty Bay, which faces the South Atlantic Ocean. The only other witnesses were the officer on watch and the helmsman, as it was an extremely cold day and all other personnel were below decks. Further the other witnesses saw only the tag end of the performance because they were both busy with charts; but what they did witness was quite enough. Enormous blocks of ice had been hurled high into the air and came cascading down all around the hole burst through the thick ice-sheet and the water was rolling, and apparently boiling, while masses of steam issued from both the hole and the descending ice. The book includes 229 pages of such reports, but does not include any of the others reported here.

The evidence available is overwhelming. Extraterrestrial intelligences are operating from our oceans and seas.

UFO Abduction From Undersea

Printed in Great Britain
by Amazon

68002299R00131